EurographicSeminars
Tutorials and Perspectives in Computer Graphics

EurographicSeminars

Tutorials and Perspectives in Computer Graphics

Edited by G. Enderle and D. A. Duce

P. R. Bono I. Herman (Eds.)

GKS Theory and Practice

With 92 Figures

Springer-Verlag
Berlin Heidelberg New York
London Paris Tokyo

EurographicSeminars

Edited by G. Enderle and D.A. Duce
for EUROGRAPHICS –
The European Association for Computer Graphics
P.O. Box 16, CH-1288 Aire-la-Ville

Editors

Peter R. Bono
Peter R. Bono Associates, Inc.
P.O. Box 648
Gales Ferry, CT 06335, U.S.A.

Ivan Herman
Insotec Consult GmbH
Franz-Joseph-Straße 14
D-8000 München 40, FRG

ISBN 3-540-18257-8 Springer-Verlag Berlin Heidelberg New York
ISBN 0-387-18257-8 Springer-Verlag New York Berlin Heidelberg

Library of Congress Cataloging-in-Publication Data.
GKS theory and practice. (EurographicSeminars) 1. Computer graphics–Standards.
I. Bono, P.R. (Peter R.) II. Herman, I. (Ivan) III. Series. T385.G57 1987 006.6 87-26397
ISBN 0-387-18257-8 (U.S.)

© 1987 EUROGRAPHICS The European Association for Computer Graphics,
P.O. Box 16, CH-1288 Aire-la-Ville
Printed in Germany

Printing: Druckhaus Beltz, Hemsbach/Bergstr.
Bookbinding: J. Schäffer GmbH & Co. KG., Grünstadt
2145/3140-543210

In Memoriam Günter Enderle

We shall not cease from exploration
And the end of all our exploring
Will be to arrive where we started
And know the place for the first time.

T. S. Eliot, *Four Quartets*

Günter Enderle, Series Editor of EurographicSeminars, died in hospital on 13 January 1987 at the age of 42, following a tragic road accident. Günter's death robbed the world of a great engineer, computer scientist, manager and above all, personality.

Günter founded the EurographicSeminars series, and since the publication of the first volume in 1984, the series has grown steadily and includes volumes covering a broad range of topics from introductory to advanced research. The high standards set by the series originate in Günter's own very high professional standards.

Günter himself made deep and lasting contributions to the development of standards for computer graphics and GKS in particular. He was deeply involved in the development of GKS from the earliest days, and many of us in the UK remember vividly the excellent tutorial he gave on GKS at the Rutherford Appleton Laboratory in 1981. It was for many people their first exposure to the thinking and concepts behind GKS and did a very great deal to promote understanding of GKS in the UK. Günter's own book on GKS, with Klaus Kansy and Günter Pfaff, *Computer Graphics Programming* is a classic in the field. Günter himself, proposed this present volume, *GKS Theory and Practice*, and it is appropriate therefore that it should be dedicated to his memory. I think that he would have been proud of the excellent job done by Peter Bono and Ivan Herman in assembling this collection of papers.

Günter will be greatly missed by his many friends and colleagues, especially by myself, co-editor of this series. *Requiescat in Pace*.

David Duce

Preface

As the first international graphics standard, the Graphical Kernel System (GKS) has influenced heavily the concepts, architectures, and algorithms associated with device-independent and machine-independent graphics programming. Several dozen implementations are available commercially; no doubt, hundreds more partial and complete implementations exist in large companies, universities, and research institutes worldwide.

The purpose of assembling this collection is to make available, in one easy-to-use reference, a handbook that can be helpful to those specialists who want to have a deeper insight into the problems that arise when trying to realize GKS in a specific environment, under practical circumstances. The book should also be valuable in supplementing university courses concerned with teaching the principles of implementing device-independent computer graphics. The book should be especially valuable outside Europe: in the U.S. and the rest of the Americas, in Asia, and in Australia, where Eurographics publications are not so widely disseminated and available.

With few exceptions, the widely available references on GKS concentrate on *describing* the standard itself, rather than on the issues associated with *implementing* the standard. Since the beginnings of the graphics standardization effort, the Eurographics Association, through its annual conferences and its journal *Computer Graphics Forum*, has promoted an open exchange of information about the design and testing of GKS and about GKS's relationship with the other components of a graphics system. However, these important papers are scattered across five years of publications. Many of the GKS papers - although important at the time - were of only transitory interest because they discussed aspects of GKS that were either made obsolete or resolved by subsequent changes to GKS as it evolved to its present form. The remaining papers are of enduring interest; the best of these we have gathered into this volume.

GKS was formally approved as an International Organization for Standardization standard (ISO 7942) on 15 August 1985; however, it has been technically frozen since late 1982. As of this writing, language bindings for GKS are in various states of standardization: FORTRAN, Pascal, and Ada are at the Draft International Standard (DIS) stage; consequently, they can be viewed as technically frozen. The C language binding has been registered only recently as a Draft Proposal (DP); consequently, it may change somewhat before being approved and published. The bibliography at the end of this introduction gives the official designations of the standards and suggests some textbooks on GKS.

This collection selected from all the papers presented at Eurographics Conferences or published in *Computer Graphics Forum* since 1981 is organized into four parts. The first section deals with architectures for GKS systems. Part two presents several extremely useful algorithms needed for the correct implementation of GKS. Part three addresses the topics of certifying and formally specifying GKS. The fourth part deals with proposals for bindings to languages - Prolog and ALGOL68 - not currently planned for standardization by ISO/TC97/SC21/WG2, the standards body responsible for computer graphics within the ISO Technical Committee on Information Processing.

We hope you will find these papers interesting, instructive, and ultimately valuable. We would like to acknowledge the generous cooperation of the editors and publishers of *Computer Graphics Forum* who assisted us in assembling this collection. We hope you find our efforts worthwhile.

We also would like to recognize the substantial contributions of David Duce and Bob Hopgood, who coordinated the production of this next volume in the EurographicSeminars series.

Peter R. Bono
Gales Ferry, Connecticut
U.S.A.

Ivan Herman
Budapest
Hungary
Current address: Munich
Federal Republic of Germany

January, 1987

Textbooks

1. F. R. A. Hopgood, D. A. Duce, J. R. Gallop and D. C. Sutcliffe, *Introduction to the Graphical Kernel System (GKS)*, Academic Press, Second Edition (1986).

2. G. Enderle, K. Kansy and G. Pfaff, *Computer Graphics Programming: GKS - The Graphics Standard*, Springer-Verlag, Heidelberg, Second Edition (1987).

The Standards	ISO Document Designation
GKS	ISO 7942 - 1985
GKS FORTRAN	ISO DIS 8651/1
GKS Pascal	ISO 2nd DIS 8651/2
GKS Ada	ISO DIS 8651/3
GKS C	ISO DP 8651/4
GKS-3D	ISO DIS 8805
GKS-3D FORTRAN	ISO DP 8806/1

Table of Contents

The original source of each paper, and year of publication, is indicated by *CGF* (*Computer Graphics Forum*) or *EG* (*Eurographics conference proceedings*) after the authors' names.

x

Part I: Concepts and Architectures

Although GKS (and its extensions to three-dimensions, GKS-3D) is a fully specified set of functions, its size and complexity means that a careful software design should be made prior to any kind of implementation, if acceptable size and speed characteristics are to be achieved. In other words, avoiding the pitfalls depends largely on the software skills and experience of the implementors. Hence, it has always been of great interest to see how other implementations are organized or structured. The actual architecture depends on the environment where GKS is expected to run. In this section, we have selected two papers which aim at a special GKS Workstation realization in a raster environment (**Lindner and Rix**; **Rix**), while three others are concerned with general software problems (**Buhtz**; **Herman and Reviczky**; **Herman et al.**). Another paper (**Encarnacao et al.**) deals with the VLSI implementation of GKS, a problem which gains more and more importance nowadays with the availability of advanced graphics chips from Intel, Thomson, National Semiconductor Corporation, Texas Instruments etc. Finally, **Reynolds'** paper gives an overview of a process-oriented graphic system architecture, an approach that also may be of great interest in the future.

Most of these papers appeared fairly early in the development of GKS. Consequently, they refer to early versions of GKS. The final GKS version was version 7.4; any earlier versions will differ from the final version in several details. Nevertheless, the architectural concepts described are still valid and useful to implementors.

A GKS Interface to a Realtime Oriented Raster Workstation for CAD Applications

R. Lindner and J. Rix

1 Introduction

Although raster graphics is becoming more and more common, graphics users are still much more familiar with vector graphics. The reason is mainly historical. For technical reasons vector graphics devices were available much earlier than raster devices. Consequently the amount of experience with raster graphics is still comparatively low.

Some extensions to a 3 dimensional graphics system to satisfy the demands of raster graphics have been described by Foley [1]. This paper will discuss how the Graphical Kernel System, GKS, can support CAD applications with realtime demands on raster workstations. Version 6.6 of the Graphical Kernel System [3] is examined with regard to these demands and suggestions made to remove potential bottlenecks.

The term "realtime operation" is used here to mean that the time delay between any specified change in the display file and the corresponding effect appearing on the screen is short enough that neither the user notices it nor any interactive functions (lightpen tracking etc.) are degraded. This means that the time delay is definitely less than 40 milliseconds.

The raster workstation considered here has a pixel refresh memory and may have realtime processors for primitives (vectors, polygons etc.) and special functions (like multiple priority evaluators etc.). The rapid progress in the field of VLSI will allow the installation of such processors even in medium and low cost devices in the near future.

CAD applications cover a wide range of different techniques. They not only include the classical techniques of 2D and 3D construction but also techniques like IC Mask Layout, Printed Circuit Design, Pattern Design and many other applications. Many of these applications have a strong requirement for raster graphics.

2   Realtime Raster Graphics

2.1   Reasons for Using Raster Graphics

Three motivations for using raster graphics are:

(1)   a raster screen, which may be TV compatible, can be used;

(2)   vector graphics can be enlarged by introducing new attributes;

(3)   new primitives can be introduced which are only viable with raster graphics.

While the first aims to enlarge the field of graphics applications and to make use of the TV technology, the second and especially the third aim to improve the quality of the pictures. However they make substantial demands on both software and hardware. This paper will attempt to define these demands.

The first important improvement of the raster format is full colour capability. Nearly the complete spectrum is accessible. As primitives are broken down into pixels, colour and intensity may change within primitives. Only the primitive "pixel" exists in raster format and more complex primitives have to be mapped onto pixels either by an intelligent device driver or the device itself.

The second important improvement is the ability to display areas. Using the vector format, this is only possible by abstraction and the use of hatching. Such filling techniques are slow and do not allow fast enough refreshing of complex pictures.

By changing to raster graphics, some primitives and in particular area filling are freed from many restrictions. On the other hand coding problems arise when the new functions are used. Compromises have to be found but there is not enough experience yet to fix these. Consequently, a Graphical Kernel System must be kept flexible to allow it to adapt to future solutions.

When using raster graphics additional problems arise, which could be neglected while using vector graphics. Overlapping of primitives may be neglected while using vector graphics because presentation conflicts are mostly limited to points (crossings of lines) and in most cases single colours are used. Thus the user does not regard the presentation faults as errors. As soon as coloured areas are used, overlappings must be specified more precisely. Conflicts must be removed in the data structure or the priority of the overlapping areas specified. In the case of 3D applications, hidden surface elimination must be done while changing from 3D to 2D and before entering the 2D GKS. The segment priority attribute is not usually sufficient to define the priority.

2.2   Requirements

The most critical requirement in using realtime raster graphics is to comply with the time limitations in spite of the huge amount of computation, which is necessary to define each single pixel of the picture. The problem with handling coloured surface objects in realtime will be discussed in detail. Not only the problems inside the 2D GKS and its workstation will be considered but also the even more severe problems in the 3D modelling layer. A demanding application is assumed and the bottlenecks in data processing and data transportation between picture data definition and picture presentation are evaluated. The results of this evaluation can be used to extract the problems relevant to simpler applications (for example, 2D applications without representation conflicts). Only graphical output is discussed here as the main bottlenecks occur in output. An algorithm for scan conversion and priority handling [2] is considered, which by its very nature allows a high degree of parallel processing and, therefore, is able to make use of VLSI technology which will be indispensable in the near future.

The validity of the following results is not limited by the particular algorithm. Other algorithms are at best equal in complexity to the algorithm considered here and consequently require less processor and memory resources.

2.2.1   Models to Estimate Minimal Computation Time

To estimate the minimal computation time, a model has to be defined for the complete system, from the properties of the graphical data, to the computation power of the arithmetic processor and the capabilities of the display device.

Figure 1 shows the model of the complete system, being a sequence of transformations through which the graphical data passes from the application data storage to the screen. The *Modelling Transformations* is the graphical part of the application program. A perspective transformation and 3D windowing separates part of the *user world* and provides a 2D data set for the GKS system to output.

The *GKS Transformations* include the normalization transformation from world coordinates into normalized device coordinates and the workstation transformation from normalized device coordinates into device coordinates (segment transformations are not taken into consideration because they do not always apply).

The *Device Transformations* convert the picture data defined in device coordinates into device specific control signals. For raster output, scan conversion and especially the solving of presentation conflicts (e.g. by segment priorities) of overlapping primitives are included in this set of transformations.

The particular model of the graphical data considered consists of 1000 facets with 3 vertices each. Most vertices will belong to several facets, which may each have front and back sides. Thus, the total number of vertices may approach 500. Only very complicated and unusual constructions have less vertices per facet. Each vertex is coded by 3 geometrical coordinates (x, y and z) and 3 colour values (R, G and B) in floating point format. The average size of a facet on the screen is considered to be 20 raster units.

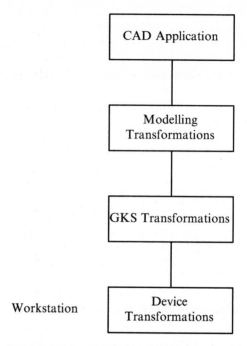

Figure 1 Data Flow in the System

The model for the computational power of the arithmetic processor is character-ized by the following features. The floating point operations addition, subtraction, multiplication and division require 5 microseconds each, the comparison 1 microsecond and data type conversion 2 microseconds. The fix point operations addition, subtraction and comparison require 0.5 microseconds each, multiplication and division (4 bytes) 4 microseconds each. Besides the time for the arithmetic operations themselves additional time is needed for program control and data flow organization. This fact is taken into account by an overhead factor of 5.

The model for the capabilities of the display device is characterized by a screen resolution of 512 by 512 raster points. Each point (pixel) is considered to be coded by 3 bytes (1 byte for red, green and blue each). The refresh rate is considered to be 25 cycles per second (40 milliseconds frame repetition rate).

2.2.2   Minimum Time Estimate for the Modelling Transformations

It is assumed that the perspective transformation is realized by a hardware 4×4 matrix. Each coordinate value requires 17 floating point operations. For 500 ver-tices with 3 geometrical coordinates each and 5 microseconds for each floating point operation, a computation time of 500×3×17×5×5 = 637,500 microseconds is required.

For the 3D windowing, each geometrical coordinate requires at least 2 comparisons with the window cube in floating point. These take a computation time of $500 \times 3 \times 2 \times 1 \times 5 = 15,000$ microseconds.

2.2.3   Minimum Time Estimate for the GKS Transformations

In the best case, the normalization transformation is reduced to a grid conversion of world coordinates. This transformation requires 1 floating point multiplication and 1 floating point addition for each geometrical coordinate. Therefore, this transformation requires a computation time of $500 \times 2 \times (5+5) \times 5 = 50,000$ microseconds.

If representation conflicts (overlappings) for primitives are to be solved in addition, a 3D system has to process the z-coordinate also. This requires $500 \times 1 \times (5+5) \times 5 = 25,000$ microseconds computation time.

The workstation transformation is another grid conversion of normalized coordinates into device coordinates, combined with 2D windowing. For each geometrical coordinate, 1 floating point multiplication, 1 floating point addition, 1 data type conversion and 2 floating point comparisons (for the 2D window checking) are required. From this results a computation time of $500 \times 2 \times (5+5+1+1+2) \times 5 = 70,000$ microseconds.

The additional computation time for the z-coordinate processing is $500 \times 1 \times (5+5+1+1+2) \times 5 = 35,000$ microseconds.

2.2.4   Minimum Time Estimate for the Device Transformations

Scan conversion may be looked upon as a pipeline of processing steps.

In the first step, for each facet it has to determine which edges are to the left and the right edges of the screen. This computation also provides the extreme coordinates (top, bottom, left and right) of the facet. The computation requires normally 5 fixed point comparisons for each facet. From this a computation time of $1000 \times 5 \times 0.5 \times 5 = 12,500$ microseconds results.

In the second step, the extreme coordinates are used to sort the facets. This sorting and the storage of the extreme coordinate values is required to organize an *active edge list* in order to avoid unnecessary computations. For the sorting a procedure of the rank $n \log(n)$ is assumed. 10,000 fixed point comparisons are required. A computation time of $10000 \times 0.5 \times 5 = 25,000$ microseconds results from this. The computation time for the active edge list organization is (optimistically) assumed to be included.

In the third step, the interpolations are initialized. These are required later to compute the location and the start values for the left facet border, the location of the right lower facet border and the values for the single pixels. As far as facets use the pen attribute, only the facet border locations have to be interpolated. Any of the 3 vectors of each facet requires an initialization for its x coordinate interpolation. Each initialization requires 2 subtractions and 1 division in fixed point. A computation time of $1000 \times 3 \times (0.5+0.5+4) \times 5 = 75,000$ microseconds results from this.

If shading of the facets is added, the initialization has to be extended to the 3 colour components. Only the left facet borders are important because they hold the start values. On average, about every second facet has 2 left edges, all the other facets have only one. For each facet the scan line interpolation increments for each of the 3 colour components must be computed. Altogether, a computation time of $1000\times(3/2+1)\times3\times(0.5+0.5+4)\times5 = 187,500$ microseconds results.

If there are presentation conflicts (overlappings) of primitives to be resolved, the interpolation increments for the z-coordinate must be computed also. For this an extra computation time of $1000\times(3/2+1)\times1\times(0.5+0.5+4)\times5 = 62,500$ microseconds is required.

In the fourth step, the line initialization of the facets is done scan line by scan line. For any active facet 2 fixed point additions are required for any change of the scan line in order to compute the facet borders in x. If the facets have an average size of 20 raster units (assumption in the model) a computation time of $1000\times20\times2\times0.5\times5 = 100,000$ microseconds is required.

If shading of the facets is required, an extra computation time of $1000\times20\times3\times0.5\times5 = 150,000$ microseconds is required for the 3 colour components.

If even presentation conflicts have to be resolved, the z-coordinate must be processed further, which requires $1000\times20\times1\times0.5\times5 = 50,000$ microseconds extra computation time.

Finally, in the fifth step the interpolation along the scan lines is performed if shading or solving of presentation conflicts have to be done. The average amount of points for a facet is 200 for the assumed size of 20 raster units. For the shading a computation time of $1000\times200\times3\times0.5\times5 = 1,500,000$ microseconds is required.

For solving representation conflicts each facet point requires 1 fixed point addition and on average 1 fixed point comparison (on average there are 40 active facets for each scan line and 2 active facets for each pixel). From this results a computation time of $1000\times200\times(0.5+0.5)\times5 = 1,000,000$ microseconds.

2.2.5   Results of the Minimum Time Estimation

Table 1 shows the computation times estimated above. In the case of the simplest but still useful 2D application modelling transformations, shading and conflict solving are not involved. The total computation time is still 332,500 microseconds.

If presentation conflicts are to be solved by making use of the segment priority, the computation time grows by 500,000 microseconds (on average 1 comparison for each pixel!) to 832,500 microseconds - nearly 1 second.

The frame rate (refresh time) in the assumed device model is 40 milliseconds. Thus, in the simplest case, the model is too slow by a factor of 8, and by a factor of 20 if presentation conflicts are resolved. If, in addition, shading has to be done, the factor increases to 65. Finally, if all the presentation conflicts of a 3D application have to be solved, the model system is too slow by a factor of about 100.

The very high data transmission rate of 3 bytes (one byte each for the 3 colour components R, G and B) for each pixel adds to all the problems of computation time. A pixel rate of 100 nanoseconds requires a data transmission rate of 30 Mbytes/sec in parallel with the extensive computation requirements. The transmission rate itself is already more than most modern minicomputers can do.

Computation Time (microseconds)	Basic Algorithms	Shading	Conflict Solving
Modelling Transformations:			
- Perspective Transformation	637500		
- 3D Windowing	15000		
GKS Transformations:			
- Normalization Transformation	50000		25000
- Workstation Transformation	70000		35000
Device Transformations:			
- Facet Border Evaluation	12500		
- Facet Sorting	25000		
- Facet Initialization	75000	187500	62500
- Scan Line Interpolation	100000	150000	50000
- Pixel Interpolation		1500000	1000000
	985000	1837500	1172500

Table 1: Minimum Computation Times

3   A GKS Interface to a Raster Workstation

3.1   Introduction

In previous sections the problems existing in raster graphics have been described and an estimation of the computation time has been produced for a conventional device configuration without using any special processors. For a CAD application for 2D and 3D objects, we will discuss the possibilities of handling the picture data in real-time using GKS.

On the one hand there is the problem of high computation time, and on the other there is the high data transfer rate. The computation cannot be done fast enough in GKS and the data cannot be transferred through GKS as long as conventional computers are used. The easiest solution will be to execute most of the calculations in the raster output device by special hardware. This will also solve the problem of the high data transfer rate.

In connection with GKS the following questions are of special interest:

(1)   To what extent can GKS support raster devices?

(2)   How can raster devices support GKS?

(3)   How might GKS be enhanced?

(4)   What are the limitations of GKS?

GKS includes primitives for vector graphics, and in addition, two primitives with attributes to support raster graphics. Experience with raster graphics has been growing steadily. GKS must be prepared to meet future demands and be kept simple at the same time. We have to discuss the details of such a compromise.

3.2 Present State of the GKS Standard

In GKS version 6.6 two output primitives (PIXEL ARRAY and FILL AREA), the modal attributes and Segment Priority are provided to support raster workstations.

3.2.1 PIXEL ARRAY

The output primitive *pixel array* is a versatile and flexible mechanism to perform unrestricted raster graphics output, and does not have any limitations worth mentioning. The calculation of all pixels has to be done within the modelling transformations before entering GKS. Then the pixel data are transformed by the GKS transformations. We have seen that a conventional computer is not even able to calculate the raster scan conversion in realtime. Transforming pixel arrays is an even heavier burden for a conventional computer.

3.2.2 FILL AREA

The output primitive *fill area* is easy to code but restricted in its effects. The representation of an area is defined by a closed polyline and its attributes.

This primitive allows us to execute the scan conversion by a special processor in the raster device. This reduces the load on the conventional computer considerably and allows faster output at the workstation.

3.2.3 Modal Attributes

Additional data information passes across the GKS interface via the attributes and allows more computation to be shifted to the special processor in the output device.

The modal attribute used with the primitive *fill area* is the *current interior style*. Currently three values are available: HOLLOW, SOLID and PATTERN. The attributes HOLLOW and SOLID are specified by the current pen number, the attribute pattern by the current pattern and the current pattern reference point.

The current pen number, specifies an index into the colour table, the current pattern is defined by a matrix of indices into the colour table, the size of the pattern rectangle and the current pattern reference point.

These modal attributes of the fill area primitive cannot be changed after definition. Independent of the modal attributes the colours in the colour table can be changed dynamically by the function SET COLOUR TABLE.

Powerful devices contain the look up table and therefore enable a reduction of the amount of data to be transferred by GKS. If not included in the device, the look up table must be simulated by GKS, as all functions are simulated which the device is unable to perform.

3.2.4 Segment Priority

The attribute *segment priority* solves conflicts of overlapping primitives within segments with different priorities. This mechanism can be realized by the device hardware and reduces computation effort in GKS.

As shown above, GKS version 6.6 allows the use of special hardware for scan conversion, for the solution of the presentation conflicts of overlapping surfaces, and for the use of a look up table (figure 2). By this it is possible to generate realtime raster output for 2D applications if a powerful raster device is available. Segment priority in a 3D application can be used to differentiate z-coordinate ranges of the objects. If a device provides a large number of priority levels, segmentation of the object can resolve most of the presentation conflicts. Some special cases are not solvable, e.g. two surfaces that penetrate each other.

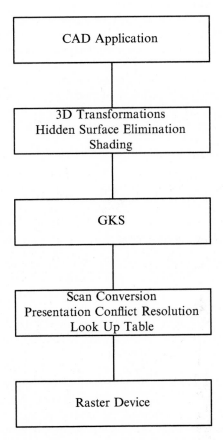

Figure 2 Data Flow in GKS Version 6.6

3.3   Possible Raster Graphics Extensions of GKS

With more information at the device interface many more expected capabilities of future raster devices can be used. Like linestyle or linewidth for vector graphics output, equivalent information for raster graphics output should pass through GKS extending the current attributes or introducing new attributes.

The introduction of a *shading attribute* is a possibility for output of shaded objects. The shading calculation could be performed inside GKS by special hardware in the raster device. For further enhancement it would be possible to introduce special functions of the GENERALIZED DRAWING PRIMITIVE. To satisfy the requirements of realtime output for extensive pictures, it can be useful to partition the object data into an active part and a passive one.

3.3.1   Shading Attribute

A shading attribute should be an extension of the interior style attribute of the Fill Area primitive. The introduction of such an attribute is discussed in a moment. It would be useful for many 2D and 3D applications, but would be difficult to implement. The use of lighting models for 3 dimensional shading is too complex for a kernel system. One possibility for 2 dimensional shading is given.

The necessary information for a shaded facet can be defined by the geometrical coordinates and the colour specification of three points, connected with the facet. By this the colour of any point of the facet is defined and is not influenced by GKS transformations. The data of the three points are used for interpolation and therefore they must not be clipped.

The shading attribute allows shaded objects to be displayed on a raster device. If the raster device has special hardware for interpolation, even realtime processing is possible. The complexity of pictures which may be processed in realtime depends on the power of the raster device hardware.

3.3.2   Generalized Drawing Primitive

The Generalized Drawing Primitive (GDP) in GKS version 6.6 is defined by an implementation dependent function code, 2 dimensional geometrical data in a fixed format and an array of data. The function with the defined parameters is interpreted by the device in a special way. On the geometric data, GKS performs all GKS transformations. The GDP may use the current GKS attributes. The data array including additional parameters or attributes, which are not influenced by GKS transformations, is useful for many applications.

For example, the approximation of a curve needs the order of approximation as additional information; the colour information for a shaded area may be passed through GKS using a parameter array. A three dimensional application with raster graphics needs visibility information at the device, if there are realtime demands. This information is derived from the z-coordinates. It can be transferred by the attribute array and can be interpreted by an intelligent workstation. Any other workstation drivers should interpret the drawing function SHADED AREA internally as the GKS function FILL AREA, using the modal attributes of the primitive instead of the supplementary information of the attribute array, or should send an error message to the user (implementation dependent).

3.3.3 Applications Using a Large Amount of Data

To work in realtime with a large number of objects the data set has to be partitioned in an active and a passive part. Figure 3 shows the data flow for such a system.

On raster workstations the passive data including visibility information are stored in the pixel memory. The active data are refreshed continuously in the modelling layer and passed through the GKS transformations to the special workstation with the raster device. There, the scan conversion, the shading and the visibility interpretation are performed. Afterwards, the calculated active pixels are combined with the passive pixels from the pixel memory dependent on their visibility values. The pixels with the higher visibility value are displayed on the display surface.

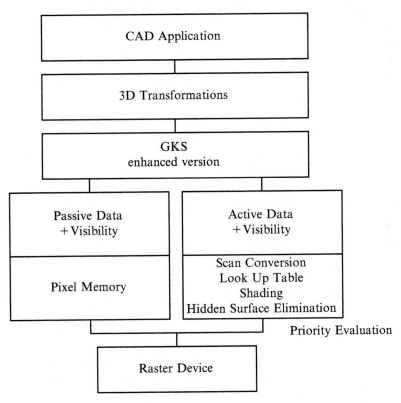

Figure 3 Processing Large Amounts of Data in the Extended GKS

4 Realtime Applications with GKS

The present GKS version 6.6 already supports many raster graphics applications. Small extensions such as the ones discussed above, can be used to meet the obvious trends in raster device development. The shading attribute and the use of special functions of the generalized drawing primitive will allow the presentation of shaded objects even with hidden surface elimination in realtime, as soon as powerful raster devices are available.

References

1.   J. Foley, J. Templeman, and D. Dastyar, "Some Raster Graphics Extensions to the Core System," *Computer Graphics* **13**(2), pp.15-24 (1979).

2.   R. Lindner, "Rasterdisplay-Prozessoren - Ihre Bedeutung, Konzepte und Verfahren," D17 Darmstadter Dissertation, Fachbereich Informatik, TH Darmstadt (1979). (In German.)

3.   ISO WG2, "Graphical Kernel System (GKS) Version 6.6," ISO TC97/SC5/WG2 (1981).

On Developing a GKS Driver Architecture for Raster Workstations

J. Rix

1 Introduction

Experience with raster graphics is still growing and more applications are taking advantage of raster device technology. A device driver is needed to support applications using the raster facilities.

The driver is the connection between the application program and the physical devices for graphical output and input. The graphics standard GKS [4] was defined because of the variety of ways of adapting a device to each different application.

The Graphical Kernel System describes the logical interface to graphical workstations. The kernel system includes a set of functions independent of devices and application programs. In GKS the functionality of each available graphical device is described in the appropriate workstation description table. Depending on this description the workstation functions of GKS are either sent directly to the device interface, or are evaluated within the workstation driver and mapped to existing device functions [2].

As figure 1 shows, each device needs a driver for its own special hardware facilities. In order to reduce the number of driver implementations, it is necessary to design a driver architecture which can handle several devices.

The ideas to be presented here arise from experience with GKS implementations on different raster graphics systems:

● the Videograph Raster Display System;

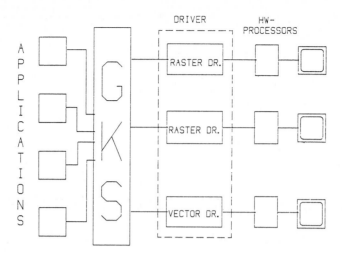

Figure 1 Structure of a Graphics System

- the PAN 30 Colour Display System;
- the PERQ Raster Device;
- the ICAN Raster Workstation;
- and the realtime Raster Workstation based on a Multi-microprocessor system that is being developed at our Institute and will be completed next year [6, 7].

These systems are examined in order to analyse the different device features that will be exploited in the raster driver.

2   Raster Device Facilities

The most important advantage of raster technology is the possibility for filling areas with the complete range of colours.

One disadvantage of raster graphics is how to handle the problem of overlapping areas. This can be solved by use of a priority attribute.

The main difference between the technology of vector and raster displays is that the former has a display file which includes segment information, whilst the picture in the latter is refreshed from the pixel memory. Only the colour value or index to the colour look-up table is stored for each pixel. There is no structure information. This means that each modification of the picture structure requires a complete update of the picture from the segment storage, and this will not be possible in real-time (in the refresh cycle) for the next few years. Thus segment handling, pick interrupts and updating of frames are not usually performed by the device (with the exception of realtime output processors).

Special hardware features have been developed to support some raster graphics functions, for example:

● dynamic colour change (look-up table);

● pattern representation;

● storage planes (pixel planes);

● writing modes (replace, xor, etc.).

The use of a colour look-up table is the only dynamic change within the pixel memory. The colour of a pixel is determined by a colour index in the refresh cycle. Most raster systems have this capability, for example, Videograph, PAN 30 and ICAN. In the PAN 30 system a pattern table will be included to allow areas to be filled with 16×16 patterns, after the segment transformation (rotation) has been applied.

To change a picture, for example to delete or to transform one object, typically requires the complete picture to be redrawn into the pixel memory. This may be quite time-consuming. To obviate this problem one can make use of different storage planes and/ or the xor writing mode instead of the replace mode [5].

1(a) If the storage planes are independent of each other, double buffering is possible, so that the interactive user does not notice the new drawing every time. The Videograph system, for example, has four independent planes.

(b) The storage planes are not independent. This means that they are combined or super-imposed during the refresh output. In this case the problem of overlapping areas can be solved, if objects are distributed to planes dependent on their segment priority. Additionally, when a picture is changed, only the objects in the affected planes need to be redrawn.

(2) When xor mode is used, the modification of an object can be achieved by redrawing the object only once (to delete) or twice (to transform, once at the old location and once at the new transformed location). However, the disadvantage is that overlapping parts of objects are drawn with an xor-mixed colour or colour index and this solution may be excluded for applications where there is a lot of overlapping. However, this undesirable effect may be acceptable for fast picture editing. After the editing session, an update to correct the picture may be needed.

A lot of devices allow the use of different modes. The combination of modes can be useful, for example, replace and xor. A static background picture is displayed with replace mode and then the dynamic or detectable picture elements are displayed with xor. Input prompts and echoes are also written into pixel memory with xor.

To gain some experience, a workstation driver for the PAN 30 system was implemented using xor mode.

Another facility is to expand the pixel memory, so that in addition to colour (index) value, each pixel stores:

(a)   the segment priority to solve overlappings during writing into memory or during the combination of storage planes, or

(b)   the segment name to facilitate fast pick input identification.

3   Use of Raster Features with GKS

After much discussion the GKS raster extensions have been included in the standard. Two output primitives are provided, CELL ARRAY and FILL AREA. CELL ARRAY allows special raster technology to make changes to sets of pixels. The primitive is mapped by grid conversion to the precision of the device or is defined directly for one device in pixel coordinates.

The FILL AREA primitive has the attribute INTERIOR STYLE. Both vector and raster presentations are then possible. The area can be filled with one colour, a defined pattern, or can be hatched on a vector device or just the boundary can be displayed.

The visual presentation of overlapping areas may be solved using segment priorities, or if xor mode is used, it is not necessary to solve the problem because areas are displayed in a mixed colour representation.

Because the picture is refreshed from pixel memory, it has to be rebuilt after every interactive picture change. To realize such an update on a raster device in an efficient way and with an acceptable response time, requires the features of the device to be taken into account. It appears that a GKS workstation driver has to be written in a special way to adapt to all these different device features.

Figure 2 explains the interfaces and parts of the driver. The virtual device (VDI) or DI/DD interface between the two parts of the driver is a flexible one. The functional extent is defined by the description of the device with its special raster facilities. The workstation driver maps the GKS functions to the described device functions.

In the output pipeline of a workstation, for example, the following functions have to be executed:

> Segment handling and transformation
> Workstation transformation and clipping
> Attribute binding (area filling or colour assignment)
> Scan or grid conversion
> Priority evaluation

This mapping of the workstation functions will be simulated by the GKS workstation driver in a similar straightforward way for all workstations; but none of the special functions will be taken into consideration other than by specific driver software.

On the other hand, with the growing functionality of graphical devices more and more driver functions will be taken over by the hardware (for example, the scan conversion of lines and areas). These functions will be useful only if their definitions conform to the GKS definitions. For example, many devices provide area filling, but often self-intersecting polygons are not supported. GKS allows self-intersecting polygons and it may be more efficient to use the software scan conversion in the standard driver, rather than to check the polygon for intersections and then divide

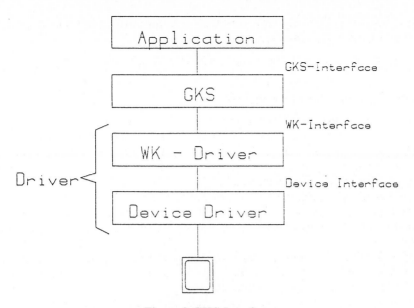

Figure 2 GKS Interfaces

into non-intersecting polygons which can be handled by the device. To achieve higher efficiency in a workstation, the device must provide functions that are similar to the standard functions. This means that device manufacturers must pay attention to the GKS functionality [3].

As an example, a driver for the PAN 30 raster display system was implemented [8]. This system uses a pixel memory with 1000×2000 pixels, each with 8 bits as an index into the colour look-up table. The PAN 30 has an LSI 11/23 as a workstation processor. The configuration of the GKS implementation is shown in figure 3.

The distribution of GKS and the driver to the host and the workstation processor allows a powerful workstation with a device dependent segment storage that reduces the data flow between GKS and the workstation. In the device, a colour table with 256 entries and a pattern table for 16×16 patterns are available. In the next development step, rotation of patterns with the object and rotation of PIXEL ARRAYs will be added. Later on, the xor mode for writing into the pixel memory will be used, in order to explore the possibilities and disadvantages. The advantages of fast picture modification, without redrawing the complete picture, must be compared with the undesirable effects in some applications which result from the mixed colour of over-lapping objects.

Because of the problem that two different writing modes cannot be addressed by GKS (other than through the ESCAPE function), this implementation only uses the xor mode. It would be possible to use combinations of modes, e.g. replace and xor, internally within the driver, for example, to write a static background picture with replace and the dynamic part with xor. In this case, it has first to be decided what is static and what is dynamic. Then the background is displayed and afterwards the dynamic part (for example, the detectable segments). To get a correct picture at the

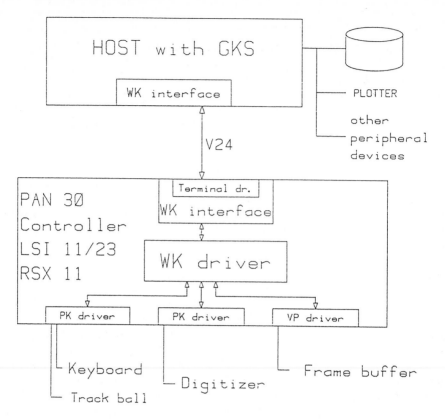

Figure 3 Configuration of the GKS - PAN 30 Workstation

end, the final version can be updated, drawn using replace mode. Only picture changes require output to be handled differently from normal.

The same difficulties occur with an implementation using different storage planes:

(a)   They can be used only inside the driver, for example to hold the update in double buffering, or the distribution of objects to different planes, combined during the output refresh. Here the decision which segment to allocate to which plane can be solved with segment priorities, but within a single plane overlappings must first be resolved.

(b)   They can be controlled with the ESCAPE function.

(c)   They can be controlled as different workstations (that requires great care on the part of the user of the GKS system to control it in a consistent way, for example the attribute settings must be the same for all planes, because there will only be one colour table).

But these solutions or their combinations always need a special workstation implementation.

4   Architecture of a GKS Raster Driver

It will be difficult to handle all these device functions in a common driver, because of
the effect on other functions. For example the use of different storage planes or the
xor mode affects segment storage and picture updating. It is possible to solve this
inside the workstation driver. However if, for example, an application programmer
wants to use different modes to write into the pixel memory in his application, he
has to use the special functions Generalized Drawing Primitive (GDP) or ESCAPE.
This means that special workstation driver functions are also needed to handle this.

As a result of this discussion the following solution can be proposed. There will
be a set of modules realizing the kernel driver functions, which will exist for each
workstation. This will be the greatest common part of all drivers. These functions
include, for example, segment transformation, workstation transformation, and attribute bundles. The goal of this driver architecture is to discover and implement as
many kernel functions as possible [5]. In addition to these kernel functions, there
will be a set of specific functions for a class of devices (here raster devices): scan
conversion, colour look-up table, pattern table, etc. The kernel and the device
specific functions are needed to define a minimal driver.

Because of the way the driver is defined, the functionality required is the same for
different devices, also the functionality of the modules implementing the drivers is
the same. The way in which a function is implemented may be different, for example, clipping a vector against a rectangle (2 points → 2 points) or clipping raster
points (n points → m points $n \geq m$).

A third layer of driver functions includes those to adapt to the special device facilities mentioned above.

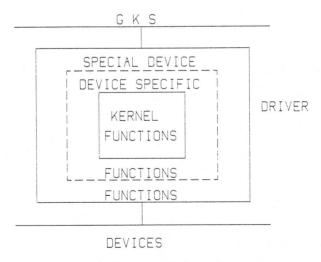

Figure 4 Layer Model of Workstation Functions

All these functions have to be implemented as isolated software modules with well-defined interfaces, so that they are independent of each other and of the order of the pipeline processes. To be able to implement all these functions will be advantageous for any new type of raster device. The implementation work will be reduced, because the existing software solutions can be used without any change, as long as these functions are defined in that function layer. That means, a driver is a specific configuration of these software modules. The necessary modules are chosen and combined depending on the requirements of the application program, the user characteristics and the hardware functions and facilities of the raster device [1, 9].

The possibility of using these special device functions mentioned above may also be dependent on the application requirements for the graphics system. Then a special driver structure will be generated, which is dependent on the functions taken over by the hardware and on the facilities to be used.

A modular structure with well-defined interfaces is also advantageous for distributing the driver functions in multi-processor architectures.

References

1.   R. Anderl, J. Rix, and H. Wetzel, "GKS im Anwendungsberieich CAD," *Informatik Spektrum* **2**(2), pp.76-81, Springer-Verlag, Heidelberg (April 1983). (In German.)

2.   G. Enderle, K. Kansy, and G. Pfaff, *Computer Graphics Programming: GKS, the Graphics Standard,* Springer-Verlag, Heidelberg (1983).

3.   P. J. W. ten Hagen, "The review of GKS version 7.0, the finishing touch," *Computer Graphics Forum* **1**(4), pp.204-212 (1982).

4.   ISO, "Information processing systems - Computer graphics - Graphical Kernel System (GKS) functional description," ISO 7942, ISO Central Secretariat (August 1985).

5.   D. Kromker, G. Pfaff, and J. Rix, "Multimikroprozessoren und Rastertreiber Arbeitsklausur Wenschdorf, Nov. 1982," GRIS-Nr. 82-12, Forschungs- und Arbeitsbericht, FG Graphisch-Interaktive Systeme, Technische Hochschule Darmstadt. (In German.)

6.   R. Lindner and J. Rix, "A GKS interface to a realtime oriented raster workstation for CAD applications," in *Eurographics '81*, ed. J. L. Encarnacao, North-Holland (1981). (Reproduced in this Volume.)

7.   R. Lindner, "Multiple-Write Bus-Access in a Multi-microprocessor System," GRIS-Nr. 81-8, Forschungs- und Arbeitsbericht, FG Graphisch-Interaktive Systeme, Technische Hochschule Darmstadt.

8.   S. Noll, "Konzept und Realisierung einer interaktiven Rasterworkstation," Diplomarbeit, Fachgebiet Graphisch-Interaktive Systeme, Technische Hochschule Darmstadt (April 1983). (In German.)

9.   G. Pfaff and G. Maderlechner, "Tools for configuring interactive picture processing systems," *IEEE Computer Graphics and Applications*, pp.35-49 (July 1982).

CGM- Concepts and their Realization

R. Buhtz

1 Requirements and Design Concepts

Common Graphics Manager (CGM) is the name given to the implementation of GKS level 2B developed at the Free University of Berlin [1,6]. This paper is a survey of the early phase of the implementation (1980-1982).

Work commenced in February 1980. At the outset some basic design decisions were necessary on account of the special scientific computer environment in Berlin. The "Berlin GKS" was to be a common graphical software package for all the machines at the Free University [4]. The design decisions were:

- The software package had to be adaptable for different machine types with minimal effort. The original host computer for CGM is a CDC Cyber 835 (before that a Cyber 172). Further installations were planned for at least Siemens 7000-series (BS 2000) and Harris H 100-series. CGM is now installed on many other machine types, for example IBM, Vax and UNIVAC. The interfaces to operating system dependent modules had to be defined on such a level as to allow installation without a deep knowledge of GKS, because many of the satellite computers in the university environment are run by users and in general there is no local graphics specialist available.

- The implementation language had to be FORTRAN. From a modern viewpoint, FORTRAN is neither an elegant nor a comfortable programming language. In addition the fact that FORTRAN is available worldwide is not a decisive argument in its favour, for by a similar argument one would drop all GKS activities in favour of an existing, well known standard package such as Calcomp. Nevertheless it was decided to use FORTRAN because interfaces between FORTRAN and higher level languages such as ALGOL 68 and Pascal may be provided rather easily, whereas the problem of providing interfaces in the reverse direction has never been solved satisfactorily. Hence a FORTRAN implementation covers a larger number of users. Taking this in conjunction with the first requirement the language chosen was ANSI FORTRAN 66. Subsequently the implementation migrated to FORTRAN 77.

The GKS standard contains some important basic concepts which have to be realized by an implementation. GKS uses a set of internal tables which are conceptually dynamically allocated, that is they may be *requested* (for example Workstation State List during OPEN WORKSTATION) or *cancelled* (for example Workstation State List during CLOSE WORKSTATION). The total number of workstations simultaneously open or of segments simultaneously stored on different workstations is unknown in advance and is conceptually limitless. These considerations lead to the conclusion that for the efficient and correct realization of GKS some basic software components are required for dynamic allocation and deallocation of memory. To ensure fast access, and to avoid the storage of redundant information, data blocks have to be stored only once and additional modules for handling pointers and chained tables had to be provided.

GKS requires output primitives of unrestricted length to be handled, for example during transformation, clipping and routing to all active workstations; and requires such primitives to be accessed from internal segment storage. This leads to further dynamic requirements for a GKS implementation. Temporary auxiliary arrays of different lengths have to be provided for:

- copying information (e.g. area clipping; the clipped polygon may have more border points than the original, or may even be split into disjoint parts);

- reading information from segment storage (e.g for picture regeneration or INSERT);

- storage of dynamic attribute changes for the next UPDATE.

Such software components may be provided very easily in a high level language like ALGOL68 or Pascal. Algorithms may be found in any textbook for such languages [7].

The decision to implement CGM in ANSI FORTRAN 66 resulted in the definition of two smaller software packages:

- CGM Memory Manager;

- CGM Table Chain Manager.

These are not a part of GKS but were necessary to enhance the functional capability of ANSI FORTRAN 66 to provide pointers and dynamic arrays. There is no loss of portability here for the packages themselves are written in ANSI FORTRAN 66.

In this paper it will be shown how CGM implements GKS. Special issues of interest are:

- portability;

- efficiency;

- closeness to the standard.

2 CGM Memory Manager

The CGM Memory Manager is a subroutine package for handling dynamic memory blocks. It contains two subroutines which provide the following basic features: *Get Block* which allocates a block of length N and delivers a start address (relative to a fixed COMMON block) to the calling program; *Release Block* which marks the specified block as no longer in use, the block is then available for later *Get Block* calls. These two routines solve all the dynamic problems of GKS, for example "how many workstations may be opened at the same time?", "how many segments may exist at the same time?", "how large can output primitives be on segment storage?". These questions are reduced to one question: "how large does the dynamic buffer area of the CGM Memory Manager have to be?". By choosing a suitable dimension for one unstructured COMMON block, all applications can be accommodated.

The standard buffer limit can be tuned for a particular installation by setting appropriate installation parameters. It is not necessary to change the source code. Equally, it is so easy to increase the buffer limits that this may be left to the application programmer. Most systems allow the length of a common block to be increased, for example by using a BLOCKDATA subprogram. The user may work with any buffer length (within machine constraints) by linking such a module and calling a special routine which causes the CGM Memory Manager to rearrange its pointer chains appropriately. Thus a computing centre may provide a standard buffer length which meets the requirements of the majority of its users, without having to consider peak requirements. Demanding users can then override the defaults.

When the CLOSE GKS function is executed, information about memory usage is written to the error file.

The dynamic buffer area is used throughout CGM, using only the two routines described above. Thus it is possible to replace them by operating system specific routines as is being done for the CDC machine [2, 5]. The CDC operating systems provide an interface for requesting new field lengths during the lifetime of an application program, the so-called *Common Memory Manager*. The two CGM routines can be replaced by calls to the Common Memory Manager, delivering the base address of the requested block relative to the same COMMON block. Thus from the point of view of the higher CGM routines nothing has changed.

This leads to a basic concept of CGM. Whenever operating system oriented optimizations are possible (and useful) they may be performed easily by local staff, because an ANSI FORTRAN solution is provided which may be used immediately, and the interfaces are small and simple, so that special knowledge about the internal CGM structure is not necessary. The optimization may be performed in due course once the system is running.

3   CGM Table Chain Manager

The CGM Table Chain Manager is a subroutine package for handling pointers and chained tables required by GKS. An example is the list of all workstation state lists for open workstations which may vary in length depending on the number of workstation. Every workstation state list itself contains further dynamic tables, for example, pen tables. In practice this means that the workstation state list contains a pointer in the first pen table entry which points to the next and so on.

The CGM Table Chain Manager consists of routines for the following basic functions: adding new members to an existing (or new) chain; removing a member from a chain and rearranging the chain; accessing specific chain members; releasing complete chains. For these purposes memory allocation and deallocation is necessary. This is performed by the CGM Memory Manager. Hence the CGM Table Chain Manager is written in ANSI FORTRAN. Machine dependent optimization is unnecessary. The CGM Table Chain Manager can be used with every memory handling package that respects the Get/ Release Block interface. CGM table chains may coexist with unstructured temporary arrays because the CGM Table Chain Manager is only one special user of the CGM Memory Manager.

The following examples illustrate the cooperation of the different CGM table chains. First, as an easy example, consider setting a pen representation. If the user defines a new pen, the CGM Table Chain Manager requests a new memory block and fits it into the workstation pen table (see figure 1). The specified attributes are then entered into the block. Such a pen table can only grow during the lifetime of a workstation because GKS does not provide a "delete all pens" functions. The chain is released when the workstation is closed.

As a more complicated example, consider segments. Segments (and workstations) can be created and cancelled during the lifetime of an application program. The data blocks (the state lists themselves) are held centrally in GKS. The cross-references between segments and workstations are performed by pointers or chains of pointers (see figure 2). For example the CLOSE WORKSTATION routine should cancel everything in GKS connected with the workstation, so that after the function is executed it is as if the workstation had never been open. This is achieved by first accessing the data block of the workstation state list and releasing its subtables, such as the pen table, with the CGM Table Chain Manager. The chain of segments stored in the workstation is checked. For every segment this subtable contains a pointer to the segment state list. The segment state list contains a chain of pointers to all workstations on which the segment is stored. This chain has to be accessed for every segment stored on the actual workstation, and the pointer to this workstation has to be cancelled. If as a result the segment is not stored on any workstation, the segment itself is cancelled, its segment state list is released and its name is cancelled from the central list of segment names in use (inside GKS).

After this process, the chain of pointers to all these segments may be released, and - last but not least - the data block of the workstation state list is cancelled as well as the name of the workstation (from the central list of workstation identifiers in use). After this, all references to the workstation are cancelled.

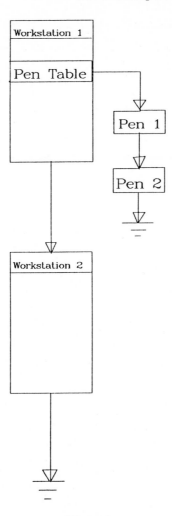

Figure 1

"Releasing" chain members is handled cooperatively: the CGM Table Chain Manager only rearranges the chain, the single memory block is passed to the CGM Memory Manager. If the neighbouring blocks to the released block are also unused, they are combined together so that the free space is maximized.

4   CGM's Segment Storage Concept

Segment storage is an internal workstation in GKS. Segments stored in segment storage can be used in the INSERT function. Segment storage in CGM is also used to hold an internal segment for simulating picture regeneration on unintelligent workstations, even without explicitly opening a segment storage workstation.

Cross References between Workstations and Segments

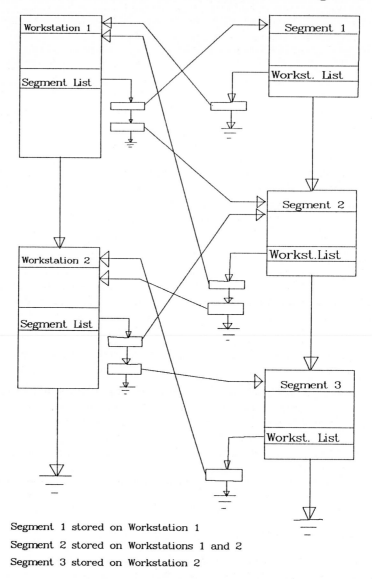

Segment 1 stored on Workstation 1

Segment 2 stored on Workstations 1 and 2

Segment 3 stored on Workstation 2

Figure 2

Interactive applications access the segment storage frequently, and so efficiency of access is important. ANSI FORTRAN 66 does not support direct access files and so it was necessary to define an interface (which was kept as simple as possible) to machine-dependent direct access routines. The interface only supports the transfer of unstructured memory blocks of fixed (installation dependent) size. There is a higher level layer (ANSI FORTRAN) which handles the decomposition (and reconstruction) of the GKS data structures at the DI/DD interface (device independent/ device dependent) into unstructured memory blocks.

It was known from the outset that it is not easy to generate modules to a special interface and localization of errors is difficult. A possibly unconventional method was used. In addition to defining the interface an ANSI FORTRAN solution was also provided by simulating direct access on a sequential binary FORTRAN file. Thus there is a reference version of CGM for comparison whilst an installation specific solution is developed. The full software can be tested immediately. The reference routines are not suitable for production use, though they are not so inefficient as one might suppose. This surprising fact is due to the way CGM uses segment storage for picture regeneration. Segments are in the main read in the same order as they were "generated" (i.e. as they were written to segment storage). Consequently in most cases segment storage is read sequentially and in such cases direct access cannot be faster than sequential access. There are only two cases in which real direct access is needed:

(1) Use of segment priorities: the user specifies explicitly the order in which segments are to be redrawn, i.e. which segments are "foreground" (high priority) or "background" (low priority). This opens up interesting applications, especially on raster devices. If the raster primitives FILL AREA and PIXEL ARRAY are used then automatic hidden surface removal is possible.

(2) Use of segment storage by the INSERT SEGMENT function. If a segment has to be copied into the open segment, direct access to the segment storage file is required.

Benchmarks on a CDC computer have shown that the ANSI FORTRAN routines are comparable in speed with assembler direct access routines for sequential reading (normal regeneration), whilst for real direct access usage (INSERT SEGMENT) there is a factor of 1:10 in favour of the assembler routines.

The same direct access interface is used by CGM to handle a second internal file, the CGM software text file.

CGM now uses FORTRAN 77 direct access i/o and no machine dependent routines are required.

5 Software Text in CGM

One of the most interesting facilities of GKS is the generation of software text using different fonts. The total number of available text fonts is implementation dependent. The storage of coordinates is carefully optimized in CGM.

There are now 9 text fonts available in CGM. These include standard text and high quality roman, italic and Greek fonts. In addition, special symbols for mathematics and natural sciences (e.g. integral and differential operators) and centred symbols are available. For CGM Version 4.0, which will implement GKS Version 7.0 (planned for the end of 1982) it is intended to implement all 21 of Hershey's character fonts including gothic fonts, cyrillic alphabet and further special symbols.

For all these fonts, an 8-bit representation for x and y coordinates is sufficient and so efficient data packing is possible as long as there is only one font in memory at a time. CGM text fonts are therefore kept on a direct access file in binary packed format. This file is accessed through the same interface as segment storage. At installation time, this file is generated from a coded data file contained in CGM, using a "CGM pre-processor". Portability was achieved because the file must be generated afresh for each installation. The modules themselves are portable. This concept is used elsewhere in CGM.

6 Pre-processors in CGM

Despite all portability considerations, two installations of CGM on different machines cannot be identical; even a package written in ANSI FORTRAN needs adaptation. Care was taken to try to reduce this adaptation work to a minimum. As this work is mainly straightforward, it is performed using pre-processors supplied with the CGM code.

One or more "files" are required for installation of a CGM component. These are either those provided with the CGM code or are supplied at installation time. A pre-processor operates on these files and generates new files in a form suitable for use on the given computer. Pre-processors are provided for the following tasks:

● *Source code tuning and setting installation parameters*: the input files are CGM code and a small data file containing the installation parameters (e.g. block lengths, dynamic buffer size, computer word length). The pre-processor produces several output files containing configured CGM source. Setting parameters by such a mechanism is not only easier than by hand, but is also safer.

● *Generating the internal software text file*: this pre-processor was mentioned in the last section. The input file is a coded text file (containing the text coordinates), the output file is a binary packed direct access file. This pre-processor can also be tuned through installation parameters (because it is a part of the CGM code) and thus it can use a machine dependent word length for packing etc. Another interesting feature is that the pre-processor is fully portable, but a binary WRITE produces different results on different computers, so that the resulting binary files are different. When this pre-processor is used after the installation of "real direct access" the software text file will be a direct access file.

● *Generating the DI/DD interface*: this pre-processor is used every time a new device driver is installed. It configures CGM for the local graphical environment. The input file is a coded file containing a data block for every graphical device, the so-called Workstation Description Tables. Entries include screen size, resolution and special features of the given workstation, for example whether it is able to change colours of primitives dynamically.

These data blocks are easy to maintain. The resulting output file contains the source for two subroutines. One subroutine is the physical DI/DD interface, in other words it contains FORTRAN CALL statements for every driver. The second subroutine contains all the workstation description tables in fast-access form. Hence, at runtime, no internal file or data conversion is required to access this frequently used data. The first subroutine contains call statements for all drivers. This implies that all drivers are linked to the application program even if they are not needed. In larger configurations this may lead to excessive memory requirements.

Following the CGM principle of allowing machine dependent optimizations, calls to dummy routines were provided in the OPEN WORKSTATION and CLOSE WORKSTATION routines which may be replaced by assembler routines for dynamic loading and unloading of drivers. Such modules are now available for CDC and IBM machines.

7   The Layer Structure of CGM

In conclusion, some remarks about the CGM code structure, especially with reference to portability, are in order (see figure 3).

The entire central code, "GKS itself", is located in the highest machine and device independent layer. The special GKS drivers for Metafile Output, Metafile Input and Segment Storage also belong to this layer. Thus CGM is immediately available on every computer, though some modules may be replaced for optimization. As soon as real devices are linked to CGM, modules must be device dependent. CGM drivers are structured such that some driver components are portable, to facilitate moving drivers to other machines and writing new drivers.

At the highest device driver interface, the central CGM code is interfaced to a device dependent but machine independent layer. Here all device dependent operations, for example conversion to ASCII-bytes, are performed. Experience has shown that such components can be written in ANSI FORTRAN without loss of efficiency. Some device independent tasks (for example workstation clipping, pick-simulation and software text generation) may be performed using a set of device independent driver utilities which are contained in this layer. Exporting a driver together with CGM code means that this second layer is included.

Connecting a file to a terminal and sending ASCII bytes to a terminal or plotter requires machine dependent modules, because they are impossible to write in ANSI FORTRAN (or at least not efficiently).

There are well-defined interfaces to be adhered to, but they are simple interfaces and do not require knowledge of the internal features of GKS. Only very simple I/O routines have to be provided and for terminals they can be provided in a device independent manner. Portability is possible in another sense, the same modules may be used for a range of drivers. This feature makes the installation of new drivers easier.

Note

Since this work was first presented in September 1982, the project has continued. As of March 1987, the implementation has been brought up to GKS Level 2B (as defined in ISO Standard 7942). It runs on a wide range of machines from IBM-PC's to the Cray-XMP. The system is designed for use in open networks (on top of the

CGM Layer Structure

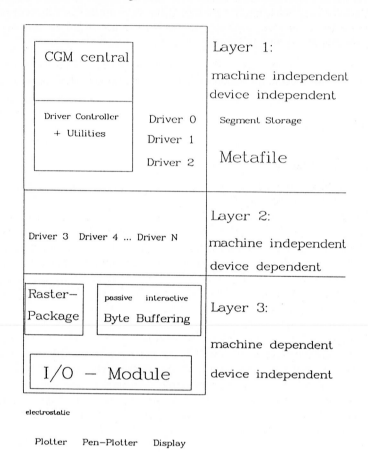

Figure 3

"Deutsches Forschungsnetz (DFN)") and is in use worldwide in universities, research centres and private industry. A further account of the system appears in [3].

References

1.   J. Bechlars and R. Buhtz, *CGM Handbook: Special Design Concepts and Installation Guide for COMMON GRAPHICS MANAGER Version 3.1,* Freie Universitat Berlin (April 1982).

2.   J. Bechlars, "Experiences with CGM, the Berlin GKS Implementation," *Conference Proceedings ECODU 33*, St. Paul, Minnesota (1982).

3.   J. Bechlars and R. Buhtz, *GKS in der Praxis,* Springer-Verlag (1986). (In German.)

4.   R. Buhtz, "Implementation Policy at the Free University of Berlin," in *Report on the Workshop on the Implementation of GKS at ECMWF*, ed. H. Watkins, ECMWF, Reading, Berkshire (UK) (1981).

5.   R. Buhtz, "The Berlin GKS-concepts and their Realization on a CYBER," *Conference Proceedings ECODU 31*, Helsinki (1981).

6.   ISO, "Information processing systems - Computer graphics - Graphical Kernel System (GKS) functional description," ISO 7942, ISO Central Secretariat (August 1985). (This paper refers to the earlier version of GKS, 6.4.)

7.   H. Rumpel and R. Buhtz, *Einfuhrung in ALGOL 68, Bd II*, Freie Universitat Berlin (1977). (In German.)

A General Device Driver for GKS

I. Herman and J. Reviczky

1 Introduction

When implementing GKS in some kind of a software environment, one is faced, sooner or later, with a major practical problem: the extreme diversity of the currently available graphic devices. If the implementor chooses the thorny path of entering the software market with a new GKS implementation, the demand for newer and newer device drivers (i.e. workstations, in GKS terminology) is steadily growing. Devices are different in local processing capabilities, in precision, in their way of coding, one has rich possibilities for text drawing but cannot do area filling, while the other one is just the opposite.

After a certain amount of time the GKS implementor will acquire the practice of writing new device drivers by making use of old drivers, changing the code here and there, adding some new code and omitting inappropriate code. This method is quite prone to errors, and it can be made only by a person who has a perfect knowledge of the code itself, in other words it cannot be made by "outsiders".

A much better solution is to have an extensive set of individual functions stored somehow and a good and, as far as possible, automatic method to "create" the new device driver. This is what we have attempted to do, and what will be presented in what follows.

2 General Outlook

Our research group began the implementation of a full level 2c GKS in Autumn 1982 and had practically finished the work in March 1984. The program has been written in the C language and it runs under UNIX-like and RSX-11 operating systems. The structure of the implementation has been presented already at the EUROGRAPHICS'83 conference in Zagreb [3]. The only relevant feature of the implementation in the present context is the fact that each workstation is a separate process (or "task" in RSX terminology) communicating with the Device Independent process/task through a communication channel ("pipe" under UNIX, a simulation of pipes under RSX). The communication goes with the help of a protocol we have called HVDI, which is more or less on the same level as the current ISO CGI proposal [5] or the WSI of the DIN-NI position paper [1].

The workstation process has to do clipping, performing the segment and workstation transformations, filling polygons, drawing STROKE precision texts etc. and finally driving directly the graphic hardware itself, that is generating the appropriate bit-patterns going for example through the communication line.

The work to be done by the process itself depends of course on the hardware capabilities; if SOLID fill area can be made locally then it should be left to the hardware; on the other hand the process is eventually to contain e.g. a hatching algorithm to perform HATCH style fill area.

Creating a new workstation is therefore equal to the creation of a new process which runs quite independently of the rest of the whole. In our system a workstation process is created by the help of the following units (all of them will be described in detail in sections to come): **Device Description File (DDF).** This is a file containing constants which are more or less equivalent to the set of data defined as the Workstation Description Table in the GKS document [4], plus some additional data. **General Device Driver (GDD).** This is a set of program files; they contain all routines which are eventually (but not necessarily) to be used for a specific new workstation, e.g. a function for hatching, for the generation of dashed lines, to draw characters in STROKE precision etc. All these files have references to the DDF and are ready for conditional compiling based on data read from the Description File. **Device Coder (DCR).** This is the only program which must effectively be written for a new device. It must contain some prescribed entry points, that is some functions which perform specific tasks (i.e. drawing a line) by sending appropriate bit-patterns to the device. These functions are invoked from the routines of the GDD.

Once these units are ready (that is the DDF and the DCR are written and the files of the GDD are at hand), all files of the GDD are to be compiled and finally linked; the constants of the DDF direct the conditional compiling of these files. This step is done by an appropriate indirect command file (used by the make utility of UNIX or by the RSX Task Builder).

In what follows, we shall give a more detailed description of these basic units. Because of lack of space we shall concentrate on some of the necessary data and functions (e.g. aimed at area filling and segmentation); however, if anyone is interested in all the details of the above process, a comprehensive document is also available [7].

Before going into details, something must be said about the basic tool of conditional compiling.

All the programs have been written in C. This is important because we have made extensive use of the so-called C pre-processor. Just briefly, this pre-processor allows the definition of constants for C programs; in contrast to usual constant definitions however, these values can also be used to perform conditional compiling.

For example a C program can contain the following lines:

```
#if (Condition)
    Code 1
#else
    Code 2
#endif (Condition)
```

where *Condition* refers to a usual logical decision involving any previously defined constants. Based on the logical value of this Condition, either *Code1* or *Code2* is added to the final code while the other one is entirely omitted. For further details see for example Kernighan and Ritchie [6].

3 The Device Description File

This file contains constants in the format required by the C pre-processor syntax. These data cover the Workstation Description Table as described in the GKS document, but some additional data have been shown to be necessary for proper device handling. These values are used in the GPD files both as constants for the routines themselves and as basic "switches" for conditional compiling.

Constants used for conditional compiling are basically those which describe device capabilities. There is, for example, a constant called "WS_CAT" which can be INPUT, OUTIN or OUTPUT; the actual value of this constant directs whether or not functions performing output or input tasks should be present in the final process. Separate constants are present to indicate which are the linetypes handled by the hardware and which are those where a software simulation is necessary (and consequently the function generating, for example, a dashed line should be added to the final driver). This is the method by which "registered" device properties may be included in a workstation.

Let's see in a greater detail the constants driving area filling and segmentation. (We give the name of the constants, the possible values and some explanation.)

```
CAN_HS      - may be YES or NO.
CAN_PT      - may be YES or NO.
CAN_SL      - may be YES or NO.
```

These constants describe the capability of the hardware to handle area filling in HATCH, PATTERN and SOLID interior style, respectively. If a given style cannot be handled directly by the device, a simulation function must be added at compile-time to the driver.

```
HOS0        - value in Device Coordinate System.
HOS1        - value in Device Coordinate System.
HOS2        - value in Device Coordinate System.
SOL1        - value in Device Coordinate System.
```

These constants are necessary when HATCH (SOLID) style area filling is done by software; these values simply give the distances which should be kept between hatch lines for different style numbers (SOLID area filling is done by very dense hatching, therefore the last value refers to SOLID simulation).

NMP_FI - some index number.
NMP_PA - some index number.

These two values give the number of pre-defined fill area and pattern indices.

PD_FIT - list of predefined fill area bundle tables.
PD_PAT - list of predefined pattern tables.

For example, the following lines will give two predefined fill area bundle tables for the workstation (we have followed the C pre-processor syntax):

```
#define NMP_FI 2
#define PD_FIT {{SOLID,1,1},{HATCH,1,1}}
```

In some cases the graphic device can handle attribute bundle tables properly, just as it is defined in GKS. We have therefore two more constants describing whether the change of a given attribute bundle table can be handled by the hardware (value is IMM) or whether a regeneration is necessary (this is represented by an IRG value).

FI_REP - may be IRG or IMM, fill area bundle table.
PA_REP - may be IRG or IMM, pattern representation.

Segmentation constants are present exclusively for describing device capabilities and hence are used for conditional compiling only.

DIN_EX - may be IRG or IMM.

This is the constant which says whether the device has any kind of segmentation by itself, that is whether a segment may be opened and deleted or not. If the value is IRG, that means that all segmentation functions must be handled by the software.

The following constants describe the segment dynamic modification possibilities according to the GKS Workstation Description Table. All constants can be either IRG or IMM; all of them direct the presence or the omission of a definite function in the final Device Driver. The constants are as follows:

DIN_ST - device can transform segments (with clipping!).
DIN_VI - device can set off segment visibility.
DIN_IV - device can set on segment visibility.
DIN_HI - device can execute segment highlighting.
DIN_SP - device can execute segment priority setting.

4 General Device Driver

The General Device Driver is, as we have already said, a set of files containing all the functions which could be necessary for the correct implementation of a workstation, usable with the rest of our GKS implementation. Some of the functions are to be present in all workstations; these are for example the routines which are responsible for the correct interfacing of the Device Independent Part, for the handling of error situations etc. These functions represent the implementation-dependent peculiarites of a workstation running in our system, and therefore interface problems are completely hidden from the author of a new workstation (these problems would represent an unnecessary burden for someone who has not yet any special knowledge about the details of our implementation).

The remaining functions are building blocks for a new workstation. They are usually short functions dealing with one specific task which is eventually to be performed by a workstation program: functions for area filling, for the creation of markers according to the Standard's requirements, drawing lines with different linetypes etc. All these functions and their eventual invocations are surrounded by C pre-processor statements to add or omit the code for the final program. These statements make use of the constants defined in the DDF (which is "included", in C terminology, into all files of the GGD).

The main problem is of course to properly interface all these functions among themselves. To give an idea of what these function structures look like, let us look at an outline for the function handling the segment transformation.

```
#if (WS_CAT != INPUT)
        /* In case of an INPUT workstation, this routine is superfluous */
sesgtr()
{
#if (DIN_ST == IMM)
        /* The device can handle segment transformation, the appropriate
            routine of the DCR is invoked! */
        transsg (segmname, seg_tr_matr):
#else
        set_transformation_data( );
        if (implicit_regeneration == ALLOWED)
#if (DIN_EX == IMM)
        /* Segment can be deleted by the hardware, appropriate routine
            of DCR is called!*/
        deletsg (segmname);
        redraw_segment( );
            /* This is done by an inner routine of GDD */
        }
#else
        {clear ( ); /* This is a call for DCR! */
        perform_implicit_regeneration();
            /* This is again done by an inner routine of GDD */
        }
#endif (DIN_EX == IMM)
        else
        {new_frame_necessary = YES;
        }
#endif (DIN_ST == IMM)
} /* End of sesgtr ( ) */
#endif (WS_CAT != INPUT)
```

5 Device Coder

This is an individual C program, which must be written for each new device; it contains some low-level functions which handle directly the graphic hardware and which are invoked from the program of the GDD.

The potential entry points of this program are of course fixed in advance. In fact, we have defined a set of functions which can be considered as a kind of a Generic Graphic Function Set (GGFS), a subset of which is in use for a given device. That is, the functions belonging to this set are effectively invoked from the rest of the workstation if and only if some conditions, described in terms of data belonging to the Device Description, are true. As we have seen before, these data describe first of all the local capabilities of the graphic device; the choice of the appropriate subset of GGFS reflects these capabilities. On the other hand, nothing is said about the inner structure of the function itself; it is up to the author of DCR to make these routines so that they should be optimal for the given hardware.

Let's see again some examples. In case of an OUTPUT or OUTIN workstation, the graphic hardware is of course supposed to be able to draw lines. Consequently the GGFS contains the following two functions:

```
move(nx,ny)
dc nx,ny;
```

```
line(nx,ny)
dc nx,ny;
```

where the first routine sets a position for line-drawing and the second one to draws a line from this position to another one. Coordinates are given in DC. (Limits of DC figure in the DDF; data are transformed so as to be within these limits.)

In some cases however, the hardware can handle polylines as well. This information is also present in the DDF; if the POLY constant has been set to YES, the polyline GKS commands will propagate through the output pipeline down to the DCR without being split into separate lines. There is therefore an entry in the GGFs which is to be used only in this case, and this function will be invoked only if the above constant has the appropriate value. The function is as follows:

```
/* if (POLY = = YES) */
pollin (points)
dc *points; /* Pointer to the set of points */
```

In case of area filling, things are a bit more complicated. If the hardware cannot do any kind of area fill, that is CAN_HS, CAN_PT and CAN_SL (see above) are all equal to NO (this is the case for a TEKTRONIX 4014), the workstation has to simulate area filling completely. This simulation is done by drawing lines at appropriate places (simulating SOLID by very dense hatching, and doing patterns by SOLID filling of small squares); therefore no further function is needed in the DCR, simulation is done by calling the move-line pair as defined above. If one of these fill area possibilities is available on the device, the DCR has to contain one of the following three functions:

filhat(m,pl); /* Hatch polygon "pl" with hatch style "m" */
filsol(c,pl); /* Fill polygon "pl" with colour "c" */
filpt(pt,pl); /* Fill polygon "pl" with pattern "pt" */

In most of the cases however, the local capabilities of the device are somewhere between the above mentioned two levels. A typical situation is when the device can handle SOLID area filling, but only in limited situations. This is the point where the implementor of a new workstation has the task of writing a possibly ingenious program. Indeed, he/she has two choices: either to leave the problem of full area filling of SOLID style to the GDD (that is CAN_SL is set to NO and the device area filling is made accessible through a GDP), or to devise a good algorithm performing general area filling making use of the hardware. In the latter case CAN_SL must be set to YES, the new algorithm has to be written in a function called "fillsol" and must be present in the DCR so as to be invoked from other functions of the GDD in appropriate places. The problem is usually the fact that even if the hardware can do some kind of area filling, it may have restrictions which are outside the Standard. Just as an example: the DATAGRAPH VTC 8002 graphic terminal has local polygon filling; however the algorithm which is used is based on the notion of a so-called secondary colour (that is the boundary of the polygon should be of different colour than the one used for filling), which may cause severe problems if different picture elements are present on the screen. For this reason in our VTC driver we had to implement a GDP for this purpose and the "official" GKS area filling is done through the "move-line" pair.

There are finally cases when the device can handle everything exactly as GKS demands: bundle table, table indices and all styles of area filling. For the use of this "highest" level you find three functions in the GGFS, namely:

```
/* if (FI_REP = = IMM) */
firep (index,struct_pointer)  /* Set fill area bundle table */
int index;
attribute *struct_pointer;
```

```
/* if (FI_REP = = IMM) */
fisty(index);  /* Set fill area index */
```

```
/* if(FI_REP = = IMM) */
filla(pl);  /* Fill "pl" polygon */
```

Thus for "intelligent" devices, only these three functions need to be present in the DCR, while all area-filling functions are omitted from the final workstation by the conditional compiling process.

6 Practical Results

Once the work for the GKS implementation had been finished, we were faced with the problem of creating a new device driver almost instantaneously. The functions of the GDD had been tested on a TEKTRONIX 4014 display, which is an ideal tool for this kind of work because of its relatively restricted local capabilities. A Hungarian refresh display called GD80, which could for example handle segments properly, had played the role of an "intelligent" device.

The first "alien" display which had to be interfaced was very much like the TEK-TRONIX, although there were minor differences for example in the Device Coordinate System, the coding itself etc. Due to the facts that on the one hand the differences were not really important and on the other hand we made the new driver ourselves, the creation of a new GKS workstation took us barely 3 hours, including compiling.

The second, and from our point of view much more interesting interfacing problem came when a DATAGRAPH graphic display had to be driven. There were major differences between the DATAGRAPH and a TEKTRONIX; it had colours, it had limited area filling possibilities etc. The situation was exciting for us, because the driver had to be made by somebody who at that time had only a very general knowledge about GKS and the peculiarites of our implementation, and no knowledge at all of our HVDI protocol. Even the DATAGRAPH display was a bit new to him. However, he managed to create a correct first version of a GKS workstation in about two weeks (which included the time needed to get acquainted with our driver generation technique).

Then other displays came. By now we could affirm, that for someone who has had practice in the use of our technique, interfacing an average graphic device does not take much more than a few days (and most of this time is spent on finding the discrepancies between the official device specification and the reality...).

7   Some General Considerations

Although our driver generating technique makes use cf the peculiarites of our implementation, there are some general consequences which could be of interest. We have made extensive use of the C pre-processor; as a matter of fact the same technique could be used in other environments as well. Some kind of a macro-processor, which is quite a standard utility in an average operating system nowadays, could easily play the role of the C pre-processor (if there is no macro-processor at hand, it seems to be much more fruitful to make a simple one instead of writing completely new code for a driver every time). The fact that our workstation is a separate process is again less important; we have stressed that our technique completely hides the interfacing of the workstation with the Device Independent Part. This cut between the Device Dependent and Device Independent levels exists in some form in all implementations and it should not be a serious problem to follow the same ideas when the whole of GKS is a single process (only linkage time becomes longer).

The problem of handling different graphic devices has already been raised several times, and the ISO CGI proposal represents for example a typical solution for it. While the use of a fixed, standardized interface can be very advantageous for the future, if it is followed by hardware vendors, it does not help to handle devices which are already on the market. In our case there is no fixed interface in the classical sense but we have the Generic Graphic Function Set instead, used as we have described in section 6: an interface of a given device corresponds to a subset of the General Function Set, a subset which is generated exclusively based on the device capabilities. In their excellent book on graphical programming, Enderle et al [2]. speak of a DI/DD function set which contains, roughly, a higher level function set called the Workstation Function Set (which is more or less equivalent to our HVDI interface), and a low level one called the Device-Oriented Function Set; our Generic Function Set is something of a mixture of the two, used to produce a device-specific function set for driving the hardware. We feel this approach is extremely fruitful. An ideal case would be to create some kind of a standard for the Generic Graphic Function Set, which could be followed to share code among different GKS implementations, but we are aware of the fact that the standardization of this function set would raise problems which are far from being easily solvable. It would however be very advantageous for the international graphic community to explore further the possibilities of this direction.

References

1. DIN-NI, "Structure of a Workstation Interface," Position Paper for the WG2 Meeting, Benodet (May 1984).

2. G. Enderle, K. Kansy, and G. Pfaff, *Computer Graphics Programming: GKS, the Graphics Standard,* Springer-Verlag, Heidelberg (1983).

3. I. Herman, T. Tolnay-Knefely, and A. Vincze, "XGKS - A Multitask Realization of GKS," in *Eurographics'83,* ed. P. J. W. ten Hagen, North-Holland (1984). (Reproduced in this Volume.)

4. ISO, "Information processing systems - Computer graphics - Graphical Kernel System (GKS) functional description," ISO 7942, ISO Central Secretariat (August 1985).

5. ISO, "Information processing systems - Computer graphics - Interfacing techniques for dialogues with graphical devices," ISO DP 9636, Parts 1 to 6 (1986).

6. B. W. Kernighan and D. M. Ritchie, *The C Programming Language,* Prentice-Hall (1978).

7. J. Reviczky, "General Device Driver," XGKS Program Descriptions (1984). (Internal document of the Computer and Automation Institute of the Hungarian Academy of Sciences.)

XGKS - A Multitask Implementation of GKS

I. Herman, T. Tolnay-Knefely and A. Vincze

1   Basic Requirements

XGKS is the name of a GKS 7.2 implementation which is under development at the Computer and Automation Institute of the Hungarian Academy of Sciences.

The project commenced in September 1982. As is the case in all implementations, there were some basic considerations arising from the particular environment which had to be bourne in mind. These requirements were fairly general, and that is why our answer to these "challenges" (to use Toynbee's terminology) may be of general interest.

- The computers we are interested in are rather small. These include PDP machines (PDP 11/40's) and desk top computers based on a standard 16 bit processor such as the Z8000, Intel 8086 or M68000. These machines and/ or the operating systems they run have one thing in common; task size is limited, typically to 64K (even if the physical memory is larger). In this context, full GKS is large and that puts an unfortunate burden on the user task.

- We wanted to find an easy way to make the GKS implementation usable from different programming languages. we had had unfortunate experiences with another, in-house, graphics package (GSS80), which had to be written in a C-like language (called GESAL) and interfaced to both GESAL and FORTRAN. This turned out to be rather clumsy.

- We had to define a DI/DD interface at a high level, in order to be able to utilize the high level local intelligence in some Hungarian made graphics hardware, for example the GD80 [1].

● The aim was to implement a full level 2C GKS, which includes both multiple workstations and event input.

2 Design Concepts

The basic concept of our GKS design is to divide GKS into several tasks. This means that the main part of the systems, the DI part, is itself a task, communicating with the application program and the workstations through some standard inter-task communication mechanism. The first requirement (small computers) gave rise to this idea, but in fact the GKS document itself suggests this approach. Event mode input presupposes some kind of multi-task structure, as does the multiple workstation concept.

The "pipe" concept is used for inter-task comunication (having in mind a Unix-like environment).

As seen from figure 1, a program using XGKS has three levels: the application program level, the DI and the workstations. The application program is linked to a thin interface (called the IF) of XGKS. This layer transforms routine calls into the commands of a communications protocol understandable by the DI part. From this perspective, the application program level is one task. Even if the application program itself is split into several tasks the IF should be present in only one of them.

Again, the DI part is one single task. It holds the GKS state list, performs normalization transformations and handles WISS functions. The DI part sends appropriate commands to individual workstations, taking into consideration the workstation's type (INPUT, OUTIN etc.).

Each workstation is an individual task from the DI part's point of view, though it can be split into smaller parts, for example for handling event input. There is a private pipe from the DI part to each workstation, through which commands are sent. There is however just one common pipe coming back from all workstations; answers cannot mix because the structure of GKS is such that a complicated answer is returned by a workstation only when a given command is sent to just that workstation.

3 The DI/DD Interface

In the above structure the DI/DD interface is actually the communication protocol used in the pipes from the DI part to the individual workstations. This protocol is at a high level; coordinates are sent in NDC, primitives are unclipped. The workstation has to apply both the segment and workstation transformations as well as the clipping operation and generating STROKE precision text. Whilst this makes the workstation task fairly large if the graphics hardware has poor capabilities, it does make it easy to exploit the local intelligence in intelligent devices. Thus it is possible to turn the GD80 device into a GKS workstation machine communicating with the host directly through the DI/DD protocol.

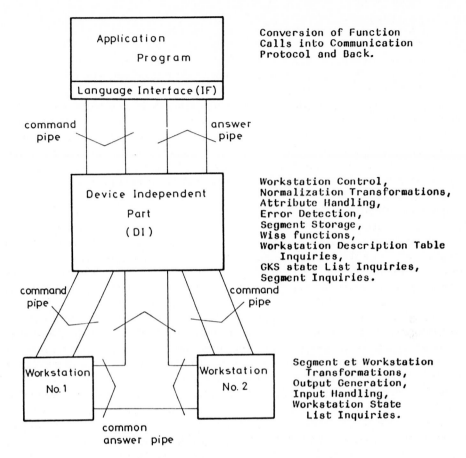

Figure 1 Overall Structure of XGKS

4 Language Bindings

The communication between the IF and the DI part and the DI part and the workstations is defined in a language independent way. That is, the only part depending on the user's language is the IF; the rest can be written in any language the implementor chooses.

This gives an effective solution to the second requirement. Since the IF is small and simple, the best way to bind a new language to XGKS is to rewrite the IF. It is not necessary to define difficult interfaces between different programming languages, a problem which rarely has a satisfactory solution.

The only drawback of this solution is that one cannot exploit special language features, for example as was done by Rosenthal and ten Hagen [3] in their C language binding. There is no problem for the proposed FORTRAN binding standard. We think that the advantages of the approach taken here outweigh this disadvantage.

5   Segment Store

Our concept of segment storage takes a similar line to the Free University of Berlin team [2] and Rosenthal and ten Hagen [3] both of which were reported at Eurographics '82. In GKS, segment storage is conceptually associated with each workstation, and a segment is stored on each workstation that was active when it was created. The stored information is however the same on each workstation, notably the output primitive data in NDC. It is a natural idea therefore to implement a common segment storage for all workstations. This common storage is, of course, handled by the DI part. It turns out that the information stored in a segment is just the commands of the high level DI/DD interface, and it is therefore quite a simple matter to store the commands in segment storage at the same time that they are sent to the workstations. Given this common segment storage, the WISS workstation is reduced to a small program containing just three routines, linked to the rest of the DI part. The file system of the local operating system is used for actual storage. The DI part opens a file when a segment is opened, stores the DI/DD commands in the file and closes it when the segment is closed. No special directory is used for these files, just the directory system of the local operating system. The workstations have the right to access these files if necessary (for example to perform an UPDATE command) and to extract the graphical information, that is the DI/DD commands.

Unlike Buthz [2], however, this segment file is not always open. It depends on the local segment storage capability of the workstations actually open. If the graphics hardware can store segments outside the host machine, the above mechanism is superfluous. To decide whether this is the case, all workstations have a datum about this capability, which becomes known to the DI part when the workstation is opened. (We believe that it would be advantageous to add this datum to the GKS Workstation Description Table.) Consequently common segment storage is only done by the DI part when there is at least one open OUTPUT, OUTIN, MO or WISS workstation having no segment storage capability.

6   Synchronous and Asynchronous Commands

The main problems arising from the use of a multi-task approach are inter-task communication and the consistency of common data. Pipes are good tools for communication, not only because they provide a means of sending data from one task to another, but also because they are treated by the operating system as resources. That is, a task waiting for information from a pipe is swapped out. In our case this means that the task of an inactive but open workstation is swapped from main memory and does not interfere with the remaining tasks.

The same happens to the DI part. If the application program does not use GKS functions for a given period, then the DI process is automatically swapped and put into a "wait" state. This is a very important feature of our system; a large graphics program, say a CAD system, using GKS as a tool for graphical input and output, can spend large amounts of time dealing with its own data, without using graphics functions. The effectiveness of the whole environment is increased because during these periods the major part of GKS does not use the processor or main memory.

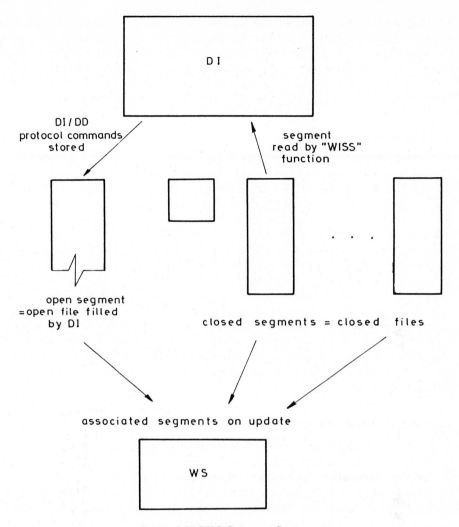

Figure 2 XGKS Segment Storage

The consistency of common data arises in connection with the segment store. The safest way is to use a "command and answer" communication protocol between the tasks. For example, after issuing a command to a workstation the DI part would wait for an answer on the answer-pipe. For reasons of efficiency, another approach has been chosen.

All functions of GKS are divided into two classes: asynchronous and synchronous. Synchronous functions are handled as above: all levels wait for an appropriate answer to ensure the data are safe. "REDRAW ALL SEGMENTS ON WORKS-TATION" and any kind of input are examples of synchronous commands. There is however a group of functions which do not need synchronization; first are the output primitives. In this case all tasks continue working without waiting for an answer.

This approach requires some careful thought in relation to error handling, but we will not go into that here. It is clear that this approach is more efficient than a simple "command and answer" protocol. The asynchronous protocol is highly advantageous if the workstation hardware is intelligent enough to perform some transformations and/ or clipping locally. The user's program can then proceed in parallel with these actions, which can significantly speed up the whole application program.

7 Optimizations

The overall structure of XGKS makes it possible to optimize GKS commands. If one of the workstation command pipes is actually a physical communication line between two devices (this arises quite frequently, for example a host and an intelligent graphics terminal) the effectiveness of the configuration can be decreased if there is too much information flow between the two devices. On the other hand, we appreciate that an application programmer using a GKS-like set of functions, prefers to invoke possibly superfluous functions in preference to keeping the actual state of the system. A good example of this is the use of attributes. It is not always trivial to know the actual current attributes for lines, markers, text etc. and it is much simpler to invoke the attribute setting functions again. As GKS 7.2 has a large number of device independent attributes, this can result in a series of superfluous flows of information through the command pipes. The DI part therefore makes an optimization and checks whether the workstation really needs a given datum and only sends new information when strictly necessary. The same kind of optimization can be done with pick identifiers and clipping windows, an optimization which is also done by the DI part.

8 Status of Implementation

At the time of writing (June 1983) only some parts of XGKS are completed, namely the DI part, the C language interface and a metafile output workstation. The DI part is quite large, about 40 Kbytes. However, both the C language interface and the metafile output workstation are small; the former is about 2 Kbytes while the latter is about 10 Kbytes. (In the case of the metafile output workstation the operating system's file handling routines represent a large part of this 10 Kbyte area.) We are currently working on device drivers for a Tektronix 4010 and a GD80; the Tektronix represents a quite simple display hardware, whilst the GD80 has a great deal of local intelligence and consequently only requires a small driver. A Pascal interface to XGKS is also planned; this is not expected to take more than one week's work. It is hoped that the first version will be running by the time of the Eurographics '83 conference and so there will be more to say about the actual implementation.

References

1. Anon, *All About GD80,* Computer and Automation Institute, Hungarian Academy of Sciences (1980).

2. R. Buhtz, "CGM-Concepts and their Realization," pp. 371-382 in *Eurographics '82*, ed. D. S. Greenaway and E. A. Warman, North-Holland (1982). (Reproduced in this Volume.)

3. D. S. H. Rosenthal and P. J. W. ten Hagen, "GKS in C," pp. 359-369 in *Eurographics '82*, ed. D. S. Greenaway and E. A. Warman, North-Holland (1982).

A VLSI Implementation of the Graphics Standard GKS

J. Encarnacao, R. Lindner, M. Mehl, G. Pfaff and W. Strasser

1 Introduction

The operation of a graphics system requires extensive computational power which currently is only just available at graphical workstations. So on many systems it is necessary to run the graphics routines on the same computer as the application program. This configuration may be justified on economic grounds but leads to inefficient operation of the general purpose single processor computer.

More demanding applications will soon reach the limits of the computational power available, especially when a high rate of interaction is required and the response times must be kept low. One method of alleviating these problems is to include a special purpose processor, capable of substantially enlarging the power for graphical computations (see figure 1).

When looking at what should be put in a VLSI chip, the obvious candidate is a VLSI-based graphical system. We have chosen GKS [1, 7, 10] because it is an international standard and in widespread use [5] and also because of our experience in implementing GKS [2].

The focus of our work is a GKS-chip which will convert a graphical device with a GKS segment storage into a GKS workstation. Thus the GKS-chip will close the gap between the interface of a physical device and the GKS workstation interface.

The main advantages resulting from a VLSI implementation are:

- The translation of GKS specific structures into hardware will give us an optimum hardware exploitation. This results in a higher computational speed and/or lower system cost in comparison with an equivalent implementation with a general purpose microprocessor.

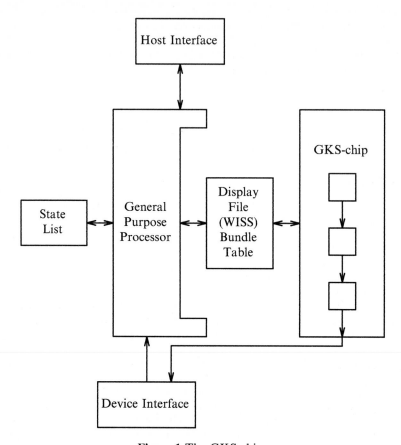

Figure 1 The GKS-chip

- Because the GKS-chip can be used with different types of output devices (vector and raster display, plotter, metafile), these devices will be made compatible with any application program using the GKS interface.

- A single chip (supported by additional memory) will make an advanced system out of simple device hardware.

There is one important overall criterion for the quality of the GKS-chip design, which is the effectiveness of the chip for most types of graphical devices. This will allow a wide range of workstations to use a GKS-chip and be compatible with suitable GKS implementations. The device-dependencies will be totally compensated for, or, at least, hidden inside the graphical workstation.

In the last few years many engineering groups consisting of software and application specialists, have shown that the complete design of a VLSI chip may be done by customers [4, 8, 9, 12]. Besides the basic knowledge of the design process that can be obtained from the Mead/Conway book [11], this work depends on the support of a CAD system consisting of a great variety of design aids and simulation programs

[14], e.g. a layout editor with cell database, logical and electrical simulators, place-ment and routing programs, circuit compactors, design rule checkers and mask file generators.

The contents of this paper results from the basic study [6], which examines the feasability and the concept of the GKS-chip.

2 Structure of GKS

Before reporting on the chip design settled upon, let us consider some features of GKS, as these influence the structure of the chip architecture.

We can distinguish 4 classes of GKS-functions:

a)   functions to set GKS-states (e.g. SET WINDOW);

b)   functions to inquire actual state values (e.g. INQUIRE SET OF ACTIVE WORKSTATIONS);

c)   output functions (e.g. POLYLINE);

d)   input functions (e.g. REQUEST LOCATOR).

They have to be embedded in a GKS system as illustrated in figure 2.

Let us consider how these function groups may be implemented in the GKS chip design. GKS includes a set of internal tables (states in figure 2). These are mainly the workstaion state lists and the segment storage. According to the design structure introduced in the previous chapter we keep these lists under the control of the general purpose processor. The workstation bundle tables are kept twice; the subset of

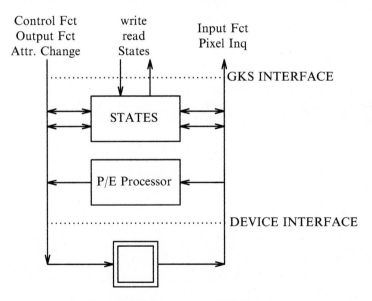

Figure 2 Distinction of GKS Functions

them containing the "realized" values is also stored within the output processor chip. Thus, with respect to SET-STATE and INQUIRE-STATE functions the general purpose processor has the tasks of

a)   Storing function values called by the application program in its internal list; providing the output processor with the "realized" bundle table values.

b)   Retrieving and returning the values requested by inquiry functions to the application program.

The set of output functions sent to the general purpose processor is stored within the segment storage logically connected to this processor. The set is stored in the device independent format defined as Workstation Independent Segment Storage (WISS) with the extension that primitives outside segments are also stored in this segment storage. From this segment storage the picture of a workstation is refreshed by the special output processor. The structure and control of the GKS output function implementation is explained in the next section. The general purpose processor thus has the additional task to

c)   keep and administrate the segment storage;

d)   insert primitives upon arrival into the segment storage.

Input functions are also handled by the general purpose micro processor. It has access to physical input devices, reads the input device dependent data from them and performs the measure and trigger mapping as explained in [13]. Thus the logical data values of the active logical input devices are provided asynchronously (implementing the highest GKS level); additionally prompting and echoing information is produced in the general purpose processor and is inserted in the segment storage at specific places from where the output processor automatically fetches and displays it on the screen. The tasks of the general purpose processor are thus extended by

e)   performing the measure/trigger process;

f)   inserting prompt/echo information into the segment storage;

g)   delivering logical input data into the application program.

3   Structure and Implementation of the GKS Output Functions

Each output function can be regarded as a 'software pipeline' constructed from functional entities. Each entity causes a transformation of the output primitives according to specific states. An example of a logical pipeline of transformations applied to the GKS POLYLINE primitive is given in figure 3.

In general each GKS output function can be constructed from a set of transformation modules. A functional software (FS) pipeline consists of a number of function blocks activated sequentially to process a primitive. The actually implemented FS pipeline (which has to be performed on the output processor hardware pipeline) depends on the following criteria:

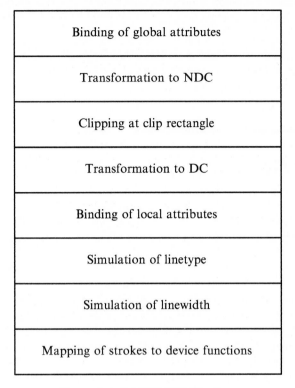

Binding of global attributes
Transformation to NDC
Clipping at clip rectangle
Transformation to DC
Binding of local attributes
Simulation of linetype
Simulation of linewidth
Mapping of strokes to device functions

Figure 3 A POLYLINE Pipeline

● The given GKS functionality; this includes the concept of coordinate transformation, clipping, attribute binding, etc.

● The set of physical device characteristics given by the scope of the intended range of devices.

● The efficiency with which the software modules can be performed in hardware.

As will be explained in the next section, the blocks in common for the six GKS output primitives have to be discovered. A hardware pipeline has to developed which can perform the hardware pipelines for all six primitives efficiently under microprogram control. The need to find a common hardware solution influences the design of the functional software pipelines.

In the following a set of transformation modules is listed that can be used to set up the software pipeline solutions for the GKS output primitives:

a) Coordinate transformations: this is to implement normalization, segment and workstation transformations for all primitives (note: scaling, rotation and translation are needed separately).

b)   Clipping: a set of clipping algorithms is needed to clip the different output prim-
     itives at a clipping rectangle.

c)   Attribute representation functions: this set of algorithms performs the genera-
     tion of states for linetype, linewidth, hatching, characters and markers; the
     filling of the interior of a polygon with patterns, the correct placing of charac-
     ters within a string, etc.

d)   Raster scan algorithms for lines, characters, polygons and raster cells.

4   Functional Design of the GKS-Chip

As stated in section 3, for each of the six GKS output primitives we develop a functional description in the form of a software pipeline. As an example, the POLYLINE
function is explained in figure 3. These software pipelines suggest adequate solutions
for the implementation as a hardware pipeline. This hardware pipeline will consist of
a set of function blocks which are configured (adjusted and connected to each other)
by a microprogram to perform the desired primitive functions. So the main task
when designing the GKS-chip will be the development or selection of algorithms
suitable to be executed by a pipeline and the design of the pipeline itself. The design
is done in a way that function blocks and interconnections remain sufficiently flexible
to allow configuring according to the different primitive functions and target devices.
This circuitry must be simple and sufficiently straightforward to be small and fast.
Space is important because of the limited chip area. The system must be tuned as in
any pipeline the slowest function block determines the overall output delay.

     As we will see later on, not all of the GKS output functions can easily be imple-
mented to fulfill the requirements stated above.

     All primitive functions require a basic set of function blocks. Since the POLY-
LINE function is the simplest one we describe the basic function blocks describing
this primitive function. For each output primitive we will now consider the necessary function blocks.

a) POLYLINE:

The function blocks necessary to perform this primitive function are directly given in
the description of the software pipeline, so that only a selection of suitable algorithms will have to take place. The function blocks and their realizations are listed
below.

Transformation: All transformations in GKS may be concatenated, resulting in
one transformation matrix. These transformations are the NORMALIZATION, the
WORKSTATION, the SEGMENT, and the ATTRIBUTE TRANSFORMATION.
Nevertheless the transformation block will have to perform 4 floating point multiplications plus 4 additions. Because of the space requirements, the multiplications will
have to be done by using a microprogrammed adder and shifter network. Another
substantial part is the conversion to a fixed point data representation. Doing this

before adding, allows the adders to work on fixed point data and consequently be very small and fast. All the following function blocks are also driven with integer data. More details about data representation are given in section 5.

Clipping: A simple and fast solution to the line clipping problem is given in [15]. With some modifications that are inherently part of the algorithm presented in [16], this clipping function block will also be applicable for polylines.

Scan Conversion: When the output is sent to a raster device, the set of vectors leaving the clipping stage is converted by a Bresenham-like algorithm [3] to produce a sequence of points. Because the conversion time of a line depends on the length of the line, a buffer between the clipper and the scan converter stages will decouple the pipeline from the scan conversion and minimize loss of pipeline throughput.

These function blocks must be completed by circuitry capable of simulating the linetype and the linewidth if it is not supported by the device hardware.

b) and c) POLYMARKER and TEXT:

The most convenient way to define these functions is to transform each primitive to a set of polylines. This primitive mapping (character and symbol generator) is situated before the transformation stage, so that only one more function block before the polyline pipeline is required. Even when driving a raster device, this has the advantage of avoiding a complete additional pipeline for primitives being defined as point arrays (raster matrix).

d) FILL AREA:

The polyline pipeline can be used for the transformation and clipping stages. Afterwards a polygon scan conversion circuit has to be inserted that will be used with some modifications for hatch simulation also. It is impossible to define this function block so that it is fast in execution because:

(1) the whole clipped surrounding polyline has to be accessible as each scan path has to be compared with every polygon edge;

(2) for each scan line the set of intersection points has to be calculated and stored;

(3) the processing of the visible vectors can only take place after sorting them.

It is not surprising that the implementation of FILL AREA places extreme demands on the implementation.

As we have shown, the coordinate oriented approach guarantees a high data throughput for line oriented devices and a feasible solution for raster devices. Further work is required to increase the effectiveness of raster scan conversion.

5 Representation of Coordinate Values

The representation of data at the application/host interface is determined by the range of the values occuring. A floating point representation is evidently necessary. For most applications, a 32-bit format with a 23-bit mantissa is sufficient. User data in the display file will be represented in this floating point format also. In order to keep the whole range of values, the resulting transformation-matrix will have to be calculated in floating-point. This operation, in common with all attribute or inquiry functions, is not very critical with respect to calculation time and may be executed by firmware using an insignificant amount of hardware.

To minimize the execution time and space requirements of the output pipeline functions, a close examination of the data representation is necessary. Considering that floating point addition is nearly as costly as multiplication (done either in a floating or fixed point representation), and much more costly than fixed point addition, real number addition in the pipeline execution is avoided. The conversion of floating- into a fixed point representation is done as early as possible. Now let us consider the data flow and representation in the pipeline.

The first function of the output pipeline (the transformation) is followed by clipping, area filling and raster scan functions. The output data of the clipper and all the subsequent units, do not need to be in floating point format as they lie in the range of the window coordinates of the output device. As we can easily provide a sufficiently wide data path we can also use fixed point coordinates for the clipper input data which are substantially larger than the window coordinate limit of the output device. The floating point to fixed point conversion may therefore be done inside the transformation block. The general form of the transformation is:

$$x' = ax + by + c$$
$$y' = dx + ey + f$$

where x and y are the non-transformed real coordinates and x' and y' are the transformed (integer) ones.

The multiplication within the transformation block, however, must be done with floating point because of the variability of the world coordinate and transformation data. So the real-integer-converter is located directly after the real multiplication circuits and works in parallel, to speed up the total transformation. The results are switched to the converter, which is implemented once only. This can be done as we use a fast barrel shifter as the most essential component. A shift of any number of bits is executed in one clock cycle. However, it requires a great deal of chip space. So our transformation circuit is a compromise as far as chip space and throughput are concerned. The output of the converter is a 2's complement 26-bit integer. It has two more valid bits than the real-mantissa, and typically only the lower significant part of the data word is utilized - the higher significant part of the word is needed for safety against pre-clipping overflow. The lower significant part is typically smaller than 20 bits. The two least significant bits are rounded after the transformation additions and serve only to reduce the rounding errors during these additions. The output of the transformation function is finally reduced to 24-bit representation, which is the input to the clipping stage. After the clipping process, the width of the data words may be reduced to the highest resolution of any intended target device, which will not be more than 18 bits.

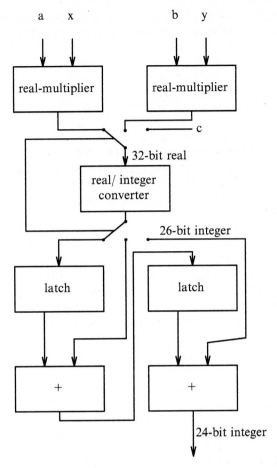

Figure 4 Data Representation in the Transformation Function

6   Scope of Application

One limitation to the use of the GKS-chip is the possible throughput for picture data. We have developed the output pipeline based on a coordinate oriented set of function blocks in order to cover a lot of functionality with a minimum set of basic functions. With regard to speed, the purely coordinate oriented algorithms (transformation, clipping) are linearly dependent on the width of the data words, that is the mantissa length of the real numbers and the integer representation. So we can execute these functions in about 25 to 30 clock cycles. Assuming another 20 cycles for data input and output (from the chip-attached display file to the pipeline and from the pipeline to the device), the total execution time of one vector will require about

40 clock cycles (a critical decision is whether to use the same set of pins for input and output). With a 100 ns (10 MHz) clock the total delay time of a vector is about

$$40 \times 100 \text{ ns} = 4 \ \mu s$$

In the simplest case of line drawings on a vector display as an output device for real time applications, with a refresh time of 20 ms and a mean vector write time of 4 μs, about 5000 vectors may be processed.

For FILL AREA functions, however, the hatch and raster scan algorithms are not mainly time-dependent on the number of vectors but, for raster devices, depend on the number of pixels to be written, and generally on the complexity of the primitives.

Within these time constraints, we intend to serve several classes of graphics devices:

a)   Real time handling of reasonably complex vector pictures will be the most impressive area of the GKS chip's utilization.

b)   A lower level of computational speed is required in dialog applications where the response time may reach one second. This large amount of time can be used to draw pictures of greater complexity to devices with refresh capabilities, as storage tube or raster devices with pixel memory.

c)   A third class is that of batch-like applications with very little interaction or even without any, e.g. plotter, microfilm or picture file generation.

7   Conclusions

The outline of the GKS-chip design presented in this paper must be seen as as further step on the way from the basic study [6] to real chip design.

Our next steps in developing the GKS-chip will be:

●   consideration of all GKS functions with respect to their integration (or not!), especially looking for an optimum balance between effort and effect;

●   the circuit design of function blocks supporting also complex algorithms like the clipping of fill area, hatch simulation, scan conversion and I/0 with respect to their usage in the output pipeline;

●   defining the micro code and designing the micro-sequencer and the micro instruction decoder, writing the micro-program;

●   final design of the chip layout;

●   implementation of the GKS interface on the general purpose processor.

The last step, the chip fabrication project, is planned for the end of 1984 in cooperation with Siemens AG, Munich.

Acknowledgement

We would like to thank Dr. Horbst and Dr. Sandweg of Siemens AG, Munich for their help and valuable suggestions during the development of the concept of the GKS-chip. We also thank the BMFT (Federal Ministry of Research and Technology) for funding the GKS-chip design and production.

References

1. P. R. Bono, J. L. Encarnacao, F. R. A. Hopgood, and P. J. W. ten Hagen, "GKS - The First Graphic Standard," *IEEE Computer Graphics and Applications* **2**(5), pp.9-23 (July 1982).

2. H.-G. Borufka, H. Kuhlmann, and G. Pfaff, "Die THD GKS-Implementierun," in *Gerateunabhangige Graphische Systeme, Drittes Darmstadter Kolloquium*, ed. J. L. Encarnacao and W. Strasser (ed.), R. Oldenburg Verlag, Munchen Wien (1981). (In German.)

3. J. E. Bresenham, "Algorithm for Computer Control of a Digital Plotter," *IBM Syst. J.* **4**(1), pp.25-30 (1965).

4. J. H. Clark, "Structuring a VLSI System Architecture," *LAMBDA* (Second Quarter 1980.).

5. J. L. Encarnacao and W. Strasser (ed.), *Gerateunabhangige Graphische Systeme, Drittes Darmstadter Kolloquium*, R. Oldenburg Verlag, Munchen Wien (1981). (In German.)

6. J. L. Encarnacao, R. Lindner, M. Mehl, G. Pfaff, and W. Strasser, *Realisierung des graphischen Systems GKS durch VLSI-Technolgie (Studie 0)*, (July 1982). (In German.).

7. G. Enderle, K. Kansy, and G. Pfaff, *Computer Graphics Programming: GKS, the Graphics Standard*, Springer-Verlag, Heidelberg (1983).

8. D. T. Fitzpatrick et al., "A RISCy Approach to VLSI," *VLSI DESIGN*, pp.14-20 (Fourth Quarter 1981).

9. J. K. Foderaro, K. S. Van Dyke, and D. A. Patterson, "Running RISCs," *VLSI DESIGN*, pp.27-32 (September/October 1982.).

10. ISO, "Information Processing - Graphical Kernel System (GKS), Functional Description," Draft International Standard, ISO/DIS 7942.

11. C. A. Mead and L. A. Conway, *Introduction to VLSI Systems*, Addison-Wesley (1980).

12. F. Mintzer and A. Peled, "A Microprocessor for Signal Processing, the RSP," *IBM J. Res. Develop* **26**(4) (July 1982).

13.   G. Pfaff, "The Construction of Operator Interfaces on Logical Input Devices," *Acta Informatica* **19**(2), pp.151-166 (1983).

14.   H.G. Schwartzel (ed.), *CAD fur VLSI - Rechnergestutzter Entwurf hochstintegrierter Schaltungen,* Springer-Verlag, Berlin, Heidelberg, New York (1982). (In German.)

15.   R. F. Sproull and I. E. Sutherland, *A Clipping Divider,* Evans and Sutherland Computer Corp.

16.   I. E. Sutherland and G. W. Hodgman, "Reentrant Polygon Clipping," *Communications of the ACM* **17**(1), pp.32-42 (January 1974).

A Token Based Graphics System

G. J. Reynolds

1 Introduction

This paper presents the development of a novel process oriented configurable graphics system architecture designed to be particularly suitable for emulating various graphics system models. The system architecture also provides a suitable vehicle for interfacing devices and workstations of varying capabilities, and for experimentation with some device dependent / device independent aspects of graphics systems. The underlying model of graphics systems on which this architecture is based is taken from an abstract reference model of computer graphics developed by Arnold et al [1, 2]. This reference model describes graphics systems in terms of graphics data states and the order of transitions between states, and as such, is independent of any specific graphics system.

The remainder of section 1 gives a brief summary of the graphics reference model and a short survey of other configurable graphics systems. Then in section 2 the configurable token based graphics system architecture is described. In section 3 an example of two different configurations is used to reflect the difference between two graphics standards. In section 4 two implementations of the graphics system architecture on different host machines are described.

1.1 A Reference Model for Graphics Systems

The underlying conceptual models of most standard graphics systems, in particular, of those existing and proposed international standards for graphics [8, 9, 10, 11], and of many existing graphics packages [3, 5], are most often seen as being graphics processing pipelines. In the case of graphics output, graphics data is refined as it passes down the pipeline, by associating graphical attributes, transforming coordinates, clipping etc., until it reaches a form which is suitable for display on a particular workstation or device. Graphical input can be viewed as a pipeline of processes transforming the data resulting from some input interaction into a form suitable for use by the application. The input interaction may also involve processes from the output pipeline in order to achieve any desired prompts and echoes. Clearly, the composition of these pipelines and the order of components within them may differ widely between models, however there are often a reasonable number of components common to most. Examples of these are transformations, attributes, clipping, storage etc. These common components play an equivalent role in each model, even though the internal detail of the components will most often differ. It can be shown that a large number of the differences between graphics system models can be expressed in terms of the different orderings (or configurations) of these components.

The abstract reference model of graphics data states has developed this processing pipeline model by isolating the smallest incremental changes to the states of graphics information (or storage areas), and by defining when graphics data undergoes transitions between these states by the application of specialized processes.

The data states are grouped together to form strands of processing, where a particular strand is concerned with a subset of the overall intended graphical effects. Five major strands can be identified in most standard graphics systems, as follows:

- Attribute strand.

- Transformation strand.

- Clipping strand.

- Dimensionality strand.

- Storage strand

The processing strands are illustrated in figure 1, which also indicates how a specific graphics pipeline can be configured by ordering the state transitions on and between strands.

1.2   Other Configurable Graphics Systems

The modular process oriented approach to building processing systems is not new and applying this approach to graphics systems is no exception. Perhaps the most evident use of this methodology is found in the UNIX [13] shell and programming environment, where well defined process modules can be readily chained together to form pipelines of processes. Output from one module can be directed as input to another using an interprocess communication mechanism called a pipe. Within the UNIX programming environment it is entirely possible to set up complex networks of pipelines which allow information to be transferred back and forth.

A. Kilgour [12] applied the UNIX methodology to the graphics field in his proposal for "a model of graphics systems as a hierarchy of communicating modules". In this model, a graphics system is constructed by forming a fixed pipeline of modules, where each module has two input ports and two output ports, allowing graphics data to flow in both directions. Each module acts as a filter, consuming graphics data

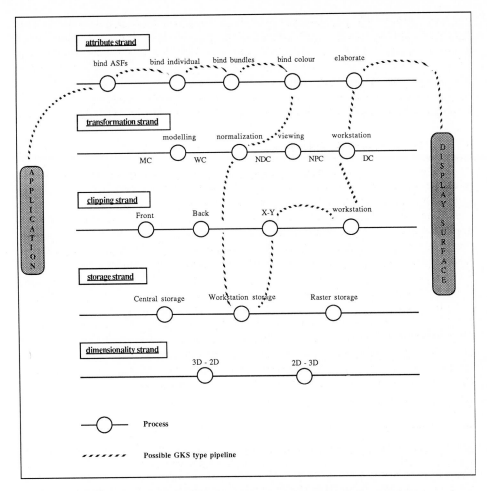

Figure 1 Processing Strands of the Graphics Reference Model

which it can deal with directly from its input ports and passing the remainder on to adjacent modules in the hierarchy.

D. Rosenthal [14] developed a similar pipeline of software filters during his work on graphics metafiles. A typical pipeline would pass a metafile picture description through several graphics refinement processes and then on to the final display surface. I. Herman [6] has taken Kilgour's proposal a stage further and developed XGKS, an implementation of the Graphics Kernel System (GKS). XGKS is a multiprocess design operating on top of the UNIX operating system.

All of the above graphics system models have used fixed or static processing pipelines. If the pipeline needed to be modified at some stage, for example, to change to a different method of hidden line hidden surface removal, the pipeline would have to be reconstructed completely. Perhaps closest to the dynamically configurable token based system model presented here is the COGS (configurable graphics system toolbox) proposal of A. van Dam et al [4]. COGS models a graphics system as a pipeline of graphics processing modules which communicate using a special type of graphics message called a packet. The configuration of a pipeline however is controlled by a special COGS module called the Administrator. This module is responsible for setting up communication links between graphics modules and for a user interface to the configuration mechanism. COGS defines a control protocol for reconfiguring the system, which can be used by any module when necessary.

2   The Token Based Architecture

As indicated in the introduction, the token based system closely follows the graphics reference model, in that there is a separate graphics process for each isolated data state. Graphics data for output primitives, attributes, etc. are packaged into tokens which are then communicated between the graphics processes, and in so doing, the graphics data undergoes a transition between states. An example graphics process might be one which binds a subset of the aspect source flag values (c.f GKS, PHIGS) to a primitive token and which maintains the current and previous settings of the ASF's.

The token based graphics system architecture is based loosely on the actor computation model of C. Hewitt [7], and consists of a number of concurrently executing graphics processes, which communicate solely by message (token) passing. Any need for sharing of data is achieved by either duplicating the data where appropriate, or by an inquiry mechanism using tokens. The term token is used to distinguish the special type of graphics messages used here from other message passing systems. Each graphics process is described by three groups of information:

- a local graphics state, actually a list of states;

- a table of acquaintances of this process, which may vary dynamically;

- a number of routines for consuming tokens.

The action of consuming a token may result in a change of the local graphics state, the removal of the token from the system, or the release of a refined token or tokens for further processing. For example, a token which altered the window to viewport mapping might be sent to a clip process, which would then modify its local state accordingly. An output primitive token arriving at this clip process may then be clipped to this window and either be removed altogether, released unaltered, or possibly be clipped into several new output primitive tokens.

This graphics system can be considered as a data driven architecture, in so far as that the content of the token passed between processes determines what action or event will occur next, and not any particular graphics process. Of course, if the token content is modified in an appropriate fashion then the next event can be prescribed.

2.1   Token Structure

Each token can conceptually be broken into two parts, a graphics data part and a pipeline configuration part (see figure 2). The graphics data part contains information relevant to the particular intended graphics effect, e.g. polyline data, a workstation inquiry, etc. This graphics information may change during the processing of a token, e.g. by transforming the polyline's coordinates, by filling in some inquired workstation details, etc.

The pipeline configuration part of a token specifies what actions are to be performed on the token, in what order the actions are to occur, and for each action, which local graphics state to use. The pipeline configuration part can be considered as a queue of actions or events, which permits the preemption of events on the queue in certain circumstances. The pipeline configuration defines an ordering of events for an individual token, coexisting tokens may use the same configuration or different ones. Note that the configuration does not refer to any internal arrangement of a process, e.g. by dynamic code loading on a set of negotiated device capabilities. The configuration or routing of a token varies during the tokens lifetime, not only by removing events from the routing as they are consumed, but also by adding new events to either the tail or the head of the queue. For example, when the precision of a text primitive token has been determined by binding the font and precision attributes, there may be a set of alternative routings, one of which may be added to the token routing in order to achieve the specified precision.

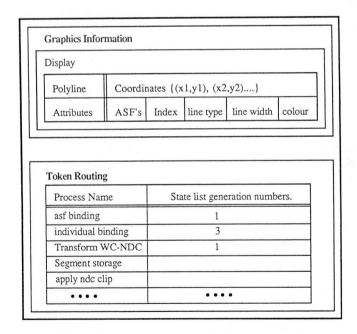

Figure 2 Sample Token for a Polyline Output Primitive

There are six different types of token which correspond to the functional grouping of most graphics interfaces, as follows:

- Control, i.e. workstation control;

- Display, i.e. output primitives;

- Storage, i.e. segment / structure manipulation;

- State change, i.e. attribute setting, transformation setting;

- Inquiry, i.e. inquire graphics state settings;

- Input, i.e. input primitives.

2.2   Control Aspects

Tokens can enter the system from a number of different points, the most obvious of these being the application interface. The application program however, is treated simply as an additional graphics process within the system which happens to be a primary producer of tokens. The application makes use of a predefined set of functions which conforms to the functional description of a particular graphics standard or system. All of these functions release tokens with appropriate routings in order to achieve the required effect. New tokens may also be entered into the system by the other graphics processes. One particular case for this is during system initialization, when a number of inquiry tokens are issued in order for processes to obtain their initial local graphics state.

A number of control problems arise because tokens can enter the system from several points and because tokens can coexist in the system with different configurations. The first of these, and perhaps the most important, is concerned with the 'current' local graphics state of a process when a token arrives. Consider the situation where the application process issues a primitive token followed by an individual attribute change token. If the configurations of each token are such that the primitive token has several processes to visit before reaching the individual attribute process, but the attribute change token can go directly to that process, then potentially, the primitive token can be overtaken by the attribute change token. In effect, the primitive would use the wrong current attribute values.

To solve this problem each process maintains a list of local graphics states, indexed by generation number. Whenever a new local state is produced it is added to the list of states and a generation number is associated with it. Each process in a token's routing is augmented by a generation number which indicates which state is to be used with the token. This solution also caters for the case when a token arrives at a process which does not, as yet, have the required state. The token is delayed until the state is created. At some stage of course, a particular graphics state will no longered be required, that is, when there are no longer any tokens left in the system referring to that state. The detection of this condition can be achieved by the use of reference counts associated with each state list. However, this could lead to a high communications overhead in incrementing and decrementing these counts in conjunction with releasing and then consuming primitive tokens.

For an output primitive token the entire graphics system state is encapsulated by the set of generation numbers contained within the token's routing. The ability to control when the generation numbers are bound to a token gives a simple method for controlling some dynamic aspects of a primitive. If the generation numbers have not been bound to a token then the token can be affected by changes to the graphics state, conversely, if the generation numbers are bound then the graphics state is fixed for that token and additional graphics state changes will have no effect (see section 3).

The control problems described earlier partly occur because the order that tokens are processed by the system can differ from the order in which tokens are generated. Clearly, this could lead to strange undesirable effects when the tokens arrive for display or for storage. A mechanism for restoring the original order of the tokens is required. One possible method for achieving this is to route all tokens through a sort process prior to display or storage. The tokens would then need to contain some form of unique ordering key which can be used by the sort process. There are two problems with this method, firstly, because tokens can be entered into the system by various processes it is difficult to generate a unique key. Secondly, the number of output tokens released into the system may differ from the number of tokens reaching the display. For example, primitive tokens can be entirely removed from the system by clipping, or split into several tokens by attribute elaboration, and hence alter the sequence of ordering keys which the sort process would have to deal with. This can be solved by replacing tokens to be removed by dummy tokens and allowing a fractional extension to the ordering key (e.g. tokens 27,27.1,27.2 etc.), but this is perhaps not entirely satisfactory.

3   A Configuration Example

Two example configurations are shown below which can be used to demonstrate whats perhaps commonly thought to be the major difference between GKS and PHIGS, that is, the difference between static and dynamic attribute bindings. The example configurations are simplified in that they ignore other differences between the standards, such as the 3D nature of PHIGS, hierarchical structures versus linear segments, deferral modes, etc.

In GKS, a primitive is created by the application issuing the appropriate function call and the primitive has attributes taken from the current GKS state bound to it at that time. If some form of segment storage is active then the primitive plus attributes may then be siphoned off into a segment. The process routing for this might be as follows:

(1)   Bind current state list generation numbers;

(2)   Bind ASF values;

(3)   Bind Individual values (e.g. line type, width, NDC clip rectangle);

(4)   Bind Index (e.g. polyline index);

(5) Perform WC to NDC transform;

(6) Segment storage (assuming the token is copied and released);

(7) Bind segment attributes (e.g. highlighting, visibility etc.);

(8) Bind bundled values (e.g. colour index);

(9) Clip to NDC;

(10) Bind colour representation;

(11) NDC to DC transform;

(12) Elaborate attributes;

(13) Display primitive.

In PHIGS a primitive element is created by the application issuing the appropriate function call and this is stored immediately in the open structure. No attribute information is bound to the primitive element at this time. In addition, attribute setting is achieved by storing attribute elements in the open structure and if the structure is currently not posted for display, these elements have no immediate effect. When the structure is posted and traversal takes place, the primitive elements have the appropriate attributes bound to them from the current PHIGS state, which is modified during traversal by the attribute setting elements. A possible configuration for PHIGS might be as follows:

(1) Structure storage;

(2) Bind current state list generation numbers;

(3) Bind ASF values;

(4) Bind Individual values (e.g. line type, width);

(5) Bind Index (e.g. polyline index);

(6) Perform WC to NDC transform;

(7) Bind bundled values (e.g. colour index, viewing parameters);

(8) Viewing;

(9) Clip to NPC;

(10) Bind colour representation;

(11) NPC to DC transform;

(12) Elaborate attributes;

(13) Display primitive.

The two configurations differ principally in the positioning of the storage module. Dynamic attribute control (editing) is possible in PHIGS because the primitives stored in structures are in an unbound state. In GKS however, primitives are stored in a bound state and hence the attributes are not controllable. Note that GKS segment attributes, which are dynamic attributes, are not bound to the primitive until after segment storage and thus changing these attributes will have the expected effect.

4   Implementation

A prototype graphics system has been implemented on two different host machines, a DEC VAX 11/780 under VMS and a ICL PERQ 2 under PNX (v4). The bulk of both these implementations has been written in Pascal, with a small machine dependent module written in either VAX assembler or C, respectively. The machine dependent module contains routines for the creation and deletion of processes, for interprocess communication and for simple process synchronization. In the PNX (UNIX) implementation, interprocess communication is achieved using pipes, this requires an additional process to be the parent of all the graphics processes. The VAX implementation uses VMS mailboxes for interprocess communication, these correspond closely to 'named pipes' or 'sockets' in other UNIX operating systems.

Tokens in the prototype vary between approximately 70 bytes and 1200 bytes depending on token type. A constant 65 bytes of this are used for pipeline configuration and the remainder for graphics data. For example, a 16x16 cell array of 4 byte colour indices would require at least 1 kbytes of data.

The prototype currently does not contain all the processes necessary for emulating a complete graphics system such as GKS or PHIGS, nevertheless, sufficient processes have been implemented to allow some reasonable graphics to be produced. The processes so far implemented include the following:

Attribute Strand	ASF binding
	Index binding
	Individual binding
	Bundle representations
	Colour representation
	Elaborate polyline
	Elaborate fill area
	Elaborate text
Transformation Strand	Modelling transform
	View Orientation
	View Projection
	Workstation transform
Clip strand	View clip
	Workstation clip
Storage strand	Structure store or WISS

5 Summary

A configurable graphics system architecture has been described, and shown to be capable of emulating the effects of various standard graphics systems. The system uses a special form of message called a token which contains not only graphics data, but also token routing information. This routing information determines what processes will act on the graphics data contained in the token, what version of the graphics system state should be used in conjunction with the graphics data, and in what order these actions should occur. The token routing information is seen to be a particularly flexible mechanism for specifying a graphics systems configuration and allows dynamic variations of the configuration.

The graphics system architecture and the reference model of graphics data states form part of the research interests of the Modular Graphics Systems research group based at the University of East Anglia, Norwich.

References

1.   D.B. Arnold, G. Hall, and G.J. Reynolds, "Proposals for Configurable Models of Graphics Systems," *Computer Graphics Forum* **3(3)**, pp.201-208 (1984).

2.   D.B. Arnold and G.J. Reynolds, "A reference model for states of graphics system data," BSI working paper (January 1986).

3.   Computer Aided Design Centre, *GINO-F User's Manual*, 1976.

4.   A. van Dam et al., *COGS: A configurable graphics system toolbox*, Brown University, Dept. of computer science (November 1981).

5.   GSPC, "Status report on the Graphics Standards planning committee," *Computer Graphics* **13(3)** (August 1979).

6.   I. Herman, T. Tolnay-Knefely, and A. Vincze, "XGKS - A Multitask implementation of GKS," pp. 215-222 in *Eurographics '83* , ed. P. J. W. ten Hagen, North-Holland, Amsterdam (September 1983). (Reproduced in this Volume.)

7.   C. Hewitt, "Viewing control structures as patterns of passing messages," *Artificial Intelligence* **8**(3), pp.323-364 (1977).

8.   ISO, "Information processing systems - Computer graphics - Graphical Kernel System (GKS) functional description," ISO 7942, ISO Central Secretariat (August 1985).

9.   ISO, "Information processing systems - Computer graphics - Metafile for the transfer and storage of picture description information," ISO/DIS 8632 (1-4) (December 1985).

10.   ISO, "PHIGS: Programmer's Hierachical Interactive Graphics System - Functional Description," TC97/SC21/N819 (September 1985).

11. ISO/TC97/SC21/WG5-2, "GKS-3D," N277 (February 1985).

12. A.C. Kilgour, *A hierachical model of a graphics sytem,* University of Glasgow, Dept. of computer science (April 1981).

13. D.M. Ritchie and K. Thompson, "The UNIX Time-Sharing System," *The Bell System Technical Journal* **57**(6), pp.1905-1929 (July 1978).

14. D.S.H. Rosenthal, "Methodology in Computer graphics re-examined," *Computer Graphics* **15**(2), pp.152-162 (July 1981).

Part II: Algorithms

One of the difficulties in implementing GKS arises from the fact that its specifications are extremely general; consequently, a good number of well-known mathematical algorithms are only partially applicable. It is, therefore, of major importance to have published algorithms that can handle absolutely general conditions such as the filling and clipping of polygons whose edges may intersect. In this section, two contributions deal specifically with this problem (**Matthew; Shinde et al.**). The exact interpretation of the GKS TEXT primitive is also not trivial; the paper of **Brodlie et al.** should be helpful in this respect. Fast transformation of pixel rectangles is very important for a rich implementation of the GKS CELL ARRAY primitive; the paper of **Schumann et al.** gives good guidance here. Finally, the paper of **Singleton** deals with a problem that has become highly relevant only in the last few years with the specification of 3D extensions to GKS, namely with the implementation of the GKS-3D viewing pipeline.

Polygonal Clipping of Polylines

A. J. Matthew

1 Purpose

There is sometimes a need to clip polylines to an irregular polygonal boundary, for example to ensure that calculated contour lines are terminated at a coastline. A similar problem is to fill a polygon with a repeating pattern.

A routine to do this task could be used to clip polylines to ensure that they do not extend beyond the physical limits of a rectangular device, or to clip them at some other rectangle parallel to the physical edges, but the general routine would be an inefficient way of performing this very common special case [2].

The routine could also be used to shade a polygon all over with a pattern of parallel lines. Again, this special case can be handled more efficiently than by the general routine. However, the routine presented here is in a form which separates the task of finding intersections between a vector and a polygon into a separate routine, which could be used by a routine for shading.

2 Specification

A polyline is defined by any sequence of points in a plane: the points will be termed "nodes" and the lines joining adjacent nodes in the sequence are "vectors". A polygon is also defined by any sequence of planar points, the points here being called "vertices" and the lines "sides". A polygon has as many sides as vertices; a polyline has one fewer vectors than nodes.

If every sequence of points is allowed to count as defining a polygon, then polygons may have intersecting sides. In this case the inside of the polygon includes any point from which a line extending infinitely in one direction would cut the polygon an odd number of times. This definition of a polygon allows some awkward cases: if several consecutive nodes are colinear and in the same direction, then all except the first and last are redundant; the point of intersection of two sides need not be listed as a vertex.

On the other hand, the definition of a polygon requires that all the sides are directly or indirectly connected, and so excludes polygons with separate internal boundaries (or boundaries that do not include each other or overlap).

Nodes and vertices may be numbered in the order in which they are listed. The nth vector or side is the one from the nth node or vertex to the next, so the mth side of a polygon with m vertices joins the mth vertex to the first.

A vector may coincide partly or wholly with a side. A clipping routine should treat all such cases consistently, and here the sides are treated as part of the inside. This applies even in the case where two sides (or any even number) themselves coincide, thus giving a portion of the polygon of zero width.

3   Using the Routine

The routine presented here is in FORTRAN and is called by:

CALL POLCLP(NVERTS,XVERTS,YVERTS,NCOORD,
                     XCOORD,YCOORD,DRAWIN,IERROR)

All parameters except IERROR must be set on entry, and only IERROR is set by the routine.

NVERT	integer, the length of arrays XVERTS and YVERTS
XVERTS	real array of length NVERTS, holds the x-coordinates of the vertices of the polygon
YVERTS	real array of length NVERTS, holds the y-coordinates of the vertices of the polygon
NCOORD	integer, the length of arrays XCOORD and YCOORD
XCOORD	real array of length NCOORD, holds the x-coordinates of the nodes of the polyline
YCOORD	real array of length NCOORD, holds the y-coordinates of the nodes of the polyline
DRAWIN	logical, set to .TRUE. if the polyline is to be drawn within the polygon, .FALSE. if it is to be drawn outside
IERROR	integer, returns the value 0 if there is no error, 1 if NVERTS is less than 3, 2 if NCOORD is less than 2, 3 if both errors are found

The routine calls a subsidiary routine NXTINT, and the GKS polyline function, called GPL in FORTRAN. The routine thus requires only level 0a of GKS, and may be adapted very easily for any other graphical system.

The example program is written in terms of GKS functions and allows the user to define a polygon of not more than ten vertices and a polyline of not more than ten nodes. It draws the parts of the polyline inside the polygon in one style and then the parts outside in another style. An example set of data illustrates an awkward case.

4 Method

Each vector is considered in turn and is rotated so that it is horizontal with the nth node on the left and the $(n+1)$th on the right, the polygon being rotated by the same amount. A point on the vector extended indefinitely to the left and moving rightwards will either miss the polygon entirely or eventually intersect a side. Only the second vertex of a side is considered for intersections, so that an intersection with a vertex is not counted for both of the two sides which meet there. If this intersection is not a vertex, then here the extended vector enters the polygon.

If the intersection is a vertex and the two adjacent vertices are both above or both below the vector, then the vector does not enter the polygon. Otherwise it does, including the case where one or both the adjacent vertices also lie on the vector, so that the vector coincides with one or more sides of the polygon (figure 1).

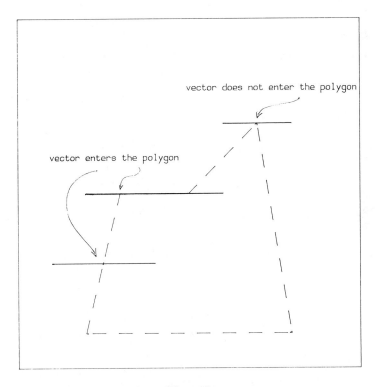

Figure 1

The point moving along the extended vector will eventually come to another intersection. In most cases it will then pass out of the polygon but there are three exceptions. One exception is where the intersection coincides with a vertex and the two adjacent vertices are both above or both below the vector (figure 2).

Another exception is where the moving point has been running along a side of the polygon, and now meets a vertex beginning a side which is not colinear. Whether it now enters or leaves the polygon depends upon the directions from which sides joined the vector at this and previous intersections.

A third exception is where the moving point had been running along a side and it meets an intersection with the polygon (which may also be a vertex), but that side continues further to the right.

5   Design Features

Intersections must be found by comparing a vector with each side of the polygon. If the sides are considered in order, the intersections that are found will not necessarily be in order from left to right (figure 3). A possible method is to store all the intersections found for one vector, and then to sort them into order [1]. There may be as many intersections as there are sides, so the storage space must be at least equal to

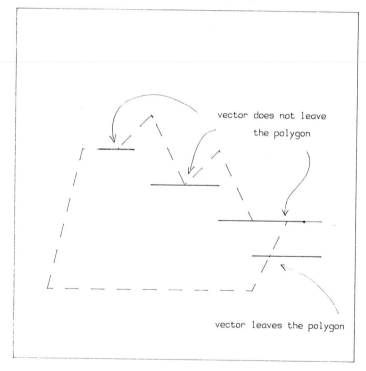

Figure 2

that required to define the polygon. However, it is not just the position of intersections which determines where the vector enters or leaves the polygon, but also whether any previous intersections were with vertices and if so from what direction the sides of the polygon joined the vector. At least one computer word would be needed to store this information for every possible intersection.

The implementation presented here attempts to minimize storage requirements, by looking each time through the polygon for the next leftmost intersection, ignoring for the time being any intersections that are further to the right or are to the left of the point currently reached. This potentially wasteful recalculation is minimized in a number of ways. The start of each side except the first is equal to the end of the previous side in the rotated coordinates. Furthermore, the y-coordinate of a side can show that it cannot possibly meet a given vector, without the need to calculate the rotated x-coordinates. When the polygon is first searched for intersections with a given vector, the number of intersections is counted; this count is decreased by one as each intersection is dealt with on successive calls, and allows the search for intersections to be terminated when all those remaining have been found, without necessarily looking at every side of the polygon. For each vector except the first, the end point of the previous vector determines whether its starting point is inside (unless the node happens to lie exactly on a side), and so any intersections further to the left can be ignored immediately.

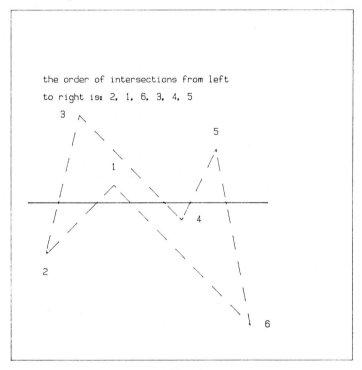

Figure 3

The calculations do not require any trigonometric functions, and the only FORTRAN function required is for one square root per vector.

6 Implementation

The clipping routine calls a subsidiary routine which returns for the current vector the intersection which is next to the right of some specified starting point. That starting point is generally the previous intersection found, but for the first intersection for a given vector it will be the left end of the vector. For the first vector of the polyline, or when the previous vector ended exactly on a side of the polygon, then no starting point is given and the subsidiary routine returns the leftmost intersection, if there is any intersection at all.

In the case where several intersections exactly coincide, the subsidiary routine will return each of them on successive calls, in order of the sides to which they belong.

When the leftmost intersection is found, then if it goes through a vertex a check is made to see whether it goes through the top or bottom of each of the two sides which meet at that vertex (figure 4). If either of the sides is horizontal then the intersection is neither top nor bottom for that side; in some cases both the adjacent sides are horizontal. There are two logical variables ("top" and "bottom"), initially false, which are reversed for each top or bottom intersection. If the intersection is not with a vertex, then both variables are reversed, since part of the side lies above the intersection and part below.

If the intersection is with a vertex and one at least of the adjacent sides is horizontal and extends to the right, then a logical variable ("right") is set to true (figure 5). If "right" is already true and the current intersection is with a vertex, then every side of the polygon is examined to see if any extends horizontally to the right through the current intersection: if none does so, then "right" is set back to false.

When an intersection is returned, the clipping routine determines whether it is one at which the vector enters or leaves the polygon; if not, then the next intersection is sought immediately. For the vector to enter the polygon, "top" or "bottom" or "right" must be true. For it to leave the polygon, they must all be false.

For clipping inside the polygon, on finding the first intersection to the right of the start of the vector, it is either the beginning of a section to be drawn (if the vector here enters the polygon), or else the end of a section to be drawn, which began with the start of the vector (if the vector here leaves the polygon). Thereafter drawing begins and ends as the vector enters and leaves the polygon. On finding an intersection to the right of the end of the vector, and at which the vector leaves the polygon, a section is drawn up to the end of the vector.

For clipping outside the polygon, on finding the first intersection to the right of the start of the vector, and if the vector there enters the polygon, a section will be drawn from the start of the vector. On finding an intersection to the right of the end of the vector at which the vector enters the polygon (or that there is no further intersection), a section is drawn up to the end of the vector.

Whenever the end of a section is found it is drawn, even though it may be contiguous with a section of the next vector and the two could form part of a polyline. (Storage space would be needed to recompose the sections into a polyline.)

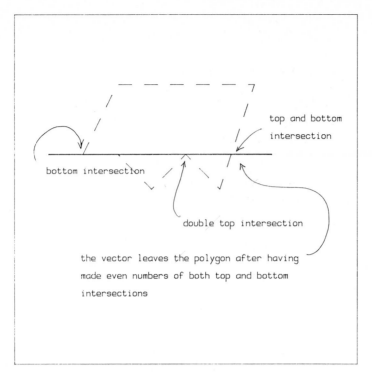

top and bottom
intersection

bottom intersection

double top intersection

the vector leaves the polygon after having
made even numbers of both top and bottom
intersections

Figure 4

On beginning another vector of the polyline, the clipping routine checks whether the previous one ended exactly on a side (figure 6). This will be so if the end of the vector and the intersection are equal. Also, if the previous vector ran along a side and ended between or on its vertices, then the test is whether the preceding intersection had "right" set to true. If either of these cases applies, then "inside", "top", "bottom" and "right" are all set to false. Otherwise "inside" and "right" are left unchanged and "top" and "bottom" are set equal to "inside" (i.e. to the value they had at the end of the previous vector, before finding any intersection further to the right of it).

References

1.   J.D. Foley and A. van Dam, *Fundamentals of Interactive Computer Graphics*, Addison-Wesley, Reading, Massachusetts (1982).

2.   W.M. Newman and R.F. Sproull, *Principles of Interactive Computer Graphics*, McGraw-Hill, New York (Second Edition 1979).

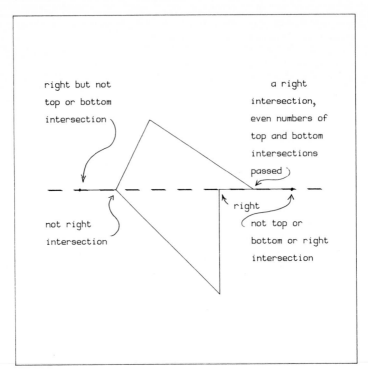

right but not
top or bottom
intersection

a right
intersection,
even numbers of
top and bottom
intersections
passed

not right
intersection

right
not top or
bottom or right
intersection

Figure 5

Appendix

```
      PROGRAM RNPLCL
C
C A PROGRAM TO GENERATE A RANDOM POLYGON
C OF 5 VERTICES AND TWO POLYLINE
C EACH OF 9 VECTORS. ONE POLYLINE IS
C CLIPPED TO THE POLYGON INTERNALLY AND
C THE OTHER EXTERNALLY. THE POLYGON AND
C THE INTERNAL AND EXTERNAL SECTIONS
C OF THE POLYLINES ARE DRAWN IN DIFFERENT
C LINE TYPES AND COLOURS.
C
      REAL XVERTS(11),YVERTS(11)
      REAL XCOORD(10),YCOORD(10)
      INTEGER IASF(13)
      DATA IASF/13*0/
         CALL GOPKS(6)
         CALL GSASF(IASF)
         CALL GOPWK(1,6,107)
         CALL GACWK(1)
```

```
        CALL GSPLR(1,1,1,1.0,1)
        CALL GSPLR(1,2,2,1.0,2)
        CALL GSPLR(1,3,3,1.0,3)
        CALL GSWN(1,-250.0,250.0,-250.0,250.0)
        CALL GSELNT(1)
C
C DEFINE THE POLYGON
C
        CALL GUWK(1,0)
        WRITE(*,100) 'POLYGON'
100     FORMAT(/,
     +  ' ENTER UP TO 10 PAIRS OF COORDINATES FOR THE '
     +  ,A,' IN THE RANGE +-250:',/,
     +  ' AN X-COORDINATE OUTSIDE THE RANGE',
     +  ' TERMINATES INPUT')
        DO 10 NVERTS = 1,10
           READ(*,*,ERR = 15) XVERTS(NVERTS),
     +     YVERTS(NVERTS)
           IF(ABS(XVERTS(NVERTS)).GT.250.0) GOTO 15
  10    CONTINUE
  15    XVERTS(NVERTS) = XVERTS(1)
        YVERTS(NVERTS) = YVERTS(1)
C
C DRAW BOUNDARY OF POLYGON
C
        CALL GSPLI(1)
        CALL GPL(NVERTS,XVERTS,YVERTS)
C
C DEFINE THE POLYLINE
C
        CALL GUWK(1,0)
        WRITE(*,100) 'POLYLINE'
        DO 20 NCOORD = 1,10
           READ(*,*,ERR = 25) XCOORD(NCOORD),
     +     YCOORD(NCOORD)
           IF(ABS(XCOORD(NCOORD)).GT.250.0) GOTO 25
  20    CONTINUE
  25    NCOORD = NCOORD - 1
C
C CLIP POLYLINE TO THE POLYGON
C
        CALL GSPLI(2)
        CALL POLCLP
     +  (NVERTS-1,XVERTS,YVERTS,NCOORD,
     +  XCOORD,YCOORD,.TRUE.,IERROR)
        CALL GSPLI(3)
        CALL POLCLP
     +  (NVERTS-1,XVERTS,YVERTS,NCOORD,
     +  XCOORD,YCOORD,.FALSE.,IERROR)
        CALL GDAWK(1)
        CALL GCLWK(1)
```

```
          CALL GCLKS
          STOP
          END
```

Example Data

```
-200,0
0,0
0,-100
-100,0
200,0
-200,100
500,0
-220,50
-200,0
-100,-100
0,0
-200,0
-200,200
200,0
0,-100
-150,10
0,100
500,0
```

```
      SUBROUTINE POLCLP
    + (NVERTS,XVERTS,YVERTS,NCOORD,
    + XCOORD,YCOORD,DRAWIN,IERROR)
C
C A ROUTINE TO DRAW THOSE PARTS OF THE POLYLINE
C DEFINED BY (XCOORD, YCOORD)
C WHICH LIE WITHIN THE POLYGON DEFINED BY
C (XVERTS, YVERTS) IF DRAWIN IS
C TRUE, ELSE THE PARTS LYING OUTSIDE.
C
C AUTHOR:    A. J. MATTHEW
C         COMPUTER LABORATORY
C         LEICESTER UNIVERSITY
C         LEICESTER
C         ENGLAND
C
      REAL XVERTS(NVERTS), YVERTS(NVERTS)
      REAL XCOORD(NCOORD), YCOORD(NCOORD)
      REAL XLINE(2), YLINE(2)
      LOGICAL DRAWIN, INSIDE, FIRST
      LOGICAL TOP, BOTTOM, RIGHT, CRIGHT
C
      COMMON /ROTCOM/ SINANG,COSANG,IDR
C
C DEFINE FUNCTIONS TO ROTATE COORDINATES
C BY THE ANGLE DEFINED BY SINANG AND
```

```
C COSANG, AND ROTATE THEM BACK AGAIN.
C IF IDR WERE -1, THEN NXTINT WOULD FIND
C INTERSECTIONS IN THE REVERSE ORDER, BUT
C IN THIS ROUTINE IDR IS ALWAYS +1.
C
       XROT(X,Y) = IDR*(X*COSANG - Y*SINANG)
       YROT(X,Y) = X*SINANG + Y*COSANG
       XBROT(X,Y) = IDR*X*COSANG + Y*SINANG
       YBROT(X,Y) = -IDR*X*SINANG + Y*COSANG
C
C CHECK THERE ARE SUFFICIENT POINTS TO
C DEFINE A POLYGON AND A POLYLINE
C
       IERROR = 0
       IF(NVERTS.LT.3) IERROR = 1
       IF(NCOORD.LT.2) IERROR = IERROR + 2
       IF(IERROR.GT.0) GOTO 99
C
C EACH VECTOR IS DRAWN HORIZONTALLY LEFT
C TO RIGHT BY ROTATING THE POLYGON
C
       DO 20 NSEG = 1,NCOORD-1
C
C SET CHARACTERISTICS OF A VECTOR FOR THE
C FIRST ONE OF THE POLYLINE OR IF THE
C PREVIOUS VECTOR ENDED ON A SIDE OF THE
C POLYGON
C
       IF(NSEG.EQ.1.OR.XINT.EQ.XREN.OR.CRIGHT)
     +     THEN
           INSIDE = .FALSE.
           TOP = .FALSE.
           BOTTOM = .FALSE.
           RIGHT = .FALSE.
           CRIGHT = .FALSE.
C
C XLAST IS IGNORED BY NXTINT IF NLAST IS ZERO
C
           NLAST = 0
C
C ELSE TOP AND BOTTOM DEPEND ON WHETHER
C THE END OF THE PREVIOUS VECTOR WAS
C INSIDE THE POLYGON
C
       ELSE
           TOP = INSIDE
           BOTTOM = INSIDE
C
C FOR THE FIRST INTERSECTION FOR A VECTOR,
C XLAST IS NOT AN INTERSECTION WITH A SIDE
C OF THE POLYGON, SO NLAST IS SET TO -1
```

```
C
          NLAST = -1
       ENDIF
C
C NOW CALCULATE THE ROTATION FOR THE CURRENT
C VECTOR TO BE CONSIDERED AS HORIZONTAL
C FROM LEFT TO RIGHT
C
     .    XDIF = XCOORD(NSEG+1) - XCOORD(NSEG)
          YDIF = YCOORD(NSEG+1) - YCOORD(NSEG)
          HYP = SQRT(XDIF**2 + YDIF**2)
C
C ALLOW FOR DOTS TO BE DRAWN AS LINES OF ZERO
C LENGTH
C
       IF(HYP.EQ.0.0) THEN
          SINANG = 0.0
          COSANG = 1.0
       ELSE
          SINANG = -YDIF/HYP
          COSANG = XDIF/HYP
       ENDIF
       IDR = 1
  C
C IN ROTATED COORDINATES, THE VECTOR
C EXTENDS HORIZONTALLY AT A HEIGHT YH
C
       YH = YROT(XCOORD(NSEG),YCOORD(NSEG))
C
C BETWEEN XRST AND XREN
C
       XRST = XROT(XCOORD(NSEG),
     +    YCOORD(NSEG))
       XREN = XROT(XCOORD(NSEG+1),
     +    YCOORD(NSEG+1))
C
C LOOK FOR THE NEXT INTERSECTION BEYOND
C THE START OF THE VECTOR, UNLESS THIS
C IS THE FIRST VECTOR OF THE POLYLINE
C
       XLAST = XRST
       FIRST = .TRUE.
```

```
      C
      C FIND NEXT INTERSECTION AFTER XLAST, IF ANY
      C
   10       IF(INTCNT.GT.0.OR.FIRST) THEN
               CALL NXTINT(NVERTS,XVERTS,YVERTS,YH,
     +         XLAST,NLAST,XINT,NINT,TOP,
     +         BOTTOM,RIGHT,INTCNT)
            ELSE
               NINT = 0
            ENDIF
      C
      C THE TOTAL NUMBER OF INTERSECTIONS TO THE
      C RIGHT OF OR ON THE STARTING POINT IS FOUND
      C ON THE FIRST CALL OF NXTINT FOR A GIVEN
      C VECTOR, AND THIS NUMBER IS DECREASED AS
      C EACH INTERSECTION IS DEALT WITH.
      C
            INTCNT = INTCNT - 1
      C
      C IF ANY INTERSECTION FOUND, THEN BOUNDARY
      C OF POLYGON HAS BEEN CROSSED
      C
            IF(NINT.NE.0.AND.XINT.LT.XREN) THEN
               CRIGHT = RIGHT
               IF(INSIDE.EQV.(TOP.OR.BOTTOM.OR.RIGHT))
     +           THEN
                  XLAST = XINT
                  NLAST = NINT
                  GOTO 10
               ENDIF
               INSIDE = .NOT.INSIDE
            ENDIF
      C
      C DRAWING MAY BEGIN IF THERE IS NO INTERSECTION
      C OF THE VECTOR WITH THE POLYGON OR AT FIRST
      C INTERSECTION TO THE RIGHT OF THE START
      C OF THE VECTOR.
      C
            IF(NINT.EQ.0.OR.XINT.GE.XRST) THEN
               IF(FIRST.AND.((DRAWIN.EQV.INSIDE)
     +         .EQV.(NINT.EQ.0.OR.XINT.GE.XREN))) THEN
                  XLINE(1) = XCOORD(NSEG)
                  YLINE(1) = YCOORD(NSEG)
               ENDIF
               FIRST = .FALSE.
            ENDIF
```

```
C
C AT INTERSECTIONS WITHIN THE LINE,
C START OR STOP DRAWING
C
            IF(NINT.NE.0.AND.XINT.GE.XRST.AND.XINT.LT.XREN)
     +         THEN
               IF(DRAWIN.EQV.INSIDE) THEN
                  XLINE(1) = XBROT(XINT,YH)
                  YLINE(1) = YBROT(XINT,YH)
               ELSE
                  XLINE(2) = XBROT(XINT,YH)
                  YLINE(2) = YBROT(XINT,YH)
C
C DRAW A SECTION OF THE VECTOR WHEN THE
C END OF THE SECTION HAS BEEN FOUND
C
                  CALL GPL(2,XLINE,YLINE)
               ENDIF
            ENDIF
C
C DRAWING MAY NEED TO BE ENDED IF NO FURTHER
C INTERSECTION IS FOUND BETWEEN THE VECTOR
C AND THE POLYGON, OR THE INTERSECTION IS
C TO THE RIGHT OF THE END OF THE VECTOR.
C
            IF(NINT.EQ.0.OR.XINT.GE.XREN) THEN
               IF(DRAWIN.EQV.INSIDE) THEN
C
C DRAW TO THE END OF THE VECTOR
C
                  XLINE(2) = XCOORD(NSEG+1)
                  YLINE(2) = YCOORD(NSEG+1)
                  CALL GPL(2,XLINE,YLINE)
               ENDIF
               GOTO 20
            ENDIF
C
C FIND NEXT INTERSECTION
C
            XLAST = XINT
            NLAST = NINT
            GOTO 10
   20    CONTINUE
   99    RETURN
         END
```

```
      SUBROUTINE NXTINT(NVERTS,XVERTS,YVERTS,YH,
     +   XLAST,NLAST,XINT,NINT,TOP,
     +   BOTTOM,RIGHT,INTCNT)
C
C THIS ROUTINE FINDS THE NEXT INTERSECTION
C OF A VECTOR WITH THE POLYGON DEFINED BY
C THE NVERTS COORDINATES IN ARRAYS XVERTS
C AND YVERTS.
C
C AUTHOR: A. J. MATTHEW
C         COMPUTER LABORATORY
C         LEICESTER UNIVERSITY
C         LEICESTER
C         ENGLAND
C
C
C THE INTERSECTING VECTOR IS HORIZONTAL AND
C INTERCEPTS THE Y AXIS AT YH, WITH THE
C POLYGON ROTATED CLOCKWISE BY AN ANGLE
C DEFINED BY SINANG AND COSANG. IF IDR IS -1,
C THEN THE POLYGON IS REFLECTED ABOUT THE Y
C AXIS AS WELL AS ROTATED, THUS ALLOWING
C INTERSECTIONS TO BE FOUND IN THE OPPOSITE
C DIRECTION.
C
C INTERSECTIONS ARE FOUND IN ORDER FROM LEFT
C TO RIGHT IN THE TRANSFORMED POLYGON.
C
C THE INTERSECTION TO BE FOUND IS THE NEAREST
C ONE TO THE RIGHT OF XLAST, OR EQUAL TO XLAST.
C THE FIRST TIME NXTINT IS CALLED FOR A GIVEN
C VECTOR, XLAST IS THE LEFT END OF THE VECTOR
C IN TRANSFORMED COORDINATES. THEREAFTER
C XLAST IS THE POINT OF INTERSECTION IN
C TRANSFORMED COORDINATES WITH THE SIDE
C OF THE POLYGON DEFINED BY THE
C NLAST-TH ELEMENTS OF XVERTS AND YVERTS
C AND THE NEXT ELEMENTS OF THOSE ARRAYS.
C
C AN INTERSECTION IS FOUND WHICH IS EQUAL
C TO THE PREVIOUS ONE ONLY IF IT BELONGS TO A
C SIDE OF THE POLYGON OF HIGHER NUMBER THAN
C NLAST. THUS IF SEVERAL SIDES OF THE POLYGON
C ALL PASS THROUGH THE SAME POINT AND THE
C INTERSECTING LINE ALSO PASSES EXACTLY
C THROUGH THIS POINT, THEN INTERSECTIONS ARE
C FOUND FOR EACH OF THESE SIDES IN ORDER.
C
C IF NLAST IS ZERO, THEN THE INTERSECTION TO
C BE FOUND IS SIMPLY THE LEFTMOST.
C
```

```
C WHEN XLAST IS THE LEFT END OF THE VECTOR
C INSTEAD OF BEING THE PREVIOUS INTERSECTION
C WITH THIS VECTOR, NLAST IS -1.
C
C THE INTERSECTION IS RETURNED AS XINT, IN
C ROTATED COORDINATES, BELONGING TO THE
C NINT-TH SIDE OF THE POLYGON.
C
C IF NO INTERSECTION IS FOUND,
C THEN NINT IS ZERO.
C
C ROTATION BACK TO THE ORIGINAL COORDINATE
C SYSTEM IS DONE IN THE CALLING ROUTINE.
C
        REAL XVERTS(NVERTS),YVERTS(NVERTS)
        COMMON /ROTCOM/ SINANG,COSANG,IDR
        LOGICAL TOP,BOTTOM,RIGHT
C
C DEFINE FUNCTIONS TO ROTATE A POINT
C
        XROT(X,Y) = (X*COSANG - Y*SINANG)*IDR
        YROT(X,Y) = X*SINANG + Y*COSANG
C
        NINT = 0
        IF(NLAST.LE.0) INTCNT = 0
        INTCHK = 0
        DO 10 NSIDE = 1,NVERTS
C
C IF THE KNOWN NUMBER OF INTERSECTIONS HAVE
C ALREADY BEEN FOUND, DO NOT LOOK AT ANY MORE
C SIDES OF THE POLYGON
C
            IF(NLAST.GT.0.AND.INTCHK.GE.INTCNT) GOTO 50
C
C LOOK FOR AN INTERSECTION WITH THE SIDE OF
C THE POLYGON, UNLESS IT IS THE SIDE ON WHICH
C THE PREVIOUS INTERSECTION WAS FOUND.
C
            IF(NSIDE.EQ.NLAST) GOTO 10
            IF(NSIDE.EQ.1.OR.NSIDE.EQ.NLAST+1) THEN
                Y1 = YROT(XVERTS(NSIDE),YVERTS(NSIDE))
            ELSE
                Y1 = Y2
            ENDIF
            NSIDE1 = NSIDE + 1
            IF(NSIDE1.GT.NVERTS) NSIDE1 = 1
            Y2 = YROT(XVERTS(NSIDE1),YVERTS(NSIDE1))
C
C THE INTERSECTING LINE MEETS THE CURRENT
C SIDE ONLY IF THE END POINTS OF THE SIDE ARE
C ABOVE AND BELOW THE INTERSECTING LINE OR
```

```
C THE SECOND END POINT IS ON IT.
C
          IF((YH-Y1)*(YH-Y2).GE.0.0.AND.YH.NE.Y2) GOTO 10
C
C THE ROTATED X-COORDINATES OF THE END POINTS
C OF THE SIDE ARE CALCULATED
C
          X1 = XROT(XVERTS(NSIDE),YVERTS(NSIDE))
          X2 = XROT(XVERTS(NSIDE1),YVERTS(NSIDE1))
C
C A POINT OF INTERSECTION IS CALCULATED.
C ONLY THE SECOND END POINT OF A SIDE IS
C CONSIDERED, SO THAT IT IS NOT CONSIDERED
C AGAIN AS THE FIRST POINT OF THE NEXT SIDE.
C
          IF(Y2.EQ.YH) THEN
             XHIT = X2
          ELSE
             XHIT = X1 + (X2-X1)*((YH-Y1)/(Y2-Y1))
          ENDIF
   20     CONTINUE
C
C CHECK THAT THE INTERSECTION IS TO THE RIGHT
C OF XLAST, OR IF EQUAL TO IT THEN THAT IT
C BELONGS TO A SIDE HIGHER IN ORDER.
C OTHERWISE IGNORE IT.
C
          IF(NLAST.NE.0) THEN
             IF(XHIT.LT.XLAST) GOTO 10
             IF(XHIT.EQ.XLAST.AND.NSIDE.LE.NLAST) GOTO 10
          ENDIF
C
C THE FIRST TIME THIS ROUTINE IS CALLED FOR
C A GIVEN VECTOR, COUNT THE TOTAL NUMBER OF
C INTERSECTIONS TO THE RIGHT OF THE STARTING
C POINT, IF ANY. FOR SUBSEQUENT CALLS, COUNT
C SUCH INTERSECTIONS AS THEY ARE FOUND, SO AS
C NOT TO LOOK FOR ANY MORE WHEN THEY HAVE ALL
C BEEN FOUND.
C
          IF(NLAST.LE.0) THEN
             INTCNT = INTCNT + 1
          ELSE
             INTCHK = INTCHK + 1
          ENDIF
C
C STORE THE FIRST INTERSECTION FOUND BY THIS
C CALL OF THE ROUTINE OR AN INTERSECTION
C WHICH IS CLOSER TO THE LEFT THAN ONE
C PREVIOUSLY FOUND.
C
```

```
            IF(NINT.EQ.0.OR.XHIT.LT.XINT) THEN
                XINT = XHIT
                NINT = NSIDE
            ENDIF
   10   CONTINUE
C
   50   IF(NINT.EQ.0) RETURN
C
C CLASSIFY THE NEXT LEFTMOST INTERSECTION
C ACCORDING AS IT IS THE TOP, BOTTOM,
C BOTH OR NEITHER OF THE SIDES OR PARTS
C OF A SIDE ON WHICH IT LIES
C
        NINT1 = NINT + 1
        IF (NINT1.GT.NVERTS) NINT1 = 1
        Y1 = YROT(XVERTS(NINT),YVERTS(NINT))
        Y2 = YROT(XVERTS(NINT1),YVERTS(NINT1))
C
C IF THE INTERSECTION IS ON A VERTEX,
C THEN IT MIGHT NOT BE BOTH A TOP AND
C BOTTOM OF ADJACENT SIDES
C
        IF(Y2.EQ.YH) THEN
            IF(Y2.GT.Y1) TOP = .NOT.TOP
            IF(Y2.LT.Y1) BOTTOM = .NOT.BOTTOM
C
C LOOK AHEAD TO THE NEXT SIDE
C
            NINT2 = NINT1 + 1
            IF(NINT2.GT.NVERTS) NINT2 = 1
            Y3 = YROT(XVERTS(NINT2),YVERTS(NINT2))
            IF(Y2.GT.Y3) TOP = .NOT.TOP
            IF(Y2.LT.Y3) BOTTOM = .NOT.BOTTOM
C
C LOOK FOR THE BEGINNING OR END OF A
C RIGHTWARD HORIZONTAL SIDE
C
            IF(.NOT.RIGHT) THEN
C
C SEE WHETHER EITHER SIDE ADJACENT TO THE
C CURRENT VERTEX CONTINUES HORIZONTALLY TO
C THE RIGHT
C
                IF(Y1.EQ.YH) THEN
                    X1 = XROT(XVERTS(NINT),YVERTS(NINT))
                    IF(X1.GT.XINT) THEN
                        RIGHT = .TRUE.
                        GOTO 40
                    ENDIF
                ENDIF
```

```
            IF(Y3.EQ.YH) THEN
                X3 = XROT(XVERTS(NINT2),YVERTS(NINT2))
                IF(X3.GT.XINT) THEN
                    RIGHT = .TRUE.
                    GOTO 40
                ENDIF
            ENDIF
        ELSE
C
C ANY SIDE MAY CONTINUE HORIZONTALLY TO THE
C RIGHT THROUGH THE INTERSECTION
C
            DO 30 MSIDE = 1,NVERTS
                YM1 = YROT(XVERTS(MSIDE),YVERTS(MSIDE))
                IF(YM1.NE.Y2) GOTO 30
                MSIDE1 = MSIDE + 1
                IF(MSIDE1.GT.NVERTS) MSIDE1 = 1
                YM2 = YROT(XVERTS(MSIDE1),
     +          YVERTS(MSIDE1))
                IF(YM2.NE.Y2) GOTO 30
                XM1 = XROT(XVERTS(MSIDE),YVERTS(MSIDE))
                XM2 = XROT(XVERTS(MSIDE1),
     +          YVERTS(MSIDE1))
                IF((XM1.GT.XINT.OR.XM2.GT.XINT).AND.
     +          (XM1.LE.XINT.OR.XM2.LE.XINT)) GOTO 40
 30         CONTINUE
            RIGHT = .FALSE.
 40         CONTINUE
        ENDIF
    ELSE
C
C AN INTERSECTION NOT WITH A VERTEX IS AT THE
C TOP AND BOTTOM OF THE TWO PARTS OF THE SIDE
C WHICH IT CUTS.
C
        BOTTOM = .NOT.BOTTOM
        TOP = .NOT.TOP
    ENDIF
    RETURN
    END
```

Algorithms for Handling the Fill Area Primitive of GKS

Y. N. Shinde and S. P. Mudur

1 Introduction

The GKS fill area output primitive is a closed polygon specified by 3 or more vertices, say N, denoted by $P(1), P(2), \ldots, P(N)$ [1]. These points define N straight edges

$$(P(i), P(i+1)) \quad \text{for } 1 \leq i < N$$

and

$$(P(N), P(1)).$$

The following points must be noted regarding this specification:

1. The polygon is nothing but a closed piecewise linear curve to be filled.

2. Usually when a 2-dimensional region is specified by its boundary, some convention regarding the orientation of the boundary curve is adopted, say anticlockwise, so that the region always remains to the left of the direction of traversal of the boundary curve. However the GKS fill area polygon specification is not oriented.

3. The boundary can be self-intersecting.

4. The definition of the interior of the fill area is based on the concept of the winding number - "For a given point create a straight line at that point and going to infinity. If the number of intersections between the straight line and the polygon is odd, the point is within the polygon, otherwise it is outside. If

the straight line passes a polygon vertex tangentially, the intersection count is not affected." However nothing is stated clearly as to what should be done if the given point lies on an edge of the polygon. The obvious interpretation that it is part of the boundary and not part of the interior however may give rise to anomalous situations such as the example of figure 1 discussed in the next observation.

5.   Multiply connected regions, that is regions with holes, cannot be specified as a single primitive. This is however being rectified through the fill area set primitive in the GKS-3D extension [2]. Sometimes it has been argued that a region with holes can be represented as shown in figure 1. We however would like our readers to note the following observations:

(i)   In a strict mathematical sense this figure has still only a singly connected boundary.

(ii)   More important, in filling the interior of such a figure, points on the coincident edges would have to be considered as interior. It may perhaps be possible to augment the inside test to handle such cases as well. However a precise redefinition of the existing definition is not really the aim of this paper.

6.   The fill area must be transformed and then clipped to a rectangular window. As a result new boundaries generated become part of the area boundaries. Multiple subareas may be generated. The resulting area or subareas are then represented on the output in one of the following styles: HOLLOW, SOLID, PATTERN or HATCH.

IndoGKS is a complete implementation of the GKS standard version 7.2 developed by the authors. All the representation styles of the fill area output primitive are supported on all devices, simulating the effect in software whenever necessary. In the rest of the paper we present the algorithms, and their implementation details, for clipping and for filling in various styles. Because of the generality of the GKS fill area specification, in some cases, existing algorithms [3, 7, 9] cannot be directly used and so entirely new algorithms or suitable extensions are discussed.

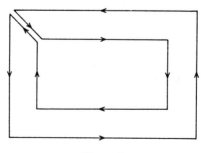

Figure 1

2   Polygon Clipping

2.1   Weiler-Atherton clipping algorithm

This algorithm basically operates by treating the given polygon and the polygon, against which clipping is to be done, as oriented graphs embedded in a plane. For a detailed discussion of this algorithm the reader is referred to [9] and to [5] for good illustrative examples. We shall discuss it briefly here to point out its inability to handle self-intersecting polygons of GKS. The algorithm first computes the intersections of all the edges of the subject polygon with the edges of the clipping polygon. It collects the resulting polygons by traversing the new subject polygon graph and clipping polygon graph (alternating at the intersection points) in one consistent direction. Consider for example the case in figure 2. Starting at I_1, you get I_3, then I_4, and I_2. At I_2 a change in direction is needed so as to reach I_1 and finish. This inability to handle self-intersecting polygons, led us to develop the bridge technique which, as we shall see, needs an additional sort per edge of the clipping polygon apart from the intersection of the subject polygon edges with the clipping polygon edges.

2.2   Bridge Technique

This is a technique for clipping a polygon against a rectangular viewport in graphics applications. Presently we shall discuss this only for the 2-dimensional space and a single subject polygon. (Later we shall discuss as to how the same technique can be extended to 3D and to many subject polygons - typically a polygon with holes.) The

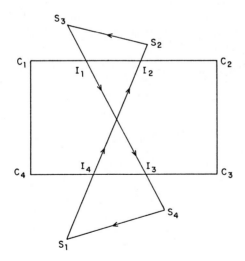

Figure 2

technique is based on the following observations made in the algorithm for polygon clipping by Sutherland and Hodgman [7].

- The Sutherland and Hodgman algorithm clips a polygon against all four edges of the screen by clipping it against one edge, then taking the resulting polygon and clipping it against the next edge and so on. This when repeated for all four edges of the clipping rectangle, generates the required output polygon. The reason we are not able to directly use this algorithm is that it always produces a single output polygon. Thus clipping a concave polygon may result in two or more regular regions (non-zero area) connected by an isthmus of zero width. Such polygons have to be classified as degenerate and have to be specifically taken care of during filling.

- The above approach reduces the clipping problem to the line/polygon classification type studied by Tilove [8]. Here the fill area polygon (connected and without holes) is specified by an ordered list of distinct points

$$(p(0),p(1),p(2), \ldots ,p(n-1))$$

Wherein each point $p(i)$ $(0 \leq i \leq n-1)$ is given by its (x,y) coordinates and is essentially a vertex of the polygon listed in its order of occurrence along the boundary. This list, can be viewed as a "vertex loop" which identifies the polygon's bounding edges (line segments in the form of an edge list).

$$([p(0),p(1)],[p(1),p(2)],[p(2),p(3)], \ldots ,[p(n-1),p(0)])$$

We will start with the hypothesis that when an infinite line passes over a polygon it intersects it at an even number of points (not considering degenerate cases like that of tangentially touching a vertex or of an edge lying on this line etc.). The clipping edge is viewed as being part of an infinite line, which divides the entire plane into two distinct regions (see figure 3a). The region in which the clipping rectangle ABCD lies is the +ve region and the one to the other side of the clipping edge is the −ve region. In fact the window/viewport region is the intersection of the +ve regions of the four infinite dividing lines corresponding to the window/viewport rectangle edges.

Based on this line/polygon intersection we form two lists: the Edge list; and the Bridge list. The following procedure is followed:

1. The edge list is initially the vertex loop representation of the subject polygon. Each entry of the edge list has an edge having, two end-points - left and right, and two pointers - one for the next edge in the vertex loop and other for the previous edge. For example, for the polygon in the figure 3b the edge list is:

	Left	Right	Next	Prev
1	$p(1)$	$p(2)$	2	8
2	$p(2)$	$p(3)$	3	1
3	$p(3)$	$p(4)$	4	2
4	$p(4)$	$p(5)$	5	3
5	$p(5)$	$p(6)$	6	4
6	$p(6)$	$p(7)$	7	5
7	$p(7)$	$p(8)$	8	6
8	$p(8)$	$p(1)$	1	7

2.   Every edge of the polygon either lies entirely in the $-$ve region (totally out) or entirely in the $+$ve region (totally in) or has one end-point in the $-$ve region and the other in the $+$ve region (assuming no end-point lies on the line L). Using this classification edges that are totally out are removed and the edge list connectivity is accordingly redefined through the next and previous pointers. Edges that are totally inside are left as they are. And edges in which one of the end-points is in the $-$ve region, have that the end-point replaced by their point

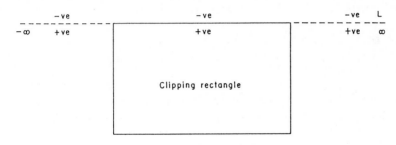

Figure 3(a)

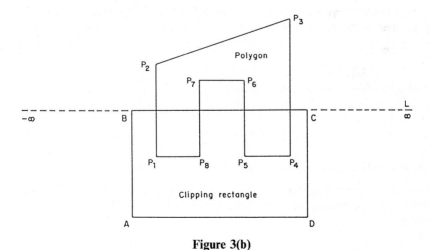

Figure 3(b)

of intersection with the line L. All such intersection points are called clip points and denoted by $c(i)$. For example, for figure 3b the modified edge list is:

	Left	Right	Next	Prev
1	$p(8)$	$c(1)$	3	8
2	–	–	–	–
3	$c(4)$	$p(4)$	4	1
4	$p(4)$	$p(5)$	5	3
5	$p(5)$	$c(3)$	7	4
6	–	–	–	–
7	$c(2)$	$p(8)$	8	5
8	$p(8)$	$p(1)$	1	7

3. The clip points lie on the line L and provide us the new line segments that are to be added. There are always an even number of points (assuming no degeneracies). These points are sorted in order of location (from left to right for horizontal edges of the clipping rectangle and bottom to top for vertical edges) and grouped in pairs of two in the sorted order:

$$[c(1),c(2)],[c(3),c(4)], \ldots ,[c(N-1),c(N)]$$

such that

● N is even

● $Xc(i) < Xc(j)$ $i < j$ for horizontal edge

● $Yc(i) < Yc(j)$ $i < j$ for vertical edge where $[Xc(i),Yc(i)]$ are coordinates of $c(i)$

This list of new segments is termed a bridge list. Every entry of the bridge list has two bridge end-points (left and right) and a next entry pointer. The next entry pointer is needed because a bridge is deleted once it is crossed or linked during the final process of winding the vertex loops. For a bridge point, along with its bridge index, a pointer to the edge list, called the edge list pointer, is also stored in the bridge list. This pointer points to the location of the bridge point in the modified edge list. The bridge list has a list head which initially points to the first entry. For example, for figure 3b the bridge list is:

	Left	Right	Next
1	$c(1)$	$c(2)$	2
2	$c(3)$	$c(4)$	0

Note: 0 in the next field indicates end of list and the first item in the list serves as the list head.

The process of generating the resulting output polygon or polygons uses the modified edge list and the bridge list. This process called 'winding the vertex loops' is discussed next.

2.2.1 Winding the Vertex Loops

Winding a vertex loop is begun by starting with the head of the bridge list. This starting bridge is termed the link bridge. In the edge list the edge containing either of the two link bridge end-points (the same result is obtained in either case, so say we choose to use the left bridge end-point) is located using the edge list pointer of that bridge end-point. The winding of the vertex loop begins at this particular edge by traversing through the edge list and collecting vertices. The loop is complete when the other end-point of the link bridge is reached.

The direction of the edge list traversal is forward or backward depending upon whether the link bridge end-point, with which the winding begins, is the left end-point or the right end-point of that edge in the edge list (connectivity direction). Thus when traversing the edge list backward all the right end-points of the edges traversed are included into the vertex loop, while for forward traversal the left end-points are included. An edge is deleted from the edge list after it has been traversed once. The winding process terminates when the edge list is empty.

During the traversal of the edge list when an edge with a bridge type end-point (left or right, irrespective of direction of traversal) is traversed, one of the following two conditions is 'TRUE':

1. This is the other end-point of the link bridge - with which the winding began - hence the vertex loop is fully wound. This other end-point of the link bridge is explicitly collected, and added in the vertex loop, if it has not already been added in the normal course of traversal. The link bridge entry is deleted from the bridge list. If the bridge list is empty after this, clipping against this window/viewport edge is over. Otherwise the next bridge of the deleted link bridge becomes the new link bridge for winding the next vertex loop.

2. The bridge end-point, say P, belongs to a bridge other than the link bridge with which the traversal started. In order to maintain the right connectivity, in the vertex loop being wound, this bridge has to be crossed by reaching its other end-point, say Q, in the edge list. Such a bridge is called a cross-over bridge. The bridge point P is explicitly collected, and is added in the vertex loop, if it has not already been added in the normal course of traversal. The traversal now restarts at the edge containing the bridge end-point Q. However the direction of traversal does not remain the same. It gets a new value based on the side on which Q is present in the restart edge (traversal direction is forward when Q is the left end-point in the restart edge and backward when it is the right end-point in the restart edge - the same logic as used when a fresh traversal starts with a link bridge). For example, when the bridge technique is applied to the polygon in figure 4a, the cross-over bridge $[c(3), c(4)]$ results in a change of the traversal direction. The cross-over bridge is deleted from the bridge list before the traversal is restarted.

The number of vertex loops wound, as a result of clipping against the clipping edge, is equal to the number of link bridges. Most of the fill area polygons are simple convex polygons, thus generating only one vertex loop, and this requires a single traversal through the edge list. This process when carried out over all four clipping edges, with the output polygon or polygons from one given as input to the next,

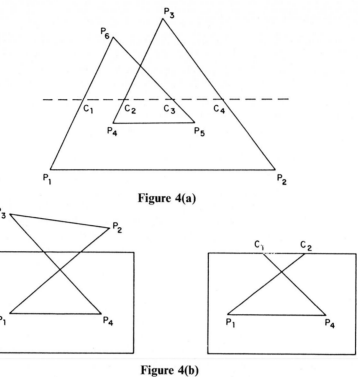

Figure 4(a)

Figure 4(b)

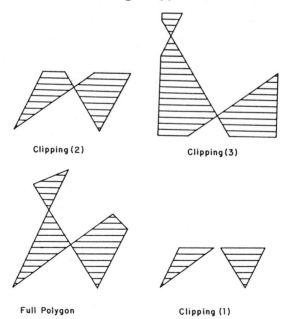

Figure 4(c)

generates the clipped fill area polygon (or polygons). All the steps except the sorting step are linear order in this algorithm. Thus the worst case computational complexity of this algorithm is $O(n \log n)$, where n is the number of edges in the subject polygon. Let us note here that self-intersecting points do not need to be computed explicitly for the clipping operations (see figure 4(b)).

An important step in this algorithm is that of deciding the direction of traversal of the edge list. This decision depends on whether the bridge point is the left or right end-point in the edge list. The algorithm therefore has to work on an edge list representation of the input polygons rather than just a list of vertices as is done in other algorithms [7, 9].

Below we describe the algorithm in a Pascal like notation. Keeping in mind that the algorithms have been successfully incorporated into IndoGKS [6], implemented entirely in FORTRAN-77, we have refrained from using pointer type variables. Instead pointers are implemented as integers referring to indices into an array. Figure 4c shows some examples of fill area clipping produced using IndoGKS.

Algorithmic Form:

Data types:

```
point = record x : real;
                y : real;
        end;
edge list record = record left  : integer;
                          right : integer;
                          next  : integer;
                          prev  : integer;
                   end;
bridge end-point = record index : integer;
                          edgelistpointer : integer;
                   end;
bridgelistrecord = record left  : bridge end-point;
                          right : bridge end-point;
                          next  : integer;
                   end;
vertexlooptype = array [1..maxvloop] of point;
bridgepointsarray = array [1..maxbridgepoints] of points;
traversaldirection  = (forward, backward);
```

The main vertex loop winding algorithm is as follows:

link_bridge := head of *bridgelist;*
WHILE (*bridgelist* not empty) DO
  BEGIN
    current-edge-pointer := *link-bridge.left.edgelistpointer;*
    bridge-point := *link-bridge.left.index;*
10:   IF (*bridge-point* the left endpoint of the current edge) THEN
    traversal := forward
    ELSE
    traversal := backward;
    collect vertex (*current-edge-pointer, traversal*);
    REPEAT (* winding loop *)
    nextstep (*current-edge-pointer,traversal*);
    collect-vertex(*current-edge-pointer,traversal*);
    UNTIL (one of the current edge's endpoints is a bridge-point);
    IF ((*traversal* = forward) and (current edge's left end-point
                         is not a bridge-point)) THEN
    (* explicitly collect the right end-point of the current edge *)
    collect-vertex (*current-edge-pointer,forward*);
    ELSE
      IF ((*traversal* = backward) and (current edge's right end-point
                         is not a bridge-point)) THEN
      (* explicitly collect the left end-point of the current edge *)
      collect-vertex (*current-edge-pointer,backward*);
    IF (*new-bridge-point* = *link-bridge.right*) THEN
    output-vertex-loop
    ELSE
      BEGIN (* cross over bridge, reach its other endpoint *)
        IF (*new-bridge-point* = *cross-over bridge.left.index*) THEN
        BEGIN
          current-edge-pointer := *cross-over-bridge.right.edgelistpointer* ;
          bridge-point := *cross-over-bridge.left.index*
        END
        ELSE
        BEGIN
          current-edge-pointer := *cross-over-bridge.left.edgelistpointer;*
          bridge-point := *cross-over-bridge.right.index*
        END;
        (* resume winding *)
        delete-bridge (*cross-over-bridge*);
        GOTO 10
      END;
    temp := *link-bridge.next;*
    delete-bridge (*link-bridge*);
    IF (*bridgelist* not empty) THEN
    link-bridge := *bridgelist* [*temp*]
  END;

Applying the bridge technique to the example of figure 3(b):

First traversal:

Edge list -				
	Left	Right	Next	Prev
1	p(1)	c(1)	3	8
2	-	-	-	-
3	c(6)	p(4)	4	1
4	p(4)	p(5)	5	3
5	p(5)	c(3)	7	4
6	-	-	-	-
7	c(2)	p(8)	8	5
8	p(8)	p(1)	1	7

Bridge list -			
Left	Right	Next	
1*	c(1)	c(2)	2
2	c(3)	c(4)	0
*	Link	Bridge	

First vertex loop: [c(1), p(1), p(8), c(2)]

Second traversal:

Edge list -				
	Left	Right	Next	Prev
1	-	-	-	-
2	-	-	-	-
3	c(6)	p(4)	4	5
4	p(4)	p(5)	5	3
5	p(5)	c(3)	3	4
6	-	-	-	-
7	-	-	-	-
8	-	-	-	-

Bridge list -			
Left	Right	Next	
1	-	-	
2*	c(3)	c(4)	0
*	List	Bridge	

Second vertex loop : [c(4), p(4), p(5), c(3)]
End of clipping; bridge and edge lists exhausted.

2.2.2 Degenerate Cases

There could be the following types of degeneracies:

1. The clipping edge just touching a vertex of the polygon (see figure 5a). An edge connecting this vertex to any other vertex lies fully outside if the other vertex is outside. When the other vertex is inside the just touching vertex is taken as the clip point.

2. The polygon edge lying entirely on the clipping edge (see figure 5b) is taken as totally inside when both its previous and next edges are inside, totally outside when both previous and next edges are outside or one end point of this edge is taken as clip point when one of its previous or next edges is inside and the other outside.

2.2.3 Anomalies in Clipping Fill Areas

Consider the example shown in figure 6. What should be the correct output? The polygon shown in figure 6b or that shown in figure 6c. The bridge technique's result is the one shown in figure 6c. The polygon shown in figure 6b is the correct output for oriented polygon clipping. For the GKS fill area definition however figure 6c is correct. In fact we would like to argue here that, for GKS, clipping resulting in the polygon of figure 6b is actually incorrect. The reason is that the line segment AB of figure 6b becomes part of the boundary of the clipped polygon even though in the unclipped polygon any point in AB is outside as per the GKS definition.

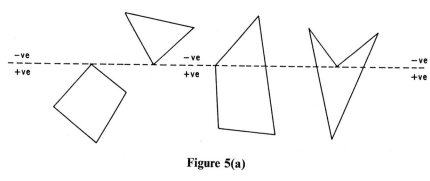

Figure 5(a)

Figure 5(b)

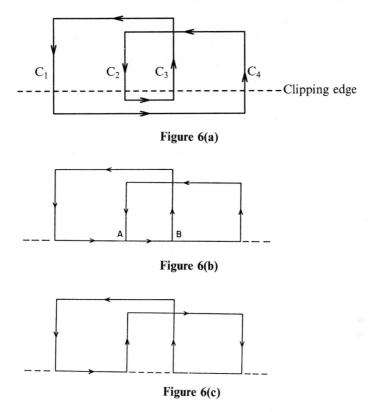

Figure 6(a)

Figure 6(b)

Figure 6(c)

2.3   Extension to 3D

The extension for 3D volume clipping is quite straightforward. Now we have six planes - left, right, top, bottom, front and back. For each plane one coordinate axis value is fixed, and other two vary. Any one of the other two varying axes could be used to sort the bridge points for ordering. But note that in non-planar subject polygons, the result obtained using one varying axis for sorting would be different from that obtained using a different varying axis for sorting.

2.4   Extension to Multiple Polygons

Multiple subject polygons, typically a polygon with holes, could result in a single polygon or multiple polygons after clipping (see figure 7). This case could be handled by processing all the polygons against an edge simultaneously, basically, merging the edge lists of all the polygons into one and processing it. With multiple polygons there may still be some unwound loops left in the edge list even after all the bridges have been exhausted. These typically are the loops corresponding to the polygons contained entirely within the clipping region. These loops can be collected very simply be ensuring that every edge in the edge list is traversed once.

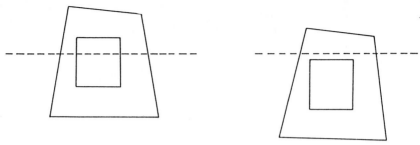

Figure 7

2.5   Extension to Clipping Against Any Polygonal Region

In the GKS-3D extension the option of removing hidden lines exists. The Weiler-Addison clipping algorithm is the heart of their hidden line removal algorithm [9, 10, 11]. GKS-3D would however require one self-intersecting polygon to be clipped by another self-intersecting polygon. For the rectangular clipping region the sorting of the bridge points is based on their x or y coordinate value, depending on the clipping edge. In case of arbitrary self-intersecting polygonal clipping regions the sorting rule is not so straightforward. The authors are continuing work on this.

3   Polygon Filling

For polygon hatching we have programmed the plane sweep algorithm of Nievergelt and Preparata [4]. The algorithm treats the display screen as an infinite plane that is swept from top to bottom (or left to right) with horizontal (or vertical) sweeps. The sweep line is invisible till it strikes a polygon vertex in the plane. Each polygon vertex, depending upon the orientation of the edges ending on it, either adds two new edges (such a pair of edges is called the Line-Segment) between which the sweep is visible (a vertex that adds a line-segment is called a Start point), or replaces an edge in the existing line-segments with a new one (called the Bend point), or removes a line-segment (called the End point), or exchanges an edge of a line segment with that of another (Self-intersection point, see figure 8). A start point can also add two new edges by way of splitting an existing line-segment into two disjoint ones (always happens in a polygon with holes). Similarly an end point can merge two line-segments into one - overall effect is of course reduction of a line-segment.

The vertices of all the polygons to be hatched in a sweep are sorted in a points list. The sorting is done on the y-coordinate value for top to bottom sweep and on the x coordinate for left to right. Each vertex point has to be classified as a START, BEND or END type. The point classifications are kept in a list in the form of classification records. The SELF INTERSECTION points are not found beforehand, avoiding the need for pairwise intersection testing of the edges, an $O(n^2)$ operation. These points are detected and computed as the sweep progresses. Thus when a new edge is added in a line-segment, its intersection with other edges in the line-segments list is tested for. If any intersection points are found, they are placed in

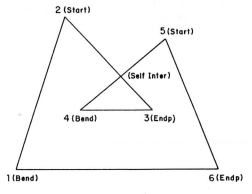

Figure 8

the POINTS list in the appropriate order based on their coordinate position.

The line segments are maintained in a linked list fashion because they need to be ordered from left to right for top to bottom sweep or vice-versa. The data types are:

```
point = record x : real; y : real
           end;
edge = record top : integer;
               bottom : integer
           end;
classification = record next : integer;
                       case class : pointtype of
                               start,bend,endp : (self,left right : integer);
                               cross : (ledg,redg : edge; crosspnt : point)
               end;
side = (left,right)
linesegment = record lnseg : array [left..right] of edge;
                     next  : integer
               end;
pointslist : array [1..maxpoints] of point;
classification-list : array [1..maxpoints] of classification;
linesegment-list : array [1..maxlinesegments] of linesegment;
```

The plane sweep algorithm is as follows:

```
sort-points;
classify-points;
scanposition := pointslist[1].y;
pointindex := 1;
REPEAT
  WHILE (new-point-in-scan(pointindex)) DO
    BEGIN
      update-linesegment-list(pointindex);
      pointindex := classification-list[pointindex].next
    END
  IF (linesegment-list is not empty) THEN
    BEGIN
      draw-hatch-line;
      scanposition := scanposition - scanstep
    END
  ELSE
    IF (pointindex < > 0) THEN scanposition := pointslist[pointindex].y;
UNTIL (pointindex = 0);
```

For the example of figure 8 the above algorithm will go through the following stages.

new point in scan	line segment
2 (start)	([2,1],[2,3])
5 (start)	([2,1],2,3]),([5,4],[5,6])
x (cross)	([2,1],[5,4]),([2,3],[5,6])
4 (bend)	([2,1],[4,3]),([2,3],[5,6])
3 (endp)	([2,1],[5,6])
1 (bend)	([1,6],[5,6])
6 (endp)	(empty)

One of the major advantages of this algorithm is that all the polygons lying in the sweep plane can be hatched in one single sweep of the plane from top to bottom (or left to right), incorporating the handling of the fill area set primitive of GKS-3D very naturally. The algorithm is of the order $(n + I)log(n)$, where I is the number of self-intersection points. It can be used for hatching on all types of devices. Angular hatching can be achieved by rotating the vertices of the polygon by the hatch angle before sweeping. Solid filling can be achieved by controlling the stepsize between consecutive sweeps. For filling on raster screens where necessary the same algorithm is used except that here instead of drawing vectors the pixels on the visible sweep path are turned ON. Figure 4c shows some examples of hatch filling, done using this algorithm that is programmed in IndoGKS, rendered on a Hewlett Packard pen plotter.

3.1   Pattern Generation using Plane Sweep

The plane sweep algorithm has been executed to perform the operation of filling a given set of polygons with vector/raster pattern. A vector pattern is described as a set of vectors within a rectangular pattern box. The lower left corner of the box is treated as its origin. The plane on which the polygons lie can be visualized as a grid of pattern boxes with the pattern reference point as the origin. Thus every box in the plane has an x index and a y index associated with it depending on its position rela-tive to the reference point (see figure 9a).

Consider the polygon shown in figure 9b which has to be filled with a given pat-tern, using the pattern reference point and the pattern size. The objective is to iden-tify the pattern boxes that lie on the edges of the polygon and inside it. To do this we use the plane sweep algorithm to slice the plane into horizontal slices. Each scan slice is as thick as the pattern height. The starting point of the scan is computed from the reference point, the pattern height, and the y coordinate value of the first point in the points classification array.

A scan slice has a line-segment list associated with it which for that y interval contains the edges of the polygons. For every edge of a line-segment it is possible to find the x intercept (lower x and higher x) within the slice. This x intercept tells us the x indices of the pattern boxes in this slice that lie on this edge. These pattern boxes are placed in a list data-structure called the pattern list.

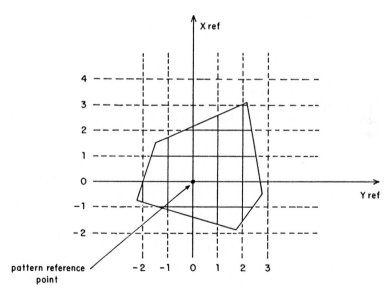

Figure 9(a)

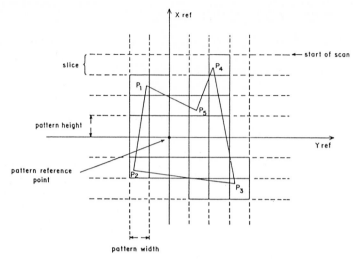

Figure 9(b)

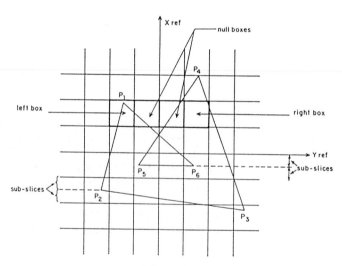

Figure 9(c)

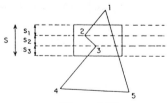

Figure 9(d)

patternlist = array [l..maxpatterns] of record xindex : integer
                                             typbox : (leftbox,rightbox,null);
                                             drawn : boolean;
                                             next : integer
                               end;

The boxes are placed in pattern list in the increasing order of their x indices (y indices for a slice are the same and need not be kept). Moreover every pattern box is classified using a box type classification - leftbox, rightbox and null. The classification acts as a tristate flag. A pattern box is a leftbox when it lies on the edge which is the left edge of a line-segment. Similarly a rightbox is one that lies on the right edge of a line-segment. There could be more than one line-segment in the line-segment list for a slice and in such a case a box might lie on the right edge of one line-segment and left edge of the other line-segment. Such a box is normally classified as null (see figure 9c) if not the first (in which case it becomes left) or the last (in which case it becomes the right) box in the slice.

For a slice all the edge boxes are identified, classified and the pattern list is formed. This list is first used to display all the in-between pattern boxes in this slice that do not have to be clipped (lie fully inside). Starting with an OFF display switch the pattern list is visited. A leftbox puts the display switch ON and all boxes with x indices between this box's x index and its next box's (next in pattern list) x index are displayed between this one and its next. A null box does not affect the switch.

The left, right and null boxes in the pattern list are to be displayed after clipping. A pattern box to be clipped can have one or more polygon vertices inside it (see figure 9d). In such a case we resort to sub-slicing of the main slice for simplifying the clipping of the pattern box vectors. Consider the case in figure 9d. Here the pattern box has two polygon vertices, 2 and 3, inside it. On the left it has to be clipped against edges [1,2], [2,3] and [3,4] whereas on the right the entire slice has one single edge namely [1,5]. So the pattern box is cut into three slices s_1, s_2 and s_3, such that in s_1 the left clipping edge is [1,2], in s_2 it is [2,3], and in s_3 it is [3,4]. In all the three sub-slices the right clipping edge however is [1,5]. Thus the main reason behind sub-slicing is to get one left clipping edge and one right clipping edge, so that the visible segment of a pattern box vector is simply the line joining its intersection with the left and the right clipping edge.

This pattern generation technique reflects the greedy nature of the plane sweep algorithm. It generates all the patterns within the current y slice and goes to the next one. Manipulation of the pattern fill by changing the reference point and pattern size is possible. This manipulation is rarely available on most pattern generators in the firmware. Moreover these patterns are transformable using the segment transformation. The application can define its own patterns by providing a list of vectors defined with reference to a rectangular box reference frame. For raster devices the vectors take the form of run length codes and are specified as in the standard. Figure 10 shows some examples of vector pattern filled areas produced using this algorithm, programmed in IndoGKS, and rendered on a dot-matrix printer.

Figure 10

Acknowledgements

The authors are grateful to the referees for their highly perceptive comments and very constructive suggestions for improving an earlier draft of this paper. The authors wish to acknowledge the interest and encouragement provided by Prof. R. Narasimhan, NCSDCT and Dr. S. Wagle, CMC Ltd. Many thanks are due to Ms. Sujata Das for testing the pattern generation algorithm.

References

1. ISO, "Information processing systems - Computer graphics - Graphical Kernel System (GKS) functional description," ISO 7942, ISO Central Secretariat (August 1985).

2. ISO, "Information processing systems - Computer graphics - Graphical Kernel System for three dimensions (GKS-3D) functional description (Draft)," ISO TC97/SC12/WG5-2 N277 Rev. (January 10, 1985).

3.   Y. Liang and B.A. Barsky, "An Analysis and Algorithm for Polygon Clipping," *Communications of the ACM* **26**(11), pp.868-877 (1983).

4.   J. Nievergelt and F.P. Preparata, "Plane Sweep Algorithm for Intersecting Geometric Figures," *Communications of the ACM* **25**(10), pp.739-747 (1982).

5.   D.F. Rogers, *Procedural Elements for Computer Graphics,* McGraw-Hill (1985).

6.   Y.N. Shinde, *Implementation and Installation Procedures for IndoGKS,* CMC Ltd. (1985).

7.   I.E. Sutherland and G.W. Hodgman, "Reentrant Polygon Clipping," *Communications of the ACM* **17**(1), pp.32-42 (1974).

8.   R.B. Tilove, "Line/Polygon Classification: A study of the Complexity of Geometric Computation," *IEEE Computer Graphics and Applications* **1**(2), pp.75-83 (1981).

9.   K. Weiler and P. Atherton, "Hidden Surface Removal Using Polygon Area Sorting," *Proceedings of Siggraph '77, Computer Graphics* **11**(2), pp.214-222 (1977).

10.   K. Weiler, *Hidden Surface Removal Using Polygon Area Sorting,* Masters Thesis, Program of Computer Graphics, Cornell University (1978).

11.   K. Weiler, "Polygon Comparison using a Graph Representation," *Computer Graphics* **14**(3), pp.10-18 (1980).

An Algorithmic Interpretation of the GKS TEXT Primitive

K. W. Brodlie and G. Pfaff

1 Introduction

The specification of text output is one of the most complex parts of the GKS standard [1]. The text "geometry" is determined by a wide variety of factors: some, such as character height, are specified directly by the user; others, such as the aspect ratio of a character in a given font, are characteristic of a particular implementation. The GKS document gives a detailed, but informal, description of the way in which these various factors combine to determine the text size and position. The purpose of this paper is to put forward a more formal description of the GKS text geometry: an algorithm is presented that calculates the size and positions of individual character bodies for any text string, under any setting of text attributes, together with the text extent rectangle and concatenation point; a realization of the algorithm as a FORTRAN 77 subroutine is also given. It is hoped that the algorithm will help implementors to interpret the GKS standard more easily.

2 The Algorithm

The algorithm is a formal interpretation of GKS text output, as described in the standard principally in section 4.4.5, and in the specification of INQUIRE TEXT EXTENT in section 5.9.5. A novel feature of the algorithm, however, is that all calculation is done in a local font coordinate system, in which the origin corresponds to the text position of the character string and in which the height of a character is one unit; a final step transforms all coordinates from this local system to world coordinates. It is believed that this leads to a more elegant and simpler algorithm. A comparison with the presentation in the GKS document is given in 2.4.

The algorithm describes the geometry that must be realized exactly for STROKE precision, and, though not considered here, to some degree of approximation for CHAR and STRING precisions.

Certain text attributes (including font and precision) are workstation dependent, and so the calculations here can be regarded as specific to a particular workstation.

The following factors determine the geometry for any instance of the TEXT primitive. The factors fall into three classes - those associated with the TEXT primitive itself; factors specified by GKS text attribute functions; and finally, font attributes which are defined internally within a GKS implementation. The following also serves to establish the notation used in the algorithm; coordinates in the local font system are shown in normal face, world coordinates are shown as bold face.

TEXT Primitive

$(\mathbf{s}_x, \mathbf{s}_y)$	text position (world coordinates)
$c^{(1)}c^{(2)} \cdots c^{(n)}$	text string (n characters)

Text Attributes

font	text font and
prec	precision
expf	character expansion factor
space	character spacing
height	character height (world coordinates)
$(\mathbf{charup}_x, \mathbf{charup}_y)$	character up vector (world coordinates)
path	text path (RIGHT, LEFT, UP, DOWN)
horiz_align	horizontal text alignment (NORMAL, LEFT, CENTRE, RIGHT)
vert_align	vertical text alignment (NORMAL, TOP, CAP, HALF, BASE, BOTTOM)

Font Attributes

f_t	font top line
f_h	font half line
f_b	font bottom line
$f_w(c)$	width of character "c" in font
f_{wmax}	width of widest character in font
$\bigcirc$	start position of character

To simplify the presentation, the algorithm in this section calculates only the start position of each character in the string (see figure 1), in world coordinates. (It is simple to extend the algorithm to calculate the position of any other fixed point on the character body; in fact the FORTRAN 77 code in section 3 calculates all four corners of each character body, rather than the start position.) The text extent rectangle and the concatenation point are also calculated. Further notation used is as follows:

$(x^{(i)}, y^{(i)})$	start position of character number i in string
$(ex_1, ey_1), (ex_2, ey_2), (ex_3, ey_3), (ex_4, ey_4)$	corner points of text extent rectangle
(cpx, cpy)	concatenation point

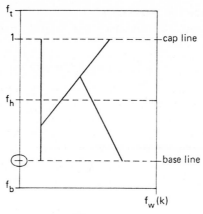

Figure 1

The three stages of the algorithm are now given in sections 2.1 to 2.3.

2.1 Interpret NORMAL Alignment According to Path

The interpretation of NORMAL values for the horizontal and vertical components of text alignment is as follows:

path	horiz align	vert align
RIGHT	LEFT	BASE
LEFT	RIGHT	BASE
UP	CENTRE	BASE
DOWN	CENTRE	TOP

In the following sections, it is assumed that this interpretation of NORMAL alignment has been made.

2.2 Calculate Start Points, Text Extent and Concatenation Point in Local Font Coordinate System

Case (a): path = (RIGHT, LEFT)

1. Calculate horizontal text length and text extent rectangle (taking origin initially as (LEFT, BASE) point in text extent rectangle)

$$\text{length} = \sum_{1}^{n} f_w(c^{(i)}) \times \text{expf} + (n-1) \times \text{space}$$

$$ex_1 = ex_4 = 0.0$$

$$ex_2 = ex_3 = \text{length}$$

$$ey_1 = ey_2 = f_b$$
$$ey_3 = ey_4 = f_t$$

2. Calculate y-coordinates of start points (no alignment adjustment)

$$y^{(i)} = 0.0 \quad i=1, \cdots ,n$$

3. Calculate x-coordinates of start points (no alignment adjustment)

If path = RIGHT,

$$x^{(1)} = 0.0$$
$$x^{(i+1)} = x^{(i)} + f_w(c^{(i)}) \times expf + space \quad i=1, \cdots ,n-1$$

If path = LEFT,

$$x^{(n)} = 0.0$$
$$x^{(i-1)} = x^{(i)} + f_w(c^{(i-1)}) \times expf + space \quad i=n,n-1, \cdots ,2$$

4. Adjust for horizontal alignment

For $i=1,2, \cdots ,n$

$$x^{(i)} = \begin{cases} x^{(i)} & \text{LEFT} \\ x^{(i)} - 0.5 \times length & \text{CENTRE} \\ x^{(i)} - length & \text{RIGHT} \end{cases}$$

with similar adjustment for x-coordinates of text extent rectangle.

5. Adjust for vertical alignment

For $i=1,2, \cdots ,n$

$$y^{(i)} = \begin{cases} y^{(i)} - f_b & \text{BOTTOM} \\ y^{(i)} & \text{BASE} \\ y^{(i)} - f_h & \text{HALF} \\ y^{(i)} - 1 & \text{CAP} \\ y^{(i)} - f_t & \text{TOP} \end{cases}$$

with similar adjustment for y-coordinates of text extent rectangle. After these alignment adjustments, the origin corresponds to the text position.

6. Calculate concatenation point

$$cpy = 0.0$$

$$cpx = \begin{cases} length + space & \text{LEFT} \\ 0.0 & \text{CENTRE} \\ -(length + space) & \text{RIGHT} \end{cases}$$

Case (b): path = (UP, DOWN)

1. Calculate vertical text length, text width and text extent (taking origin initially as (CENTRE, BOTTOM) point in text extent rectangle)

$$\text{length} = n \times (f_t - f_b) + (n-1) \times \text{space}$$

$$\text{width} = f_{wmax} \times \text{expf}$$

$$ex_1 = ex_4 = -0.5 \times \text{width}$$

$$ex_2 = ex_3 = 0.5 \times \text{width}$$

$$ey_1 = ey_2 = 0.0$$

$$ey_3 = ey_4 = \text{length}$$

2. Calculate x-coordinates of start points (no alignment adjustment)

$$x^{(i)} = -0.5 \times f_w(c^{(i)}) \times \text{expf} \quad i = 1, \cdots, n$$

3. Calculate y-coordinates of start points (no alignment adjustment)

If path = UP,

$$y^{(1)} = -f_b$$

$$y^{(i+1)} = y^{(i)} + (f_t - f_b) + \text{space} \quad i = 1, \cdots, n-1$$

If path = DOWN,

$$y^{(n)} = -f_b$$

$$y^{(i-1)} = y^{(i)} + (f_t - f_b) + \text{space} \quad i = n, n-1, \cdots, 2$$

4. Adjust for horizontal alignment

For i = 1, 2, $\cdots$, n

$$x^{(i)} = \begin{cases} x^{(i)} + 0.5 \times \text{width} & \text{LEFT} \\ x^{(i)} & \text{CENTRE} \\ x^{(i)} - 0.5 \times \text{width} & \text{RIGHT} \end{cases}$$

with similar adjustments for x-coordinates of text extent rectangle.

5. Adjust for vertical alignment

For i = 1, 2, $\cdots$, n

$$y^{(i)} = \begin{cases} y^{(i)} & \text{BOTTOM} \\ y^{(i)} + f_b & \text{BASE} \\ y^{(i)} - 0.5 \times ((f_h - f_b) + \text{length} - (f_t - f_h)) & \text{HALF} \\ y^{(i)} - (\text{length} - (f_t - 1)) & \text{CAP} \\ y^{(i)} - \text{length} & \text{TOP} \end{cases}$$

with similar adjustment for y-coordinates of text extent rectangle. After these alignment adjustments, the origin corresponds to the text position.

6. Calculate concatenation point

$$cpx = 0.0$$

$$cpy = \begin{cases} \text{length} + \text{space} & \text{BOTTOM/BASE} \\ 0.0 & \text{HALF} \\ -(\text{length} + \text{space}) & \text{TOP/CAP} \end{cases}$$

2.3   Convert from Local Font Coordinate System to World Coordinates

1. Normalize character up vector

$$n_x = \text{charup}_x / (\text{charup}_x^2 + \text{charup}_y^2)^{1/2}$$

$$n_y = \text{charup}_y / (\text{charup}_x^2 + \text{charup}_y^2)^{1/2}$$

2. Transform to world coordinates

$$(x, y) \rightarrow (w_x, w_y)$$

$$\begin{bmatrix} w_x \\ w_y \\ 1 \end{bmatrix} = \begin{bmatrix} \text{height} \times n_y & \text{height} \times n_x & s_x \\ -\text{height} \times n_x & \text{height} \times n_y & s_y \\ 0 & 0 & 1 \end{bmatrix} \begin{bmatrix} x \\ y \\ 1 \end{bmatrix}$$

this transformation to be applied to:

$(x^{(i)}, y^{(i)})$	start points of characters
$(ex_1, ey_1), (ex_2, ey_2), (ex_3, ey_3), (ex_4, ey_4)$	corner points of text extent rectangle
(cpx, cpy)	concatenation point

2.4   Comparison with GKS Document

To complete this section, it is worth comparing the above algorithm with the presentation in the GKS document. There the first step is to transform the workstation independent height and width vectors (derived from CHARACTER HEIGHT and CHARACTER UP VECTOR) from world coordinates to device coordinates, giving a character "box", or "parallelogram". At this point, the workstation dependent text aspects are incorporated in a transformation from font coordinates to device coordinates, so as to fit the character in the required box. The document nicely distinguishes the workstation independent and workstation dependent aspects of text, but equally this separation imposes an order on the calculation that can be hard to follow.

The approach here has been to fix on one particular workstation at the outset, and perform the calculations just for that workstation. This allows the various attributes to be considered together in one operation, and all calculation to be done in one simple coordinate system - font coordinates.

The final step in our algorithm is to convert from font coordinates to world coordinates. This was partly influenced by our application (see the footnote at the end of the paper). If device coordinates are preferred, it is a simple matter to apply a further transformation matrix composed of the current normalization, segment and workstation transformations.

3 FORTRAN 77 Subroutine

The FORTRAN 77 subroutine in the Appendix implements the algorithm of section 2 with the following exception: instead of calculating the start position of each character in the string, all four corner points of each character body are calculated and returned to the calling program by the parameters

(CBLLX,CBLLY), (CBLRX,CBLRY), (CBURX,CBURY), (CBULX,CBULY)

Note that the start point of each character lies on the line joining (CBLLX,CBLLY) to (CBULX,CBULY), displaced from (CBLLX,CBLLY) by the amount f_b in the direction of (CBULX,CBULY). This subroutine relies on the existence of five external functions delivering the font-dependent values of

font top line	FTTOP(FONT)
font half line	FTHALF(FONT)
font bottom line	FTBOT(FONT)
width of character C in font FONT	KARWI(FONT, C)
width of widest character in font FONT	MAXKWI(FONT)

References

1.   ISO, "Information Processing - Graphical Kernel System (GKS) - Functional Description," ISO DIS 7942 (November 1982).

Footnote

This work was carried out as part of a project on the certification of GKS implementations. It was clear that in order to validate text output, it was first necessary to have a sound algorithmic interpretation of the GKS text model. As a visual check, it is intended that the algorithm described in this paper be used to draw the outline of the character bodies against which the text generated by the GKS implementation can be displayed and compared. The algorithm also gives a means of checking the results returned by the INQUIRE TEXT EXTENT function.

Figure 2 shows the use of subroutine CXTEXT in certification of a GKS implementation. The text "CG Forum" is drawn using a GKS implementation under test, with non-default text attributes as shown. Superimposed on the text are the character boxes (in dotted lines) and the text extent rectangle (in solid lines) as generated by a call of CXTEXT. The start point and concatenation point are also marked. Remember that the text extent rectangle has the width of the widest character in the font (here lower case m).

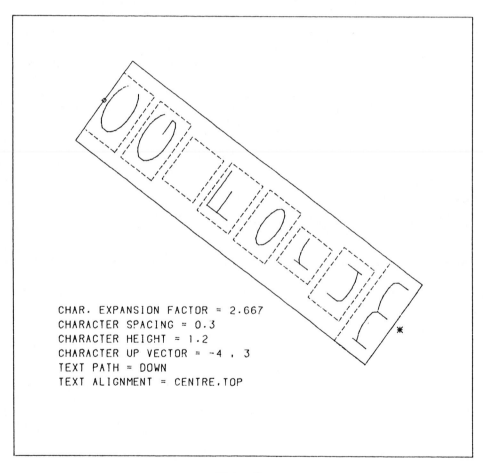

Figure 2

Acknowledgement

The work was largely done at a workshop held at INRIA, France, and sponsored by the EEC. Our thanks are due to both organisations for their support.

We are also grateful to Martin Maguire and Geoff Tolton for their help in testing the algorithm and subroutine.

Postscript

This paper was originally written at the time when GKS was a Draft International Standard. A small change was made in the International Standard that affects the way text is specified. The notions of character width and character base vector are introduced. Normally, the character width is equal to the height, and the character base vector is orthogonal to the character up vector; indeed these settings are made initially, and whenever the functions SET CHARACTER HEIGHT and SET CHARACTER UP VECTOR, respectively, are called. In this situation, the algorithm described in this paper remains valid.

However, it is possible during metafile interpretation, for a value of character width which is different to character height to be generated, or for a character base vector to be created which is not orthogonal to the character up vector. In this situation, a more general transformation matrix is needed in section 2.3, namely

$$\begin{bmatrix} \text{width} \times b_x & \text{height} \times n_x & s_x \\ \text{width} \times b_y & \text{height} \times n_y & s_y \\ 0 & 0 & 1 \end{bmatrix}$$

where

width   = character width (world coordinates)
$(\mathbf{b_x, b_y})$ = character base vector (world coordinates)

This more general matrix will cover all cases; it reduces to the matrix of section 2.3 when

$$\text{width} = \text{height}$$

$$(\mathbf{b_x, b_y}) = (\mathbf{n_y, -n_x})$$

Appendix

```
      SUBROUTINE CTXEXT (SX,SY,LCH,STR,KUPX,KUPY,KXP,KHEI,SPACE,TXPA,
     +            TXALH,TXALV,FONT,PREC,CPX,CPY,EX,EY,
     +            CBLLX,CBLLY,CBLRX,CBLRY,CBURX,CBURY,CBULX,CBULY)
C
C *** *********************************************************
C
C *** PARAMETER:   (I)- SX,SY        - TEXT START POSITION
C ***          (I)- LCH,STR(LCH) - NUMBER OF CHARS, STRING
C ***          (I)- KUPX,KUPY    - CHARACTER UP VECTOR IN WC
C ***          (I)- KXP        - CHARACTER EXPANSION FACTOR
C ***          (I)- KHEI        - CHARACTER HEIGHT
C ***          (I)- SPACE        - CHARACTER SPACING
C ***          (I)- TXPA        - TEXT PATH
C ***          (I)- TXALV,TXALH  - TEXT ALIGNMENT VERT & HORIZONTAL
C ***          (I)- FONT,PREC    - FONT & PRECISION
C ***          (O)- CPX,CPY      - CONCATENATION POINT
C ***          (O)- EX(4),EY(4)  - TEXT EXTENT RECTANGLE
C ***          (O)- CBLLX,CBLLY,CBLRX,CBLRY,CBURX,CBURY,
C ***              CBULX,CBULY(LCH) - CHAR BODY RECTANGLE POINTS
C ***
C *** *********************************************************************
      INTEGER   LCH,TXPA,TXALV,TXALH,FONT,PREC
      CHARACTER*(*) STR
      REAL      SX,SY,KUPX,KUPY,KXP,SPACE,KHEI,CPX,CPY,EX(4),EY(4)
     +        ,CBLLX(LCH),CBLLY(LCH),CBLRX(LCH),CBLRY(LCH)
     +        ,CBULX(LCH),CBULY(LCH),CBURX(LCH),CBURY(LCH)
      INTEGER   TV,TH,I
      REAL      WIDTH,HEIGHT,LENGTH,XH,VR,HR,KUX,KUY,L,SWIDTH,Z
C * DECLARE FUNCTIONS FOR ACCESS TO GLOBAL FONT ATTRIBUTES
      REAL      FTTOP,FTHALF,FTBOT,MAXKWI,KARWI
C * DECLARE SOME MNEMONIC NAMES
      INTEGER   RIGHT,LEFT,UP,DOWN,NORMAL,ALEFT,ACENTR,ARIGHT
      INTEGER   ATOP,ACAP,AHALF,ABASE,ABOTTM
      DATA      RIGHT/0/,LEFT/1/,UP/2/,DOWN/3/,NORMAL/0/,ALEFT/1/
      DATA      ACENTR/2/,ARIGHT/3/,ATOP/1/,ACAP/2/,AHALF/3/,ABASE/4/
      DATA      ABOTTM/5/
C   *********************************************************************
C * CALCULATE NORMALIZED CHAR UP VECTOR
      L = SQRT (KUPX*KUPX + KUPY*KUPY)
      KUX = KUPX/L
      KUY = KUPY/L
```

```
C  *  INTERPRET ALIGNMENT IF SET TO NORMAL (0)
         IF (TXALH .NE. NORMAL) THEN
           TH = TXALH
         ELSE
           IF (TXPA .EQ. RIGHT) TH = ALEFT
           IF (TXPA .EQ. LEFT) TH = ARIGHT
           IF (TXPA.EQ.UP .OR. TXPA.EQ.DOWN) TH= ACENTR
         ENDIF
         IF (TXALV.NE.NORMAL) THEN
           TV = TXALV
         ELSE
           IF (TXPA .EQ. DOWN) THEN
             TV = ATOP
           ELSE
             TV = ABASE
           ENDIF
         ENDIF
C *** TEXT PATH LEFT OR RIGHT
         IF (TXPA.EQ.RIGHT .OR. TXPA.EQ.LEFT) THEN
C  *  CALCULATE HORIZONTAL TEXT LENGTH AND TEXT EXTENT
C  *  RECTANGLE
         SWIDTH = 0.
         DO 100 I = 1,LCH
         SWIDTH = SWIDTH + KARWI (FONT,STR(I:I)) * KXP
         Z = KARWI(FONT,STR(I:I))
100        CONTINUE
         LENGTH = SWIDTH + (LCH-1)*SPACE
         HEIGHT = FTTOP(FONT) - FTBOT(FONT)
         EX(1) = 0.
         EX(2) = LENGTH
         EX(3) = EX(2)
         EX(4) = EX(1)
         EY(1) = FTBOT(FONT)
         EY(2) = EY(1)
         EY(3) = FTTOP(FONT)
         EY(4) = EY(3)
C  *  CALCULATE LOWER LEFT AND UPPER RIGHT POINTS OF THE CHAR
C  *  BODIES
         IF (TXPA.EQ.RIGHT) THEN
           CBLLX(1) = 0.
         ELSE
           CBLLX(1) = LENGTH - KARWI(FONT,STR(1:1)) * KXP
         ENDIF
         DO 200 I = 1,LCH
         CBLLY(I) = FTBOT(FONT)
         CBURY(I) = FTTOP(FONT)
         IF (I.NE.1) THEN
C  *  CALCULATE NEXT LOWER LEFT POINT ONLY IF NOT THE FIRST
C  *  CHARACTER
            IF(TXPA.EQ.RIGHT) THEN
              CBLLX(I) = CBURX(I-1) + SPACE
```

```
          ELSE
             CBLLX(I) = CBLLX(I-1) - KARWI(FONT,STR(I:I))*KXP - SPACE
          ENDIF
       ENDIF
       CBURX(I) = CBLLX(I) + KARWI(FONT,STR(I:I))*KXP
200     CONTINUE
C * ADJUST FOR HORIZONTAL AND VERTICAL TEXT ALIGNMENT
       IF (TH.EQ.ALEFT)   HR = 0.
       IF (TH.EQ.ACENTR)   HR = LENGTH/2.
       IF (TH.EQ.ARIGHT)   HR = LENGTH
       IF (TV.EQ.ATOP)    VR = FTTOP(FONT)
       IF (TV.EQ.ACAP)    VR = 1.
       IF (TV.EQ.AHALF)    VR = FTHALF(FONT)
       IF (TV.EQ.ABASE)    VR = 0.
       IF (TV.EQ.ABOTTM)   VR = FTBOT(FONT)
C * CALCULATE CONCATENATION POINT
       CPY = 0.
       IF (TH.EQ.ARIGHT) CPX = -(LENGTH + SPACE)
       IF (TH.EQ.ACENTR) CPX = 0.
       IF (TH.EQ.ALEFT) CPX = LENGTH + SPACE
C *** TEXT PATH IS UP OR DOWN
       ELSE
C * CALULATE VERTICAL TEXT LENGTH AND TEXT EXTENT RECTANGLE
       LENGTH = LCH * (FTTOP(FONT)-FTBOT(FONT)) + (LCH-1)*SPACE
       WIDTH = MAXKWI(FONT) * KXP
       EX(1) = -.5 * WIDTH
       EX(2) = .5 * WIDTH
       EX(3) = EX(2)
       EX(4) = EX(1)
       EY(1) = 0.
       EY(2) = EY(1)
       EY(3) = LENGTH
       EY(4) = EY(3)
C * CALCULATE LOWER LEFT AND UPPER RIGHT POINTS OF THE CHAR
C * BODIES
       IF (TXPA.EQ.UP) THEN
          CBLLY(1) = 0.
       ELSE
          CBLLY(1) = LENGTH - (FTTOP(FONT) - FTBOT(FONT))
       ENDIF
       DO 300 I = 1,LCH
       CBLLX(I) = -.5 * KARWI(FONT,STR(I:I))*KXP
       CBURX(I) = -CBLLX(I)
```

```
         IF (I.NE.1) THEN
C *  CALCULATE NEXT LOWER LEFT POINT ONLY IF NOT THE FIRST
C *  CHARACTER
           IF (TXPA.EQ.UP) THEN
              CBLLY(I) = CBURY(I-1) + SPACE
           ELSE
              CBLLY(I) = CBLLY(I-1) - (FTTOP(FONT)-FTBOT(FONT))-SPACE
           ENDIF
         ENDIF
         CBURY(I) = CBLLY(I) + (FTTOP(FONT) - FTBOT(FONT))
300      CONTINUE
C *  ADJUST FOR HORIZONTAL AND VERTICAL TEXT ALIGNMENT
         IF (TH.EQ.ALEFT)   HR = -0.5 * WIDTH
         IF (TH.EQ.ACENTR)  HR = 0.
         IF (TH.EQ.ARIGHT)  HR = 0.5 * WIDTH
         IF (TV.EQ.ATOP)    VR = LENGTH
         IF (TV.EQ.ACAP)    VR = LENGTH - (FTTOP(FONT)-1.)
         IF (TV.EQ.AHALF)   VR = 0.5*((FTHALF(FONT)-FTBOT(FONT))+LENGTH-
     *            (FTTOP(FONT)-FTHALF(FONT)))
         IF (TV.EQ.ABASE)   VR = -FTBOT(FONT)
         IF (TV.EQ.ABOTTM)  VR = 0.
C *  CALCULATE CONCATENATION POINT
         CPX = 0.
         IF (TV.EQ.ABOTTM) CPY = LENGTH + SPACE
         IF (TV.EQ.ABASE) CPY = LENGTH + SPACE
         IF (TV.EQ.AHALF) CPY = 0.
         IF (TV.EQ.ATOP)  CPY = -(LENGTH + SPACE)
         IF (TV.EQ.ACAP)  CPY = -(LENGTH + SPACE)
       ENDIF
C *  MOVE CHAR BODY POINTS AND EXTENT RECTANGLE POINTS BY HR,VR
       DO 400 I=1,LCH
       CBLLX(I) = CBLLX(I) - HR
       CBLLY(I) = CBLLY(I) - VR
       CBURX(I) = CBURX(I) - HR
       CBURY(I) = CBURY(I) - VR
400    CONTINUE
       DO 500 I=1,4
       EX(I) = EX(I) - HR
       EY(I) = EY(I) - VR
500    CONTINUE
C *  COMPLETE CHAR BODY RECTANGLE POINTS
       DO 600 I=1,LCH
       CBLRX(I) = CBURX(I)
       CBULX(I) = CBLLX(I)
       CBLRY(I) = CBLLY(I)
       CBULY(I) = CBURY(I)
600    CONTINUE
C *  TRANSFORM ALL POINTS TO WORLD COORDINATES
       DO 700 I=1,LCH
       XH = KHEI*KUY*CBLLX(I) + KHEI*KUX*CBLLY(I) + SX
       CBLLY(I) = -KHEI*KUX*CBLLX(I) + KHEI*KUY*CBLLY(I) + SY
```

```
        CBLLX(I) = XH
        XH = KHEI*KUY*CBLRX(I) + KHEI*KUX*CBLRY(I) + SX
        CBLRY(I) = -KHEI*KUX*CBLRX(I) + KHEI*KUY*CBLRY(I) + SY
        CBLRX(I) = XH
        XH = KHEI*KUY*CBURX(I) + KHEI*KUX*CBURY(I) + SX
        CBURY(I) = -KHEI*KUX*CBURX(I) + KHEI*KUY*CBURY(I) + SY
        CBURX(I) = XH
        XH = KHEI*KUY*CBULX(I) + KHEI*KUX*CBULY(I) + SX
        CBULY(I) = -KHEI*KUX*CBULX(I) + KHEI*KUY*CBULY(I) + SY
        CBULX(I) = XH
700     CONTINUE
        XH = KHEI*KUY*CPX + KHEI*KUX*CPY +SX
        CPY = -KHEI*KUX*CPX + KHEI*KUY*CPY + SY
        CPX = XH
        DO 800 I=1,4
        XH = KHEI*KUY*EX(I) + KHEI*KUX*EY(I) + SX
        EY(I) = -KHEI*KUX*EX(I) + KHEI*KUY*EY(I) + SY
        EX(I) = XH
800     CONTINUE
C   ************************************************************
        RETURN
        END
```

A Method of Displaying Transformed Picture Rectangles Using GKS Raster Functions

H. Schumann and A. Kotzauer

1 Introduction

Current raster graphics systems have quite variable efficiency, and there is a lot of correspondingly variable hardware. Intelligent raster graphics systems allowing manipulation of images use efficient computers. The use of specialized hardware is required above all for the display and manipulation of raster images in real-time. For example typical systems use many processors for manipulations on the frame buffer [5]. Besides these highly efficient systems, there are simpler systems with a limited range of functions which are suitable and sufficient for many applications, for example business graphics. But even in this field, hardware solutions are progressively used for the implementation of some functions.

In the GKS-Standard [3], the functions FILL AREA and CELL ARRAY are raster graphics output primitives.

FILL AREA represents an area which is limited by any polygon and could be hollow, filled with a colour or grey value, hatched or covered with any pattern.

CELL ARRAY represents a rectangle which is divided into $M \times N$ cells which are filled with the appropriate values of a given "cell" matrix.

Many algorithms for area filling with a colour are well known (for example, see Pavlidis [6] or Newman and Sproull [4]). They are also suitable for hatching areas and provide good results if they are implemented on systems of low to middle efficiency.

On the other hand, more expensive algorithms are required to cover an area with a pattern or to display a CELL ARRAY in the general case defined in GKS. They generally require efficient systems to obtain acceptable computing time and image quality.

In this paper a method is given with acceptable computing time and image quality for systems of lower efficiency (100,000 operations per sec, 64 Kbytes of memory, and a simple raster output device such as a matrix printer).

2   Transformation of Picture Rectangles

The pattern for FILL AREA and the colours of the cells of a CELL ARRAY are described by means of matrices which we call picture matrices. Each element of a picture matrix specifies a colour or grey value. Therefore, a picture matrix with $M \times N$ elements describes the picture contents of a rectangle which is defined, to conform to GKS, parallel to the coordinate-axes in World Coordinates (WC). This rectangle is called the picture rectangle. It is divided in $M \times N$ pieces called picture cells. Each picture cell corresponds exactly to one element of the picture matrix.

During the GKS output process, the picture rectangle is subjected to several transformations. Therefore, in the general case, it can be transformed to a parallelogram in device coordinates (DC). The same applies to picture cells. The processing required to map the elements of the picture matrix to the pixels of the output raster is comparable to that required for the scaling and rotation of pictures which are described by points. This is a complicated expensive process which requires specialized hardware support and digital filters to achieve good image quality.

For the point-by-point (or pixel-by-pixel) transformation of pictures different methods are known [1, 2, 9]. The rules fixed in GKS for the transformation of picture rectangles [3] demand the examination of each pixel to see which element of the picture matrix is mapped to it. Therefore, a ray starting from pixel centre is constructed and how often it intersects the edges of the given picture cell is calculated. If only one intersection point exists, the element of the picture matrix is assigned to the pixel. If there is no intersection or two intersection points exist, the examination is repeated with the next picture cell from the picture rectangle.

This process is expensive. Therefore, a GKS-implementation is allowed to restrict the transformation applied to the picture rectangle, using, for example, only patterns which are unscaled and parallel to the coordinate axis. In the case of a CELL ARRAY this means one cell corresponds exactly to one element of the picture matrix. The execution time for the FILL AREA and CELL ARRAY depends on the transformation applied to the picture rectangle and the contents of the corresponding picture matrix to be displayed. We will therefore discuss in the following a method for a simple implementation of this process.

This method will be introduced in three steps:

● Picture rectangle in axis-parallel position.

● Picture rectangle in general position.

● Picture rectangle as parallelogram.

The complete implementation of FILL AREA and CELL ARRAY is not discussed.

3   The Method

3.1   Picture Rectangles Parallel to Axes

With the picture rectangle parallel to the axes of the output raster, each element of the picture matrix corresponds to a (not necessarily integer) number of pixels of the output raster. That means a scaling of the picture contents described by means of the picture matrix.

The basis for the solution of this problem consists of the division of scaling by a real factor into two scalings by integer factors, relating both the picture matrix and the pixels covered by the picture rectangle to a virtual raster. In what follows the picture matrix consists of $M \times N$ elements and the picture rectangle covers $M' \times N'$ pixels in the output raster.

1st Scaling: Producing the virtual raster

The virtual raster consists of $M_1 \times N_1$ with

$$M_1 = LCM(M, M')$$
$$N_1 = LCM(N, N')$$

(LCM = Lowest Common Multiple) In this raster, a picture cell consists of $K \times L$ pixels with

$$K = M_1/M \quad (K, L \text{ integer})$$
$$L = N_1/N$$

There is not necessarily a special place in the memory for the virtual raster.

2nd Scaling: Transmission of the virtual raster to the output raster

The transmission takes place in the following steps:

- Mapping of $K_1 \times L_1$ pixels of the virtual raster to one pixel of the output raster with

$$K_1 = M_1/M'$$
$$L_1 = N_1/N'$$

- Computing the value of the pixel (grey scale or colour) of the output raster by the $K_1 \times L_1$ pixels of the virtual raster (for example by averaging).

If $K, L >> K_1, L_1$ the value of many pixels is known and the second scaling can be done very efficiently.

3.2   Picture Rectangles at Arbitrary Orientations

For displaying picture rectangles at arbitrary orientations in the output raster, four steps are necessary:

1st Step: Producing two binary sequences

Two adjoining sides of the picture rectangle are scan-converted into the output raster. Let M_2 be the number of pixels for one side and N_2 be the number of pixels for the other. For one side a binary sequence is produced in which a 1 represents a row jump and a zero continuation on the same row (a column only jump). A similar sequence is produced for the second side with a 1 representing a column jump and a zero representing continuation to the next pixel on the same column [5].

2nd Step: Producing the pixel matrix

A pixel matrix with $M_2 \times N_2$ elements is produced from the picture matrix by the method described in 3.1.

3rd Step: Filling the picture rectangle

According to the both binary sequences, the picture rectangle in the output raster is filled with the values of the pixel matrix [5].

4th Step: Filling the uncovered pixels

Step 3 does not necessarily assign values to all pixels within the picture rectangle [5]. The number and location of these pixels can be determined by examining the binary sequences. To improve the quality of an image, these pixels can be given a value depending on their neighbours.

The examples in section 4 show that this technique provides sufficient picture quality for many applications.

3.3   Picture Rectangles Transformed to Parallelograms

The picture rectangle in the output raster changes to a parallelogram if a scaling which is non-uniform in x and y follows a rotation.

In filling the picture rectangle transformed to a parallelogram, using the method described in 3.2, there are both uncovered and double-covered pixels (figure 2). The number and location of double-covered pixels can be also exactly determined by examining the binary sequences.

Note that the picture contents of the picture matrix will be distorted when displayed in a parallelogram, by any method.

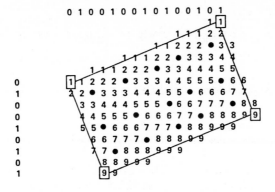

Legend: 1-9   - rows of the pixel matrix
       ●   - uncovered pixels

Figure 1 Covered and Uncovered Pixels of a Rotated Rectangle

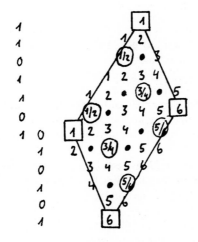

Legend: 1-6   - rows of the pixel matrix
       ●   - uncovered pixels
       ∅   - double-covered pixels

Figure 2 Covered, Uncovered and Double-covered Pixels of a Rotated Rectangle

4   Examples

Using known fill algorithms [4] and the method discussed above for transformation of picture rectangles, the GKS raster functions FILL AREA and CELL ARRAY have been implemented on the hardware configuration characterized in section 1.

Figure 3 Rotation of CELL ARRAY Rectangles

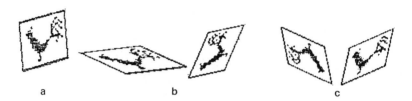

a   b   c

Figure 4 Picture Rectangles as Parallelograms

The program system [7, 8] produced does not use a frame-buffer and also implements the remaining GKS-output functions.

The pictures in figures 3 - 5 were produced with this program system described in Urban et al [8]. They give an impression of the image quality attained by means of the GKS raster functions implemented and the hardware used.

5   Conclusions

Implementations of GKS functions can be expensive in computing time and memory. An implementation therefore has to adapt to the efficiency of the available hardware configuration to obtain acceptable images. This is especially true for the GKS raster functions FILL AREA and CELL ARRAY when they are implemented on configurations of low to middle efficiency. Therefore, algorithms different from those used on highly efficient systems are necessary.

The filling and display of transformed picture rectangles is one of the principal ingredients in the implementation of the GKS raster functions. For their implementation on systems of low to middle efficiency, a method has been described which was used in the program system GDA 1600 [8]. In this software the picture has to be described as a GKS Metafile. After a phase of refinement of the picture, the time for displaying a picture will be determined by the printing speed of the matrix printer. This means the time taken to generate a picture row is proportional to the speed of the printer (max. 792 pixels per row).

The choice of the GKS Metafile as interface has retained the device independence and the full range of GKS output functions, although a device dependent implementation took place.

The methods presented for use of the raster functions are sufficient for many applications.

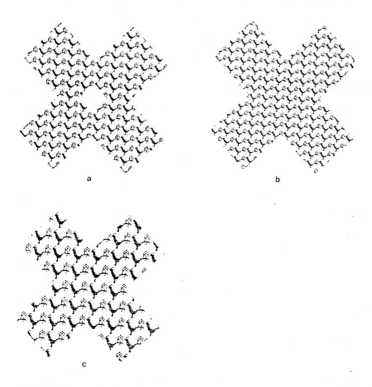

(a) Filling a polygon with a hole, scaling factors of the picture rectangle are 1:1.
(b) Filling a polygon without a hole, scaling rectangle are 0.85:0.86.
(c) Filling a polygon without a hole, scaling factor of the picture rectangle are 1.35:1.64.

Figure 5 Scaling Picture Rectangles

Acknowledgements

We are indebted to Mr. J. Hartmann for an effective implementation of the scaling of picture rectangles and to Mrs. S. Mueller for some help in connection with the implementation of the rotation of picture rectangles.

References

1. K.A. Clarke and H.H.-S. Ip, "A parallel implementation of geometric transformation," *Pattern recognition letters* **1**, pp.51-53 (1982).

2. J.B. Hanson and P.J. Willis, "A method of rotating areas on a raster scan graphics display," *Displays* **3**(4), pp.219-222 (October 1982).

3. ISO, "Information processing systems - Computer graphics - Graphical Kernel System (GKS) functional description," ISO 7942, ISO Central Secretariat (August 1985).

4. W.M. Newman and R.F. Sproull, *Principles of interactive computer graphics,* McGraw-Hill, New York (1979).

5. H. Niimi, Y. Imai, M. Murakami, S. Tomita, and H. Hagiwara, "A parallel processor system for three dimensional color graphics," *Computer Graphics* **18**(3), pp.67-76 (July 1984).

6. T. Pavlidis, *Algorithms for graphics and image processing,* Springer-Verlag, Berlin-Heidelberg (1982).

7. H. Schumann, "Realisierung der GKS Rasterfunktionen," *Rostocker Informatik-Berichte* **Heft 2**, pp.100-104 (1985). (In German.)

8. B. Urban, H. Schumann, A. Kotzauer, and W. Eckhardt, "Das Softwaresystem GDA 1600 zur graphischen Ausgabe auf dem Seriendrucker SD 1157-269," *Neue Technik im Buero* **30**(3), pp.94-96 (1986). (In German.)

9. C.F.R. Weiman, "Continuous anti-aliased rotation and ZOOM of raster images," *Computer Graphics* **14**(3), pp.286-293 (1979).

An Implementation of the GKS-3D/PHIGS Viewing Pipeline

K. Singleton

1 Introduction

GKS-3D [10] and PHIGS [9] provide functions for three-dimensional graphics programming. In both systems, the mapping of user-defined 3-D graphical output onto physical graphics devices is performed by an *output pipeline*. The appearance of any 3-D object depends on the position of the viewer with respect to the object, as demonstrated in figure 1. The view required is specified in a section within the output pipeline called the *viewing pipeline*.

The first part of this paper reviews the output pipelines of GKS-3D and PHIGS. Subsequent sections describe the functionality of the viewing pipeline and the details of a test implementation. Finally, the viewing parameter settings required to produce the standard projections are derived. As work described in this paper neared completion, the viewing mechanism in PHIGS was revised [1]. In terms of implementation, these changes are minor and are not reflected in the paper. Details of the changes can be found in the appendix.

2 Notation

In this paper 4×4 homogeneous matrices are used to represent transformations, see Foley and Van Dam [7], and column vectors are used to represent points. The point $(x,y,z)^{\mathrm{T}}$ is therefore transformed by a matrix $\underline{M}$ onto the point $(x',y',z')^{\mathrm{T}}$ as follows:

$$\begin{bmatrix} x'' \\ y'' \\ z'' \\ w'' \end{bmatrix} = \underline{M} \begin{bmatrix} x \\ y \\ z \\ 1 \end{bmatrix}$$

where

$$x' = x''/w''$$
$$y' = y''/w''$$
$$z' = z''/w''$$

The x, y and z components of a vector, $\mathbf{v}$, are denoted as v_x, v_y and v_z respectively. The transpose of the vector is written as $\mathbf{v}^T$. $\hat{\mathbf{v}}$ is used to denote a unit vector.

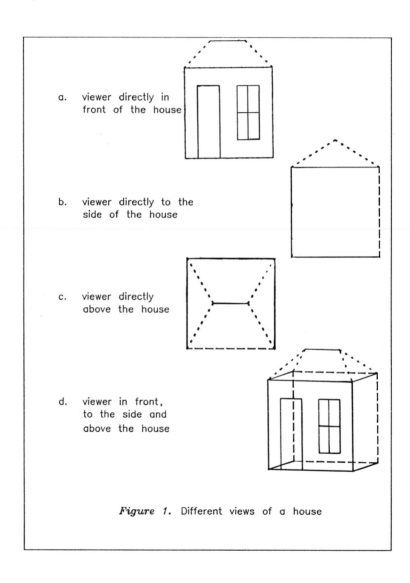

a. viewer directly in
    front of the house

b. viewer directly to the
    side of the house

c. viewer directly
    above the house

d. viewer in front,
    to the side and
    above the house

Figure 1. Different views of a house

3   GKS-3D and PHIGS Output Pipelines

The graphical output pipelines of GKS-3D and PHIGS are illustrated in figures 2 and 3 respectively. Figure 4 lists the functions provided in the two systems which allow the application programmer to specify the parameters for each stage in the pipeline.

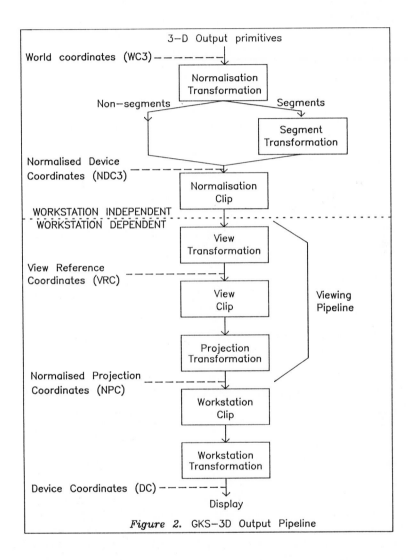

Figure 2. GKS-3D Output Pipeline

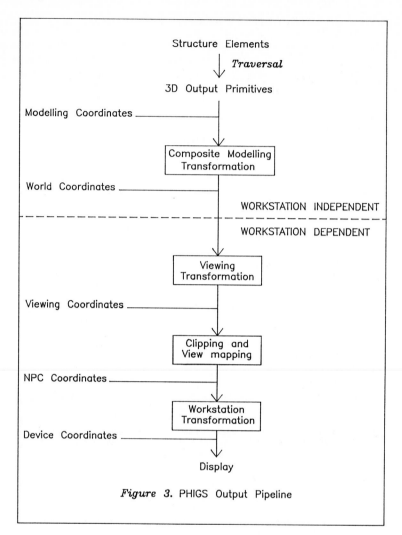

Figure 3. PHIGS Output Pipeline

3.1   The GKS-3D Output Pipeline

In GKS-3D, an output primitive is specified in World Coordinates (*WC3*). It is mapped to Normalized Device Coordinates (*NDC3*) by a *normalization transformation*. The normalization transformation is specified by defining a cuboid in the world coordinate system which is to be mapped onto a specified cuboid in normalized coordinate space. The functions SET WINDOW 3 and SET VIEWPORT 3 are used to define the respective volumes in *WC3* and *NDC3* for a given normalization transformation. SELECT NORMALIZATION TRANSFORMATION sets the current normalization transformation. In this way, the application programmer is able to construct a picture from separate parts, each defined in a convenient coordinate system. The different world coordinate systems are combined into the

	GKS-3D	PHIGS
Normalisation *Transformation*	SET WINDOW SET VIEWPORT SELECT NORMALIZATION TRANSFORMATION	———
Segment *Transformation*	SET SEGMENT TRANSFORMATION (INSERT SEGMENT) (ASSOCIATE SEGMENT WITH WORKSTATION)	———
Modelling *Transformation*	———	SET LOCAL TRANSFORMATION SET GLOBAL TRANSFORMATION
Viewing *Pipeline*	SET VIEW INDEX	SET VIEW INDEX
1. Utility *Functions*	EVALUATE VIEW MATRIX	SET VIEW REFERENCE POINT SET VIEW PLANE NORMAL SET VIEW UP COMPUTE VIEW MATRIX
2. View *Representation* *a. View* *Transformation*	SET VIEW REPRESENTATION	SET VIEW MATRIX
b. View Clip	"	SET VIEW CHARACTERISTICS
c. Projection *Transformation*	"	SET VIEW MAPPING
Workstation *Transformation*	SET WORKSTATION WINDOW SET WORKSTATION VIEWPORT	SET WORKSTATION WINDOW SET WORKSTATION VIEWPORT

Figure 4.
The GKS—3D and PHIGS functions used
to define the Output Pipeline

normalized coordinate space by appropriate normalization transformations, as shown in figure 5a.

Depending upon the level of GKS-3D in use, a *segment transformation* may be applied. This is a mapping from *NDC3* to *NDC3* which may translate, scale, shear and rotate primitives contained in a segment. The transformation affects all primitives in the segment and is defined using the function SET SEGMENT TRANSFORMATION. A similar effect is induced by the functions INSERT SEGMENT and ASSOCIATE SEGMENT WITH WORKSTATION. Animation effects can be achieved by repeatedly changing the segment transformation.

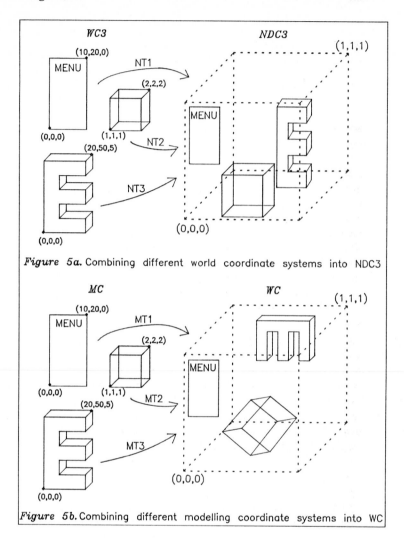

Figure 5a. Combining different world coordinate systems into NDC3

Figure 5b. Combining different modelling coordinate systems into WC

The *normalization clip* is performed on a primitive according to the value of its associated clipping indicator. Primitives are clipped against the cuboid in *NDC3* defined by the current normalization viewport. Figure 6 illustrates a possible effect of changing the segment transformation with the normalization clip enabled. The clipping boundary is *not* affected by the transformation and this may lead to an unexpected result for the user.

The action of the pipeline up to this point is workstation independent. Following the normalization clip, the workstation takes charge and hence subsequent stages may vary between workstations.

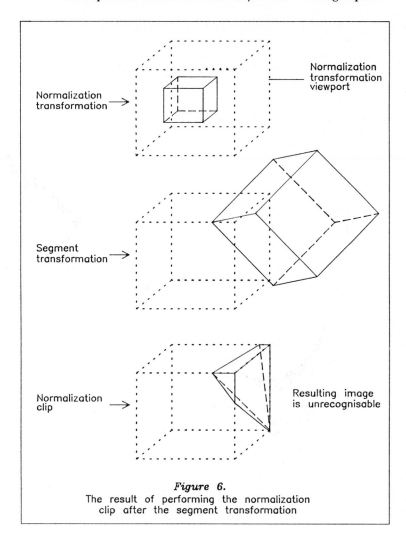

Figure 6.
The result of performing the normalization
clip after the segment transformation

When primitives are created, a set of viewing parameters is associated with them by means of a *view index*. This index refers to an entry in a table of values stored in the workstation state list. A view of the primitive is created using the current representation in the workstation state list corresponding to the view index bound to that primitive. The view representation defines two transformations and a view volume. The *view transformation* is the first transformation which maps from *NDC3* to the View Reference Coordinate system (*VRC*). *VRC* is an intermediate coordinate system introduced in order to simplify specification of the projection required. It is equivalent to a shifted and rotated version of the *NDC3* coordinate system. The view volume, to which the primitive may be optionally clipped, is defined in *VRC*. The second transformation defined in the view representation is the *projection transformation*. A view specified in *VRC* is projected into Normalized Projection Coordinate space (*NPC*). Hidden-line or hidden-surface removal takes place in *NPC*. The view representation, corresponding to a given view index for a particular workstation, is set by the function SET VIEW REPRESENTATION.

Finally, a portion of *NPC* space is selected for display. The *workstation clip* is mandatory. All primitives are clipped against a cuboid defined in *NPC* space known as the workstation window. The window is defined for a given workstation using the function SET WORKSTATION WINDOW 3. The *workstation transformation* is used to map *NPC* to device coordinates (*DC3*). The workstation window is mapped onto a cuboid defined in the workstation's physical display space. The workstation viewport is specified by the function SET WORKSTATION VIEWPORT 3.

3.2   The PHIGS Output Pipeline

In PHIGS, output elements are specified in Modelling Coordinates (*MC*), which are converted to World Coordinates (*WC*) by the current *composite modelling transformation*. This transformation is represented as a homogeneous transformation matrix which is the concatenation of the local and global modelling transformations defined using the functions SET LOCAL TRANSFORMATION 3 and SET GLOBAL TRANSFORMATION 3. The application programmer can use different modelling coordinate systems to define separate parts of a picture which are subsequently combined by the composite modelling transformation into world coordinate space. This is very similar to the mechanism in GKS-3D whereby world coordinates are mapped to normalized device coordinates by the normalization transformation. The normalization transformation, however, specifies a mapping from one cuboid to another which involves only translations and scaling, whereas the composite modelling transformation could be any affine transformation. This is demonstrated in figure 5b.

Following the modelling transformation, the view transformation is performed. From this point, the functionality of the PHIGS output pipeline is identical to that of the GKS-3D pipeline.

In the following, wherever the terminology differs, GKS-3D names are used. It is expected that these differences will be cleared up in future technical reviews of GKS-3D and PHIGS.

4   The Viewing Pipeline

In GKS-3D, a view index is bound to each graphical output primitive on creation. This index specifies an entry in the workstation view table which in turn specifies a view comprising the transformation from *NDC3* to *NPC*. A GKS-3D function, SET VIEW REPRESENTATION, is provided in order to define the table entry for a specific workstation and view index. Since the view representation is workstation dependent, the view of a primitive on one workstation will not necessarily be the same as the view on a different workstation. Different views of the same primitive, however, cannot be displayed together on a single workstation unless the primitive is despatched twice.

In PHIGS, the current view index is bound to graphical output primitives at traversal time. A structure may be traversed more than once and therefore if the current view index is different at each traversal, different views of the structure could be displayed at a single workstation. Further details of structure traversal, beyond the scope of this paper, can be found in the PHIGS Working Draft [9]. View table entries are defined using three functions:

1. SET VIEW MATRIX - defines the mapping from *WC* to *VRC*.

2. SET VIEW MAPPING - defines the mapping from *VRC* to *NPC* and also the clipping volume.

3. SET VIEW CHARACTERISTICS - sets the clipping status on or off.

Like GKS-3D, the view representation is workstation dependent.

The viewing pipeline performs the mapping between *NDC3* and *NPC*. It consists of three stages:

1. The View Transformation. A new coordinate system, the view reference coordinate system (*VRC*), is defined in which to view an object. The view transformation is the mapping from *NDC3* to *VRC* and is specified by a 4×4 matrix which must be supplied by the application program. GKS-3D and PHIGS both provide a utility function to compute the matrix from the parameters for a model, to allow arbitrary positioning and orientation of the *VRC* system with respect to the *NDC3* system. A description of how this matrix can be determined is given in section 5.

2. The View Clip. A clipping or view volume is defined in *VRC* space. Three planes, the *front*, *back* and *view* planes, parallel to the *xy* plane in *VRC*, are specified as *VRC z* values. A rectangular window, known as the *view window*, is defined on the view plane. Four projectors passing through the four corners of the view window, and their intersections with the front and back planes, describe the clipping volume. The orientation of each projector depends on the type of projection. If a parallel projection is required, the projectors are parallel to the line joining the projection reference point to the centre of the view window, as shown in figure 7. If a perspective projection is specified, all the projectors will pass through the given projection reference point, as shown in figure 8. Clipping is performed against the front and back planes and the view window independently and is optional in each case. Section 6 details an implementation of the view clip.

3. The Projection Transformation. This transformation creates the view required and maps the view volume onto the projection viewport which is a cuboid in *NPC* space. The term *projection* implies that vectors in three space are mapped onto vectors in two space. The projection transformation, however, is a mapping from three-space onto three-space since the third dimension must be maintained for 3-D workstations and to facilitate hidden-line and hidden-surface removal. The derivation of the matrix to perform the projection transformation is described in section 7.

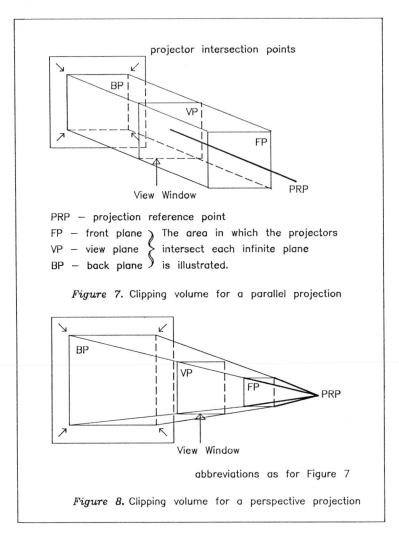

projector intersection points

PRP — projection reference point
FP — front plane ⎫ The area in which the projectors
VP — view plane ⎬ intersect each infinite plane
BP — back plane ⎭ is illustrated.

Figure 7. Clipping volume for a parallel projection

abbreviations as for Figure 7

Figure 8. Clipping volume for a perspective projection

5   Evaluation of the View Transformation

The view transformation maps from $NDC3$ to VRC. VRC is an intermediate coordinate system which is introduced to simplify specification of the view required. In the definition of a view, three parallel planes, the front, back and view planes, are specified. The orientation of these planes is arbitrary and hence their specification can be complex. The position and orientation of the view reference coordinate system axes is therefore defined so that the planes are parallel to the VRC xy plane. In this way, the front, back and view planes can be described as signed distances along the VRC z-axis.

The matrix to perform the view transformation is known as the *view matrix*. The utility functions EVALUATE VIEW MATRIX (GKS-3D) and COMPUTE VIEW MATRIX (PHIGS) compute the view matrix from parameters for a model, to allow arbitrary positioning and orientation of the view reference coordinate system with respect to *NDC3*. This section will discuss the derivation of the view matrix.

The x, y and z axes in *VRC* are, by convention, referred to as the u, v and n axes respectively.

The parameters required are specified in either *NDC3* or *WC3* and a coordinate switch is set accordingly. The parameters are:

- View Reference Point (**VRP**). This is the origin of the view reference coordinate system. It is usually chosen to be a point on or near the object to be viewed.

- View Plane Normal (**VPN**). **VPN** is a vector relative to **VRP** and defines the n-axis of the view reference coordinate system.

- View Up Vector (**VUV**). **VUV** is a vector relative to **VRP** which is used to compute the direction of the v-axis in the view reference coordinate system. The v-axis is defined as an orthogonal projection of **VUV** onto the plane through **VRP** with plane normal **VPN**, as shown in figure 9. Lines parallel to the projected **VUV** in *NDC3* will appear vertical on the screen.

Given the view plane normal and the view up vector, an orthonormal set of unit vectors parallel to the u, v and n axes can be generated. These are written as $\hat{u}$, $\hat{v}$ and $\hat{n}$ respectively, where $\hat{n}$ is parallel to **VPN**, $\hat{u}$ is parallel to the cross product of **VUV** with $\hat{n}$ and $\hat{v}$ is parallel to the cross product of $\hat{n}$ with $\hat{u}$.

$$\hat{n} = \frac{\mathbf{VPN}}{|\mathbf{VPN}|}$$

$$\hat{u} = \frac{\mathbf{VUV} \times \hat{n}}{|\mathbf{VUV}|}$$

$$\hat{v} = \hat{n} \times \hat{u}$$

If **VPN** and **VUV** are parallel or zero vectors, one or more of the unit vectors will be undefined. GKS-3D and PHIGS return an error in this case.

Consider a point **P** in *NDC3*, as in figure 10a (for clarity, only the xy plane is illustrated). The view reference coordinate system axes are added in figure 10b. The view transformation converts the original *NDC3* coordinates of **P**, x_p and y_p, into coordinates relative to the *VRC* axes, u_p and v_p in Figure 10c.

$$\begin{bmatrix} u_p \\ v_p \\ n_p \end{bmatrix} = \begin{bmatrix} \text{view} \\ \text{matrix} \end{bmatrix} \begin{bmatrix} x_p \\ y_p \\ z_p \end{bmatrix}$$

The view transformation has the effect of transforming the coordinate axes whilst keeping the object fixed. This is known as a *coordinate transformation*. In figure 11a the coordinates (x_p, y_p) and (x_p', y_p') are different representations of the same

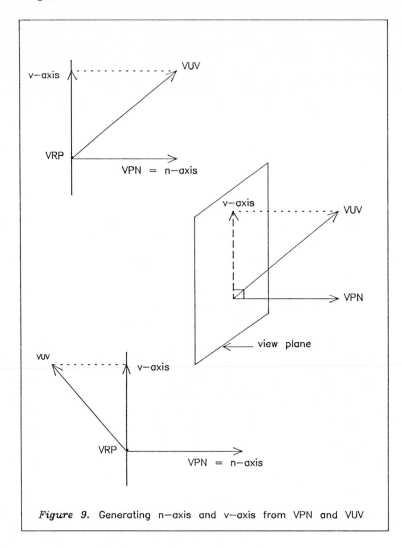

Figure 9. Generating n-axis and v-axis from VPN and VUV

point **P**. An *object transformation* will transform the point **P** itself, as illustrated in figure 11b.

Faux and Pratt [6] show that the inverse of a coordinate translation and rotation is equivalent to an equal object translation and rotation. Hence the inverse view transformation is an object transformation which translates and rotates points in *NDC3*.

To derive the view transformation, we derive an expression for its inverse. The inverse view transformation maps unit vectors along the *NDC3* axes to be coincident with the corresponding *VRC* axes, as shown in figure 12. This transformation is a three-point to three-point transformation [12].

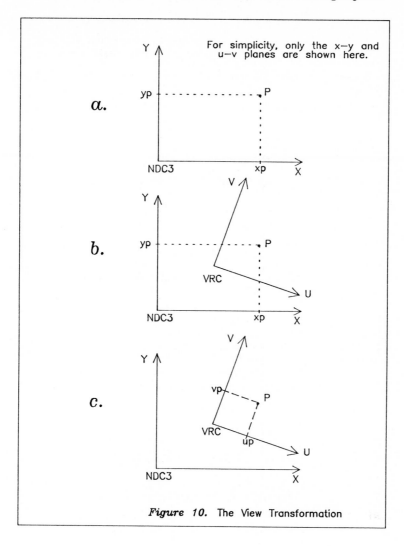

Figure 10. The View Transformation

The transformation can be represented by

$$\mathbf{p}' = \underline{R}\mathbf{p} + \mathbf{T}$$

where $\underline{R}$ is a 3×3 rotation matrix and $\mathbf{T}$ is a vector representing a translation. Clearly, unit vectors along the x, y and z axes in *NDC3* will be mapped by $\underline{R}$ onto unit vectors along the respective *VRC* axes, $\hat{\mathbf{u}}$, $\hat{\mathbf{v}}$ and $\hat{\mathbf{n}}$. Hence

$$\hat{\mathbf{u}} = \underline{R} \begin{bmatrix} 1 \\ 0 \\ 0 \end{bmatrix}$$

$$\hat{\mathbf{v}} = \underline{R} \begin{bmatrix} 0 \\ 1 \\ 0 \end{bmatrix}$$

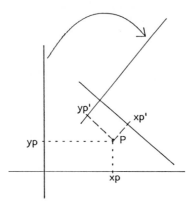

For simplicity, only the x—y and
u—v planes are shown here.

Figure 11a. A Coordinate Transformation

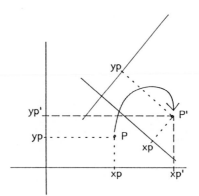

Figure 11b. An Object Transformation

$$\hat{\mathbf{n}} = \underline{R} \begin{bmatrix} 0 \\ 0 \\ 1 \end{bmatrix}$$

and therefore

$$\underline{R} \begin{bmatrix} 1 & 0 & 0 \\ 0 & 1 & 0 \\ 0 & 0 & 1 \end{bmatrix} = \begin{bmatrix} \hat{\mathbf{u}} & \hat{\mathbf{v}} & \hat{\mathbf{n}} \end{bmatrix}$$

$$\Rightarrow \underline{R} = \begin{bmatrix} \hat{\mathbf{u}} & \hat{\mathbf{v}} & \hat{\mathbf{n}} \end{bmatrix}$$

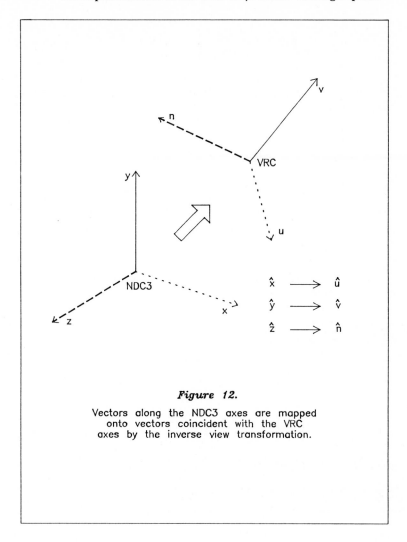

Figure 12.

Vectors along the NDC3 axes are mapped
onto vectors coincident with the VRC
axes by the inverse view transformation.

The *NDC3* origin will be transformed onto the origin in *VRC* which is defined by
the view reference point (**VRP**).

$$
\begin{bmatrix} VRP_x \\ VRP_y \\ VRP_z \end{bmatrix} = \underline{R} \begin{bmatrix} 0 \\ 0 \\ 0 \end{bmatrix} + \mathbf{T}
$$

$$
\Rightarrow \mathbf{T} = \begin{bmatrix} VRP_x \\ VRP_y \\ VRP_z \end{bmatrix}
$$

The entire transformation can now be written:

$$
\begin{bmatrix} x' \\ y' \\ z' \end{bmatrix} = \begin{bmatrix} \hat{\mathbf{u}} & \hat{\mathbf{v}} & \hat{\mathbf{n}} \end{bmatrix} \begin{bmatrix} x \\ y \\ z \end{bmatrix} + \begin{bmatrix} VRP_x \\ VRP_y \\ VRP_z \end{bmatrix}
$$

Using homogeneous representation, it is possible to express the transformation as a multiple of two 4×4 matrices:

$$
\begin{bmatrix} x' \\ y' \\ z' \\ 1 \end{bmatrix} = \begin{bmatrix} 1 & 0 & 0 & VRP_x \\ 0 & 1 & 0 & VRP_y \\ 0 & 0 & 1 & VRP_z \\ 0 & 0 & 0 & 1 \end{bmatrix} \begin{bmatrix} & & & 0 \\ \hat{\mathbf{u}} & \hat{\mathbf{v}} & \hat{\mathbf{n}} & 0 \\ & & & 0 \\ 0 & 0 & 0 & 1 \end{bmatrix} \begin{bmatrix} x \\ y \\ z \\ 1 \end{bmatrix}
$$

$$
= \underline{T}_1 \, \underline{R}_1 \begin{bmatrix} x \\ y \\ z \\ 1 \end{bmatrix}
$$

Since the matrix denoted by $(\underline{T}_1 \, \underline{R}_1)$ is the inverse of the view matrix, the view matrix is therefore equivalent to $(\underline{R}_1^{-1} \, \underline{T}_1^{-1})$. $\underline{R}_1$ has only a rotational effect and thus $\underline{R}_1^{-1}$ is the transpose of $\underline{R}_1$. $\underline{T}_1$ describes a translation, and therefore its inverse is a translation in the opposite direction. Hence:

$$
view\ matrix = \underline{V} = \begin{bmatrix} & \hat{\mathbf{u}}^T & & 0 \\ & \hat{\mathbf{v}}^T & & 0 \\ & \hat{\mathbf{n}}^T & & 0 \\ 0 & 0 & 0 & 1 \end{bmatrix} \begin{bmatrix} 1 & 0 & 0 & -VRP_x \\ 0 & 1 & 0 & -VRP_y \\ 0 & 0 & 1 & -VRP_z \\ 0 & 0 & 0 & 1 \end{bmatrix}
$$

6   Implementing the View Clip

The view parameters which define the clipping action are:

- Projection type: PARALLEL or PERSPECTIVE.

- Projection Reference Point (**PRP**).

- View Plane Distance (*VPD*). *VPD* is the z coordinate of the view plane which is parallel to the xy plane in *VRC*.

- Front Plane Distance (*FPD*). *FPD* is the z coordinate of the front plane which is parallel to the xy plane in *VRC*.

- Back Plane Distance (*BPD*). *BPD* is the z coordinate of the back plane which is parallel to the xy plane in *VRC*.

- View Window Limits. A rectangular view window is defined on the view plane by (U_{min}, V_{min}) and (U_{max}, V_{max}), which represent the bottom left and top right hand corners respectively of the window.

- Window Clipping Indicator. This enables or disables clipping against the four planes defined by the view window.

- Back Clipping Indicator. This enables or disables clipping against the back plane.

- Front Clipping Indicator. This enables or disables clipping against the front plane.

The Cyrus Beck [5] three dimensional clipping algorithm was chosen for implementation. This algorithm clips lines against an arbitrary convex volume which may be open or closed. Hence clipping to parallel, perspective and irregular volumes can be accommodated without prior transformation into a rectangular parallelepiped (parallel projections) or a right pyramid (perspective projections). Since one or more of the clipping planes in the volume may be disabled, it is also necessary that the algorithm works for open as well as closed clipping volumes.

The algorithm determines a segment of the given line such that no point on the segment lies outside the infinite plane defining a boundary. Lines to be clipped are represented in parametric form as the weighted sum of two end points, P1 and P2:

$$P = (1 - a)P1 + aP2 \qquad a \text{ in } [0,1]$$

The minimum and maximum values of a for which the line segment is within the enabled clipping boundaries are returned. If no part of the given line is visible it is rejected. The algorithm requires, for the six bounding planes, the plane normals ($\mathbf{n}_f$, $\mathbf{n}_b$, $\mathbf{n}_1$, $\mathbf{n}_2$, $\mathbf{n}_3$ and $\mathbf{n}_4$) and a point on each plane ($\mathbf{p}_f$, $\mathbf{p}_b$, $\mathbf{p}_1$, $\mathbf{p}_2$, $\mathbf{p}_3$ and $\mathbf{p}_4$). The following describes how this information, for each of the planes making up the clipping volume, is derived from the parameters.

6.1   The Front and Back Planes

Since the front and back planes are parallel to the xy plane, the normals must be parallel to the z-axis. The front plane is defined as the plane nearest positive infinity and therefore its normal will point in the negative z direction. Hence, the front plane normal and a point on the front plane for both parallel and perspective clipping volumes are:

$$\mathbf{n}_f = \begin{bmatrix} 0 \\ 0 \\ -1 \end{bmatrix}$$

$$\mathbf{p}_f = \begin{bmatrix} 0 \\ 0 \\ FPD \end{bmatrix}$$

The back plane normal points in the positive z direction:

$$\mathbf{n}_b = \begin{bmatrix} 0 \\ 0 \\ 1 \end{bmatrix}$$

$$\mathbf{p_b} = \begin{bmatrix} 0 \\ 0 \\ BPD \end{bmatrix}$$

Once again, these values apply for both parallel and perspective clipping volumes.

6.2   The View Window Planes

The four *view window* planes are defined by four projectors which pass through the corners of the view window. Convenient points on each of the planes are therefore the corners of the view window which are the same for parallel and perspective clipping volumes. Since adjacent planes contain the same view window corner, two opposite corners are sufficient to specify one point on each plane.

$$\mathbf{p_1} = \begin{bmatrix} U_{min} \\ V_{min} \\ VPD \end{bmatrix}$$

$$\mathbf{p_2} = \mathbf{p_1}$$

$$\mathbf{p_3} = \begin{bmatrix} U_{max} \\ V_{max} \\ VDP \end{bmatrix}$$

$$\mathbf{p_4} = \mathbf{p_3}$$

The normal of a given plane is obtained from the cross product of two non-collinear vectors lying in the plane. Each plane contains a projector and a side of the view window. These can easily be derived and are therefore used in this calculation. Since one projector forms an edge on two adjacent planes, two opposite projectors are sufficient to specify a projector in each of the four planes. The sides of the view window are aligned to the x and y axes and therefore $(1,0,0)$ and $(0,1,0)$ respectively can be used in each normal calculation. The cross products of the view window and projection vectors generate normal vectors for the planes in the clipping volume as follows:

$$\mathbf{n_1} = (0,1,0) \times \mathbf{d_1} \qquad \text{(see (a) in figure 13)}$$
$$\mathbf{n_2} = \mathbf{d_1} \times (1,0,0) \qquad \text{(see (b) in figure 13)}$$
$$\mathbf{n_3} = (0,-1,0) \times \mathbf{d_2} \qquad \text{(see (c) in figure 13)}$$
$$\mathbf{n_4} = \mathbf{d_2} \times (-1,0,0) \qquad \text{(see (d) in figure 13)}$$

where $\mathbf{d_1}$ and $\mathbf{d_2}$ are vectors parallel to projectors extending from the bottom left and top right hand corners of the view window. Calculation of these vectors depends on whether the projection type is parallel or perspective.

1. Parallel Projections

The projectors for a parallel projection are all parallel to the line joining the projection reference point to the centre of the view window. A vector $\mathbf{d}$, parallel to the projectors, is calculated as follows:

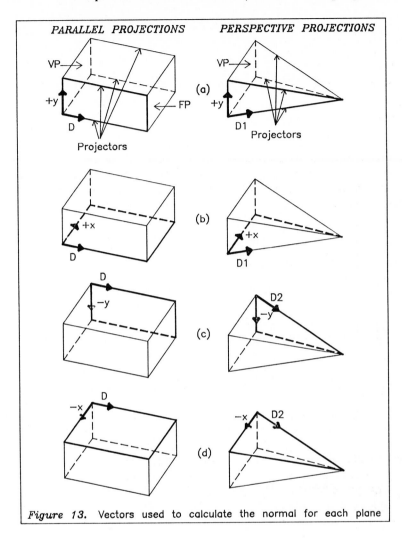

Figure 13. Vectors used to calculate the normal for each plane

$$\mathbf{d} = \mathbf{PRP} - \begin{bmatrix} (U_{min} + U_{max})/2 \\ (V_{min} + V_{max})/2 \\ VPD \end{bmatrix}$$

Thus $\mathbf{d}_1 = \mathbf{d}_2 = \mathbf{d}$

2. Perspective Projections

A perspective projection generates four non-parallel projectors which pass through the projection reference point and a corner of the view window. Vectors $\mathbf{d}_1$ and $\mathbf{d}_2$ are parallel to the projectors extending from the bottom left and top right hand corners of the view window and are calculated as follows:

$$\mathbf{d}_1 = \mathbf{PRP} - \begin{bmatrix} U_{min} \\ V_{min} \\ VPD \end{bmatrix}$$

$$\mathbf{d}_2 = \mathbf{PRP} - \begin{bmatrix} U_{max} \\ V_{max} \\ VPD \end{bmatrix}$$

In the viewing pipeline, the view clip is performed before the projection transformation. The clip can also be applied in homogeneous coordinate space after the projection transformation but before any perspective division [3] and therefore combined with the workstation clip.

7   Evaluation of the Projection Matrix

The projection matrix has two functions:

1.   A parallel or perspective projection transformation. The matrix to perform this function will be called $\underline{M}_1$ and will be derived in section 7.1.

2.   A mapping from the projected clipping/view volume onto the projection viewport. The corresponding matrix will be called $\underline{M}_2$ and will be derived in section 7.2.

The projection matrix is obtained by multiplying the two transformation matrices $\underline{M}_1$ and $\underline{M}_2$ together as follows:

$$\text{Projection Matrix} = \underline{M}_2 \times \underline{M}_1$$

7.1   Derivation of $\underline{M}_1$

The view parameters required to compute $\underline{M}_1$ are:

● Projection Type: PARALLEL or PERSPECTIVE.

● Projection Reference Point (**PRP**). For a parallel projection, the vector joining **PRP** and the centre of the view window specifies the direction of the projectors. In the case of a perspective projection, **PRP** represents the point through which all projectors pass.

● View Window Limits.

● View Plane Distance (*VPD*).

The techniques used in this section are based on those in Faux and Pratt [6]. For convenience, u, v and n coordinates are respectively referred to as x, y and z coordinates.

Parallel and perspective projection transformations are considered separately.

7.1.1   Parallel Projections

A parallel projection (3-D to 2-D) will transform a point $\mathbf{P}$ onto $\mathbf{Q}$, where $\mathbf{Q}$ lies on the view plane and the line PQ is parallel to the line joining the centre of the view window and $\mathbf{PRP}$, as shown in figure 14. From the figure, similar triangles, PTQ and $CAPRP$, can be used to derive an expression for the y coordinate of $\mathbf{Q}$, as follows:

$$\frac{P_y - Q_y}{VPD - P_z} = \frac{C_y - PRP_y}{PRP_z - VPD}$$

where $\mathbf{C}$ represents the centre of the view window. Hence:

$$Q_y = P_y + \frac{P_z(PRP_y - C_y)}{VPD - PRP_z} + \frac{VPD(C_y - PRP_y)}{VPD - PRP_z}$$

Similarly, the x coordinate of $\mathbf{Q}$ can be expressed as:

$$Q_x = P_x + \frac{P_z(PRP_x - C_x)}{VPD - PRP_z} + \frac{VPD(C_x - PRP_x)}{VPD - PRP_z}$$

The z coordinate of all projected points is VPD. However, GKS-3D and PHIGS need to retain the z information and therefore perform a projection transformation which maps three-space onto three-space. The actual transformed point required, $\mathbf{T}$ in figure 14, will have the same z coordinate as the original point $\mathbf{P}$.

The matrix $\underline{M}_1$ to perform the parallel projection transformation must therefore be such that:

$$\underline{M}_1 \begin{bmatrix} P_x \\ P_y \\ P_z \\ 1 \end{bmatrix} = \begin{bmatrix} Q_x \\ Q_y \\ P_z \\ 1 \end{bmatrix}$$

$$\Rightarrow \underline{M}_1 = \begin{bmatrix} 1 & 0 & -G_x & (VPD \times G_x) \\ 0 & 1 & -G_y & (VPD \times G_y) \\ 0 & 0 & 1 & 0 \\ 0 & 0 & 0 & 1 \end{bmatrix}$$

where

$$G_x = \frac{C_x - PRP_x}{VPD - PRP_z}$$

and

$$G_y = \frac{C_y - PRP_y}{VPD - PRP_z}$$

Notice that G_x and G_y will be undefined if the projection reference point lies in the view plane (i.e. $VPD = PRP_z$). Both GKS-3D and PHIGS generate an error if the projection reference point is positioned in the view plane.

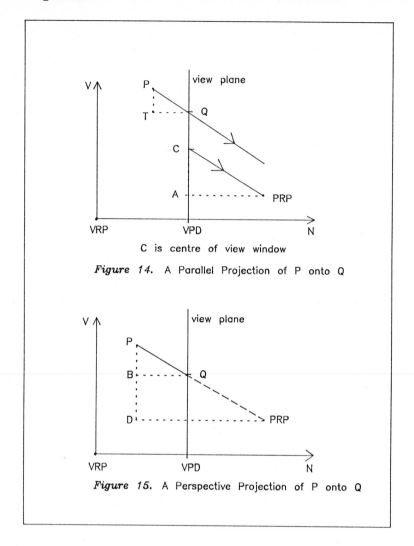

C is centre of view window

Figure 14. A Parallel Projection of P onto Q

Figure 15. A Perspective Projection of P onto Q

7.1.2 Perspective Projections

A perspective projection (3-D to 2-D) will transform a point **P** onto **Q**, where **Q** lies on the view plane and the (extended) line PQ passes through **PRP**, as shown in figure 15. From the figure, similar triangles, PBQ and $PD\,PRP$, can be used to derive an expression involving the y coordinate of **Q** as follows:

$$\frac{P_y - Q_y}{VPD - P_z} = \frac{P_y - PRP_y}{PRP_z - P_z}$$

$$\Rightarrow Q_y = \frac{P_y \times (PRP_z - VPD) - (P_z \times PRP_y) + (PRP_y \times VPD)}{PRP_z - P_z}$$

$$\text{and } Q_x = \frac{P_x \times (PRP_z - VPD) - (P_z \times PRP_x) + (PRP_x \times VPD)}{PRP_z - P_z}$$

The final expression for each of Q_x and Q_y includes a division by $(PRP_z - P_z)$. To calculate the matrix which will transform the point $\mathbf{P}$ onto $\mathbf{Q}$, the homogeneous representation of $\mathbf{Q}$ is written as:

$$Q_x = P_x \times (PRP_z - VPD) - (P_z \times PRP_x) + (PRP_x \times VPD)$$

$$Q_y = P_y \times (PRP_z - VPD) - (P_z \times PRP_y) + (PRP_y \times VPD)$$

$$Q_w = PRP_z - P_z$$

Once again a true projection is not required since the projection transformation retains the third dimension. The actual transformed point, $\mathbf{T}$, will have the same x, y and w components as $\mathbf{Q}$ but the z component should be such that the z coordinate of $\mathbf{T}$, T_z/T_w, increases and decreases with the z coordinate of the original point, P_z. With T_z/T_w as a monotonically increasing function of P_z (as P_z increases), relative z information is maintained by the transformation, and straight lines are transformed onto straight lines.

T_z is derived from the homogeneous matrix multiplication of the vector $\mathbf{P}$ and is therefore constrained as follows:

$$T_z = a P_x + b P_y + c P_z + d$$

where a, b, c and d are the elements of the third row in the matrix M_1. The constants a, b, c and d may take any value which maintains T_z/T_w as a monotonically increasing function of P_z, a and b can therefore be set to zero leaving

$$\frac{T_z}{T_w} = \frac{c P_z + d}{PRP_z - P_z}$$

Figure 16 shows two graphs of T_z/T_w against P_z from the equation above using different values for c and d. From the graphs, it is clear that for any combination of values for c and d, T_z/T_w is undefined when P_z is equal to PRP_z. Furthermore T_z/T_w is a monotonically increasing function of P_z only for values of P_z on the same side of PRP_z. However, since $\mathbf{PRP}$ represents the position of the eye, and only points at one side of the eye point should be visible, those on the opposite side need not be taken into account. In this case '$T_z = c P_z + d$' is acceptable for non-negative values of c and d.

The matrix M_1 required to map $\mathbf{P}$ onto $\mathbf{T}$ is such that:

$$M_1 \begin{bmatrix} P_x \\ P_y \\ P_z \\ 1 \end{bmatrix} = \begin{bmatrix} T_x \\ T_y \\ T_z \\ T_w \end{bmatrix}$$

where $T_x = Q_x$, $T_y = Q_y$ and $T_w = Q_w$. By setting $c = 0$ and $d = 1$ we have

$$M_1 = \begin{bmatrix} (PRP_z - VPD) & 0 & -PRP_x & (VPD \times PRP_x) \\ 0 & (PRP_z - VPD) & -PRP_y & (VPD \times PRP_y) \\ 0 & 0 & 0 & 1 \\ 0 & 0 & -1 & PRP_z \end{bmatrix}$$

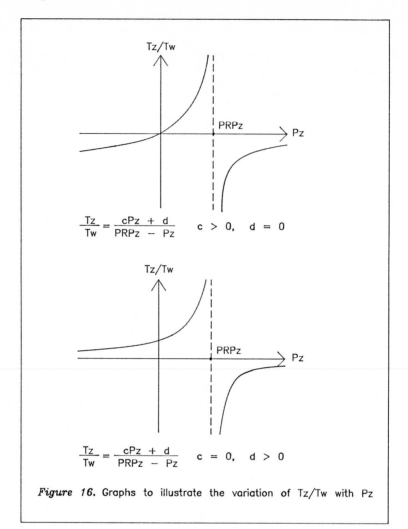

$$\frac{Tz}{Tw} = \frac{cPz + d}{PRPz - Pz} \qquad c > 0, \quad d = 0$$

$$\frac{Tz}{Tw} = \frac{cPz + d}{PRPz - Pz} \qquad c = 0, \quad d > 0$$

Figure 16. Graphs to illustrate the variation of Tz/Tw with Pz

Unfortunately GKS-3D and PHIGS do not constrain positioning of the projection reference point between the front and back planes. Accordingly, there could be visible points both behind and in front of the eye. The corresponding view volume, a double pyramid, is illustrated in figure 17. It is impossible to obtain an expression for T_z such that the requirements for T_z/T_w are satisfied for all P_z values. Thus the transformation cannot be expressed by a matrix multiplication. The BSI Graphics Panel [2] have recognised this as a deficiency in GKS-3D and PHIGS and these comments have been forwarded to ISO TC97 SC21 WG2 3D Subgroup. (This has now been resolved, see Appendix.)

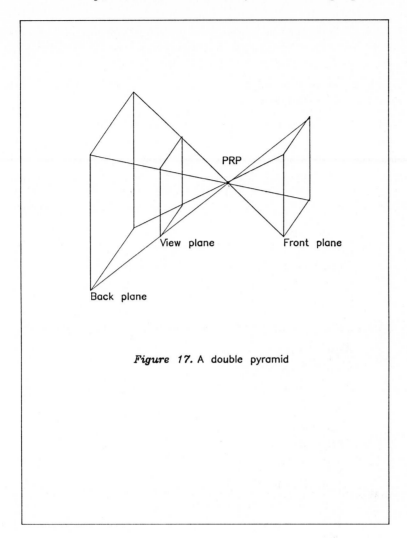

Figure 17. A double pyramid

7.2   Derivation of $\underline{M}_2$

The view parameters required to compute $\underline{M}_2$ are as follows:

- View Window Limits (U_{min}, U_{max}, V_{min}, V_{max}).

- Front Plane Distance (*FPD*).

- Back Plane Distance (*BPD*).

- Projection Viewport Limits.   A cuboid is defined within the range $[0,1]\times[0,1]\times[0,1]$ in *NPC* space.   Two corners of the volume are specified: (X_{min}, Y_{min}, Z_{min}) and (X_{max}, Y_{max}, Z_{max}).   These correspond to the back lower left hand and front top right hand corners respectively.

The view volume is mapped by M_2 onto the projection viewport such that the front and back planes defined by the view volume coincide with the projection viewport planes, Z_{max} and Z_{min} respectively. M_2 comprises:

1. Translation of the view volume corner (U_{min}, V_{min}, BPD) onto the corresponding corner of the projection viewport $(X_{min}, Y_{min}, Z_{min})$.

2. Scaling of the view volume about this corner to match the size of the projection viewport.

The above can be partitioned into three simple transformation matrices. The view volume is first shifted to place its back lower left hand corner at the origin. The volume is scaled about the origin and then shifted so that it is coincident with the projection viewport. Matrix M_2 is therefore the product of the corresponding set of matrices.

$$M_2 = \begin{bmatrix} 1 & 0 & 0 & X_{min} \\ 0 & 1 & 0 & Y_{min} \\ 0 & 0 & 1 & Z_{min} \\ 0 & 0 & 0 & 1 \end{bmatrix} \begin{bmatrix} X_{sf} & 0 & 0 & 0 \\ 0 & Y_{sf} & 0 & 0 \\ 0 & 0 & Z_{sf} & 0 \\ 0 & 0 & 0 & 1 \end{bmatrix} \begin{bmatrix} 1 & 0 & 0 & -U_{min} \\ 0 & 1 & 0 & -V_{min} \\ 0 & 0 & 1 & -BPD \\ 0 & 0 & 0 & 1 \end{bmatrix}$$

where X_{sf}, Y_{sf} and Z_{sf} are the scale factors required in x, y and z respectively.

$$X_{sf} = \frac{X_{max} - X_{min}}{U_{max} - U_{min}}$$

$$Y_{sf} = \frac{Y_{max} - Y_{min}}{V_{max} - V_{min}}$$

$$Z_{sf} = \frac{Z_{max} - Z_{min}}{FPD - BPD}$$

$$\Rightarrow M_2 = \begin{bmatrix} X_{sf} & 0 & 0 & T_x \\ 0 & Y_{sf} & 0 & T_y \\ 0 & 0 & Z_{sf} & T_z \\ 0 & 0 & 0 & 1 \end{bmatrix}$$

where

$$T_x = X_{min} - (X_{sf} \times U_{min})$$

$$T_y = Y_{min} - (Y_{sf} \times V_{min})$$

$$T_z = Z_{min} - (Z_{sf} \times BPD)$$

8   Summary

The output pipeline maps a point $\mathbf{p}_u$ in user coordinates onto a point $\mathbf{p}_d$ in device coordinates.

The GKS-3D user coordinates (world coordinates) are transformed first by the normalization transformation, $\underline{N}$, and the segment transformation, $\underline{S}$ then by the view transformation, $\underline{V}$ (see section 5), followed by the two components of the projection transformation, $\underline{M}_1$ and $\underline{M}_2$ (see section 7). Finally the workstation transformation, $\underline{W}$, maps the transformed point onto device coordinates. The whole operation can be summarized as follows

$$\mathbf{p}_d = \underline{W} \; \underline{M}_2 \, \underline{M}_1 \, \underline{V} \, \underline{S} \, \underline{N} \; \mathbf{p}_u$$

PHIGS user coordinates (modelling coordinates) are transformed first by the composite modelling transformation, $\underline{C}$ and then by the view, projection and workstation transformations as in GKS-3D. Hence

$$\mathbf{p}_d = \underline{W} \; \underline{M}_2 \, \underline{M}_1 \, \underline{V} \, \underline{C} \; \mathbf{p}_u$$

9   Examples

This section examines the GKS-3D/PHIGS viewing parameters for functional completeness by deriving the parameter settings required for the standard set of planar geometric projections classified in figure 18, see Carlbom and Paciorek [4].

It is assumed throughout that the principal faces of the object under consideration are aligned with the principal *NDC3* axes. Those parameters not mentioned do not affect the resulting projection type.

9.1   Parallel Projections

The following projections require the Projection Type parameter to be set as PARALLEL.

9.1.1   Orthographic Projections

In an orthographic projection, the projectors must be perpendicular to the view plane. The projector direction is determined by the vector joining the projection reference point and the centre of the view window. Since the view plane is parallel to the *uv* plane in *VRC*, this vector must be parallel to the *VRC* *n*-axis. The *x* and *y* coordinates of the projection reference point and the centre of the view window are therefore related as follows

$$PRP_x = (U_{min} + U_{max})/2$$
$$PRP_y = (V_{min} + V_{max})/2$$
$$PRP_z \neq VPD$$

Orthographic projections may be subdivided into two further classes of parallel projections, multiview orthographic and axonometric.

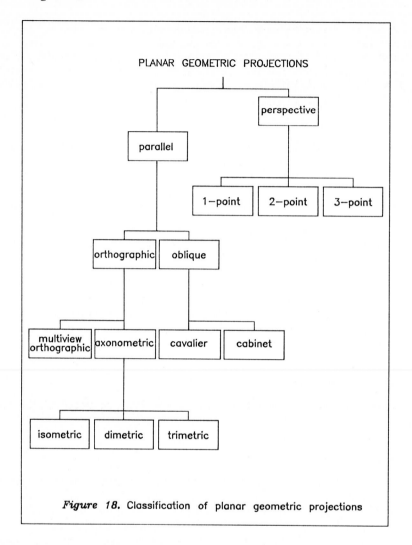

Figure 18. Classification of planar geometric projections

(a) Multiview Orthographic Projections

A number of different views of an object are formed using mutually perpendicular view planes. Usually the view planes are chosen parallel to the main faces of the object. A convenient way of creating a multiview orthographic projection is to surround the object with a cuboid. Each face of the cuboid can be taken, in turn, as a view plane to create up to six different orthographic projections of the object. In figure 19 the front face of the cuboid is to be used as the view plane. The corresponding view plane normal (**VPN**) and view up vector (**VUV**) must be aligned along the edges of the cuboid and can easily be obtained from the orientation of the cuboid. Values of the remaining parameters depend on the position of the view reference point (**VRP**). Figure 19 shows how they could be chosen in the most simple case with **VRP** at the bottom left hand corner of the cuboid face representing the current view plane.

(b) Axonometric Projections

In an axonometric projection, the object is positioned so that none of its principal faces is parallel to the view plane. These projections are classified according to the orientation of the view plane which is determined by the view transformation.

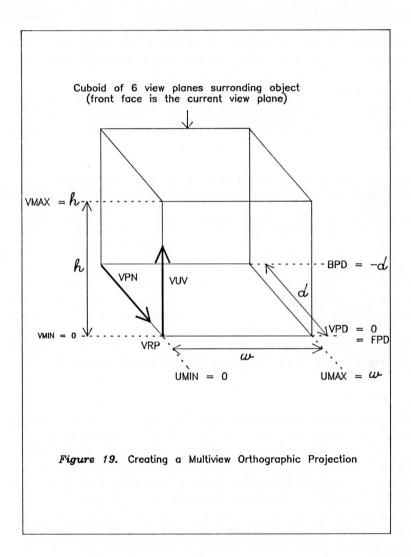

Figure 19. Creating a Multiview Orthographic Projection

1. Isometric Projections. If the angles between the view plane and the *NDC3* coordinate axes are all equal the projection is isometric. The view plane normal must therefore be parallel to one of the four lines $\pm x = \pm y = \pm z$ in *NDC3*. This is true if the absolute values of the components of the view plane normal are all equal. In an isometric projection the coordinate axes are equally foreshortened and the angles between the projected axes are all equal.

2. Dimetric Projections. If exactly two angles between the view plane and the coordinate axes are equal the projection is dimetric. The view plane normal must therefore be parallel to one of the planes $x = \pm y$, $x = \pm z$ or $y = \pm z$ in *NDC3*. In this case two of the absolute values of the components of the view plane normal will be equal. In a dimetric projection two of the coordinate axes are equally foreshortened and two of the angles between the projected axes are equal.

3. Trimetric Projections. If all the angles between the view plane and coordinate axes are different the projection is trimetric. This produces different foreshortening of the three coordinate axes and different angles between the projected axes.

Carlbom and Paciorek [4] show that the view plane normal can be calculated given the required properties of the axonometric projection in terms of either the foreshortening ratios of the three axes or the angles between the three projected coordinate axes.

For example, the foreshortening ratio of an axis is $\cos\theta$ where θ is the angle of intersection between the axis and the view plane. The angles between the axes and view plane can therefore be obtained from the required foreshortening ratios of the principal axes. Given the angle between an axis and the view plane, the angle between the axis and the view plane normal can be calculated. The cosine of the angle between a principal axis and the view plane normal is the corresponding view plane normal direction cosine. If a dimetric axonometric projection is required with foreshortening ratios of 0.5, 0.5 and 1 along the x, y and z axes respectively, the corresponding direction cosines of the view plane normal will be $\sin(\cos^{-1}0.5)$, $\sin(\cos^{-1}0.5)$ and $\sin(\cos^{-1}1)$. This projection is illustrated in figure 20.

9.2 Oblique Projections

The view plane in an oblique projection makes an oblique angle with the projectors. In general, the view plane normal is set perpendicular to a face of the object to project the given face without distortion. An oblique projection is determined by the angle between the projectors and the view plane and the orientation of the projectors with respect to the plane normal. Carlbom and Paciorek [4] derive formulae for the projector direction, **PD**, given one of the following sets of parameters:

1. α, the angle of intersection of the projector with the view plane and β, the angle of rotation of the projector about the view plane normal relative to the x-axis, as shown in figure 21. Values for the projector direction are

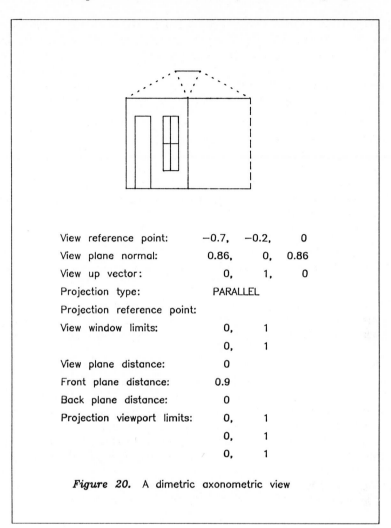

View reference point:	−0.7,	−0.2,	0
View plane normal:	0.86,	0,	0.86
View up vector:	0,	1,	0
Projection type:	PARALLEL		
Projection reference point:			
View window limits:	0,	1	
	0,	1	
View plane distance:	0		
Front plane distance:	0.9		
Back plane distance:	0		
Projection viewport limits:	0,	1	
	0,	1	
	0,	1	

Figure 20. A dimetric axonometric view

$$PD_x = a \cos\beta \cos\alpha$$

$$PD_y = a \sin\beta \cos\alpha$$

$$PD_z = -a \sin\alpha$$

where a is an arbitrary non-zero constant.

2. γ, the foreshortening ratio of the projected view plane normal and δ, the angle at which this projected normal intersects a coordinate axis in the view plane. These are illustrated in figure 22. In this case

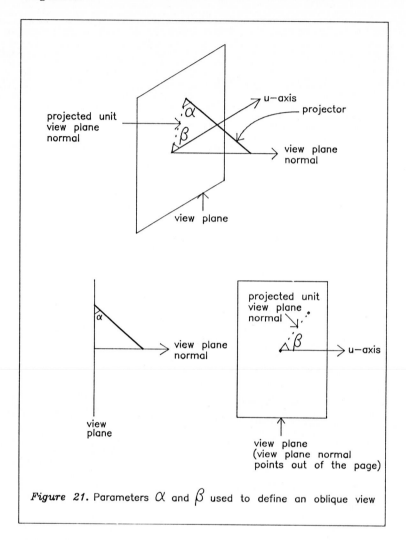

Figure 21. Parameters α and β used to define an oblique view

$$PD_x = a\ \gamma\ \cos\delta$$
$$PD_y = a\ \gamma\ \sin\delta$$
$$PD_z = -a$$

The projector direction is determined by the vector joining the projection reference point, **PRP**, and the centre of the view window, **C**. Hence

$$\mathbf{PD} = \mathbf{PRP} - \mathbf{C}$$

The coordinates of the projection reference point, given the view window limits and the view plane distance, VPD, are therefore:

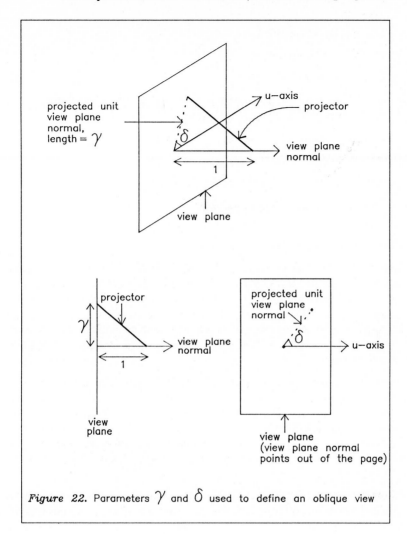

Figure 22. Parameters γ and δ used to define an oblique view

$$PRP_x = PD_x + (U_{min} + U_{max})/2$$

$$PRP_y = PD_y + (V_{min} + V_{max})/2$$

$$PRP_z = PD_z + VPD$$

One type of oblique parallel projection is the *cavalier* projection where the angle between the projectors and the projection plane is 45°. For a cavalier projection, where the angle of rotation of the projectors about the view plane normal is 30°, the projector direction vector would be

$$PD_x = a \cos30° \cos45°$$

$$PD_y = a \sin30° \cos45°$$

$$PD_z = -a \sin45°$$

A projection of this type can be obtained by assigning values to a, **PRP**, VPD and the view window limits which satisfy the equations given below.

$$PRP_x = a \cos30° \cos45° + (U_{min} + U_{max})/2$$

$$PRP_y = a \sin30° \cos45° + (V_{min} + V_{max})/2$$

$$PRP_z = VPD - a \sin45°$$

One such projection is illustrated in figure 23.

9.3   Perspective Projections

Projection Type parameter to be set as PERSPECTIVE. In a perspective projection only lines parallel to the view plane remain parallel. Parallel lines that are not parallel to the view plane converge to a single point, called a *vanishing* point A *principal vanishing point* is the vanishing point of a principal axis. Perspective projections are classified according to the number of principal vanishing points. This is equivalent to the number of principal *NDC3* coordinate axes that intersect, but do not lie within, the view plane.

1.   One-Point Perspective Projections. A one-point perspective projection has one principal vanishing point and hence only one principal coordinate axis intersects the view plane. The view plane normal vector, **VPN**, must therefore be parallel to the intersecting axis. This vector can be represented by ($a\ b\ c$) where exactly one of a, b and c is non-zero. For example, the value of **VPN** when the view plane is required to intersect the z-axis is ($0\ 0\ c$) for any non-zero value of c.

2.   Two-Point Perspective Projections. A two-point perspective projection has two principal vanishing points, and thus the view plane must intersect two of the principal coordinate axes. This is achieved by placing the view plane parallel to one axis but not parallel to any coordinate plane. Hence, VPN is perpendicular to exactly one principal axis and can be represented by ($a\ b\ c$) where exactly one of a, b and c is zero. The value of **VPN** when the view plane is placed parallel to the x-axis is ($0\ b\ c$) for any non-zero values of b and c. A two-point perspective view is illustrated in figure 24.

3.   Three-Point Perspective Projections. A three-point perspective projection has three principal vanishing points. This means that the view plane must intersect all three of the principal coordinate axes and thus cannot be parallel to any axis. **VPN** is chosen accordingly as the vector ($a\ b\ c$) where a, b and c all have non-zero values.

In any given transformation matrix, $\underline{M}$, where

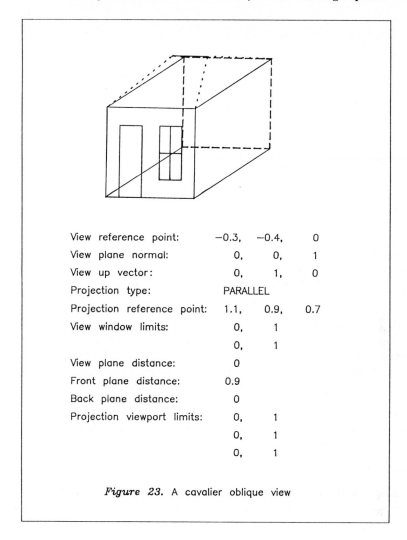

View reference point:	−0.3,	−0.4,	0
View plane normal:	0,	0,	1
View up vector:	0,	1,	0
Projection type:	PARALLEL		
Projection reference point:	1.1,	0.9,	0.7
View window limits:	0,	1	
	0,	1	
View plane distance:	0		
Front plane distance:	0.9		
Back plane distance:	0		
Projection viewport limits:	0,	1	
	0,	1	
	0,	1	

Figure 23. A cavalier oblique view

$$
\underline{M} = \begin{bmatrix} a & b & c & d \\ e & f & g & h \\ j & k & l & m \\ n & p & q & r \end{bmatrix}
$$

the matrix elements n, p and q determine the perspective transformation effect of the matrix. The vanishing points of the x, y and z axes are $(1/n,0,0)$, $(0,1/p,0)$ and $(0,0,1/q)$ respectively. Only two matrices, $\underline{M}_1$ and $\underline{V}$, contribute to the n, p and q values from which the vanishing points of the principal *NDC3* axes can be calculated. The bottom row of the concatenation of these two matrices is derived as follows:

$$(n\ p\ q\ r\ ) = (\ 0\ 0\ -1\ PRP_z\ )\ \underline{V}$$

$$= (\ 0\ 0\ -1\ PRP_z\ )\ \begin{bmatrix} \hat{\mathbf{u}}^T & -\hat{\mathbf{u}}.\mathbf{VRP} \\ \hat{\mathbf{v}}^T & -\hat{\mathbf{v}}.\mathbf{VRP} \\ \hat{\mathbf{n}}^T & -\hat{\mathbf{n}}.\mathbf{VRP} \\ 0\ \ 0\ \ 0 & 1 \end{bmatrix}$$

$$= (\ -n_x\ \ -n_y\ \ -n_z\ (\hat{\mathbf{n}}.\mathbf{VRP} + PRP_z))$$

where $(\ 0\ 0\ -1\ PRP_z\ )$ is the bottom row of $\underline{M}_1$.

10 Conclusion

This paper has described an implementation of the GKS-3D/PHIGS viewing pipe-line. The viewing pipeline is capable of generating all of the standard geometric planar projections. The corresponding viewing parameters, expressed in terms of GKS-3D/PHIGS functionality, have been derived. However, there exists a need for a utility layer [8] so that these projections can be described in a more natural manner, conforming with methods traditionally used [11]. Different types of projec-tion are described in different ways. For example, a perspective projection is specified in terms of the eye point and projection plane, whereas an oblique parallel projection is defined by the direction of the projected axes and the foreshortening ratios along the axes. It would therefore be useful to provide routines to generate different projection types from an appropriate set of parameters in each case.

Acknowledgements

I am very grateful to Terry Hewitt, Toby Howard, Tony Arnold and Roger Hubbold for their valuable suggestions and help. This work is supported by the UK Science and Engineering Council, grant number GR/D/20533.

References

1.   Anon, "Minutes of 3D Group Meeting at Frankfurt," ISO TC97/SC21/WG2 PHIGS/15 (3-7 March 1986).

2.   Anon, "BSI Position Paper on Viewing in GKS-3D and PHIGS," ISO TC97/SC21/WG2 3D/107.

3.   J. F. Blinn and M. E. Newell, "Clipping Using Homogeneous Coordinates," *Siggraph '78 Conference Proceedings* 12(3), pp.245-251.

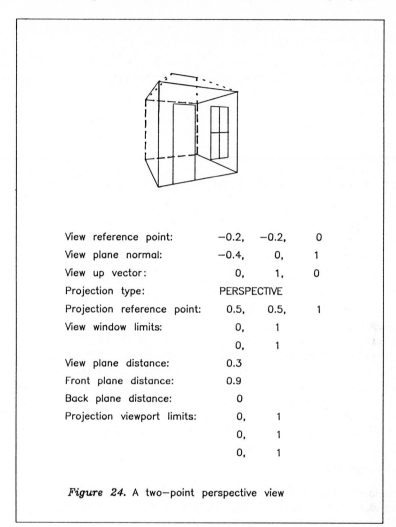

View reference point:	−0.2,	−0.2,	0
View plane normal:	−0.4,	0,	1
View up vector:	0,	1,	0
Projection type:	PERSPECTIVE		
Projection reference point:	0.5,	0.5,	1
View window limits:	0,	1	
	0,	1	
View plane distance:	0.3		
Front plane distance:	0.9		
Back plane distance:	0		
Projection viewport limits:	0,	1	
	0,	1	
	0,	1	

Figure 24. A two−point perspective view

4. I. B. Carlbom and J. Paciorek, "Planar Geometric Projections and Viewing Transformations," *Computing Surveys* **10**(4), pp.465-502 (December 1978).

5. M. Cyrus and J. Beck, "Generalised Two- and Three-Dimensional Clipping," *Computer and Graphics* **3**(1), pp.23-28 (1978).

6. I. D. Faux and M. J. Pratt, *Computational Geometry for Design and Manufacture,* Ellis Horwood (1979).

7. J. D. Foley and A. van Dam, *Fundamentals of Interactive Computer Graphics,* Addison-Wesley (1982).

8.   W. T. Hewitt and K. M. Singleton, *A Viewing and Transformation Utility Package for 3-D Graphics*, (In Preparation.).

9.   ISO, "Information processing systems - Computer graphics - Programmer's Hierarchical Interactive Graphics System," Working draft ISO/TC97/SC21 N819 (1985).

10.   ISO, "Information processing systems - Computer graphics - Graphical Kernel System (GKS) for three dimensions (GKS-3D) functional description," ISO DP 8805.

11.   J. C. Michener and I. B. Carlbom, "Natural and Efficient Viewing Parameters," *Computer Graphics* **14**(3), pp.238-245 (July 1980).

12.   M. E. Mortenson, *Geometric Modelling,* Wiley (1985).

Appendix

This section details a number of changes which were made to the specification of the viewing mechanism in PHIGS [9] at an ISO meeting in Frankfurt during March 1986 [1]. The set of viewing definition functions has been revised, although the functionality of the viewing pipeline is not affected. It is expected that these changes will be reflected in GKS-3D.

1. EVALUATE VIEW ORIENTATION MATRIX
    This utility routine, previously called COMPUTE VIEW MATRIX, returns the view matrix. The name has been changed to more accurately reflect the function of the returned matrix.

2. EVALUATE VIEW MAPPING MATRIX
    This utility routine has been added to compute the projection transformation matrix from the required parameters (described in section 7). Calculation of the projection transformation matrix was previously hidden from the user. The issue raised in section 7.1.2 is now resolved since the function generates an error if the projection reference point is between the front and back planes. The function name refers more appropriately to the 'projection transformation' as the 'view mapping'.

3. SET VIEW REPRESENTATION
    This function replaces the three functions SET VIEW MATRIX, SET VIEW MAPPING and SET VIEW CHARACTERISTICS. It defines the mapping from *NDC3* to *NPC* and sets the clipping status. The mapping is specified by two matrices whereas previously the view matrix and a set of projection parameters were used. The first matrix is the 'view matrix' or 'view orientation matrix' and maps from *WC* to *VRC*, while the second matrix, the 'projection matrix' or 'view mapping matrix', maps from *VRC* to *NPC*.

Part III: Specification and Certification

The question of validating an implementation is a very complex, and only partly solved, aspect of graphics standardization. Several different approaches have been proposed; we are still far from a full solution. Two approaches are examined in this section. One very pragmatic possibility is to create certification test suites and/or other certification software; two of these approaches are presented by **Brodlie et al.**, and by **Goebel et al**. A different approach uses formal specification of the notions contained with the standard itself, a method that could also lead to some kind of automatic (or semi-automatic) certification process. This section presents two contributions on this topic (**Gnatz**; **Duce et al.**).

A Practical Strategy for Certifying GKS Implementations

K. W. Brodlie, M. C. Maguire and G. E. Pfaff

1 Introduction

The recent emergence of GKS as a draft international standard [6] raises an important question: how can one be sure that an implementation of GKS adheres to the standard? This certification, or validation, question is crucial to every area of standardization: one could argue that a standard can be ignored (and is therefore worthless) unless adherence to it can be verified.

Unfortunately the problem of certification seems particularly hard to solve in the area of computer software - and especially so in the case of computer graphics. Ideally one wishes to *verify* that a GKS implementation conforms exactly to the standard. This might be done, for example, by taking a formal specification of GKS as "The Standard", and developing implementations from this specification by a series of program transformations. Some have high hopes that this can indeed be achieved, for example, with the aid of the wide spectrum language CIP-L [5].

Realistically however, formal verification must be seen as a distant target, some ideal that might be achieved in the future - yet surely there is an immediate requirement for some means of validating implementations. A more practical alternative is to consider, not methods of verification (whose aim is to prove the correctness of an implementation), but rather methods of *falsification*, where strenuous efforts are made to prove an implementation is incorrect. Of course this process yields no guarantee of correctness, but confidence is at least inspired in any implementation which survives the rigours of the test procedures.

Indeed it is falsification procedures that have been adopted in the validation of standards for programming languages. Typically a compiler is subjected to a large suite of test programs, specially designed to uncover likely errors, or possible misinterpretations of the standard. This process has been particularly successful in the case of Cobol [4]. Certification of a Cobol compiler by the US Federal Compiler Testing Service is now taken into account in the awarding of US government contracts to hardware manufacturers - one sure way of making certain the Cobol standard is not ignored! In the UK the BSI is set to initiate a pilot project for Pascal compiler validation.

There is growing interest in developing a falsification procedure for the validation of GKS. The EEC has recognized the importance of certification and has agreed to sponsor a number of workshops with the aim of developing a feasible validation strategy. The first meeting, held in May 1981 at Rixensart, near Brussels [1], brought together experts in computer graphics and experts in the certification of other software standards, including compilers. The meeting laid a good foundation for a series of five workshops which are being held in 1982.

This paper explains some of the current thinking on the validation of GKS; it outlines a basic strategy for testing GKS implementations and describes a pilot test suite.

2   A Model for GKS Certification

2.1   Basic Strategy

A simple model of a falsification procedure is shown in figure 1. The test program is applied to the implementation to be validated (the candidate implementation) and the results obtained are verified by the suite itself. This simple model is adequate in the case of compiler testing, where the results can be returned as variables to the test program and easily checked, and indeed some parts of graphics validation can also be handled in this way. Often however the results are in the form of a picture, or description of a picture, and the details will depend on the workstation used to produce the picture. In these circumstances the test suite cannot be expected to judge correctness.

Instead a more complicated model is required, as shown in figure 2. Here the test suite is also applied to some *reference* implementation, and corresponding results from the candidate and reference implementations evaluated by some *comparator* process.

2.2   Interfaces for Testing

There are three key interfaces at which results from the candidate implementation can be verified. These are illustrated in figure 3.

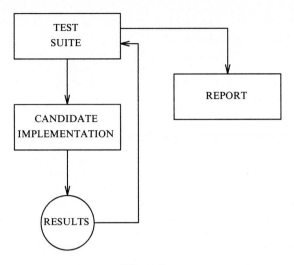

Figure 1

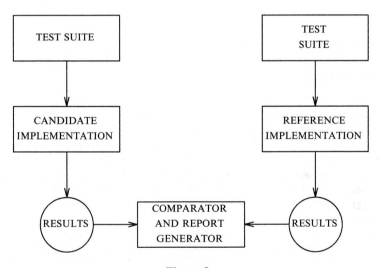

Figure 2

Application Interface

This interface, lying between GKS and the application program, is the appropriate point at which to verify the data returned by the GKS inquiry functions, input functions and error handling function.

Testing at this interface fits the simple model of figure 1: the results returned are in the form of simple variables that can easily be verified by the test program itself. Indeed a fair amount of progress has been made in the design of a test suite for checking at this interface, and this is reported in section 3.

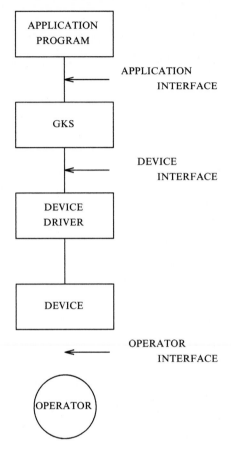

Figure 3

Device Interface

The testing of graphical output is a more difficult task. Certainly there is a need for some visual checking of pictures produced on actual graphical devices, and the importance of testing at this "operator interface" is stressed in the next section. However visual checking demands manual effort, and as such is subject to human judgement and human error. It is seen as a necessity for certification that there be some well-defined internal interface at which data passing to and from a graphical device can be intercepted and verified. Data at this point can be expressed as simple character strings and written to a file for automatic checking.

Indeed it is reasonable to expect that nearly all GKS implementations will have some such internal interface, through which a device driver is connected to the main part of the system (- the exception will be special-purpose implementations wholly in firmware). However, different styles of implementation, and the varying capabilities of actual devices, will mean that the position, or logical level, of this interface will be peculiar to a particular implementation, and a particular device within that implementation. This variability of the device interface is the key problem: either the comparator must be capable of handling this variability (in which case the reference implementation can be fixed), or else the reference implementation must be configurable to match precisely the device interfaces of any candidate, or perhaps some compromise between these two extremes might be more suitable. Indeed the extremes are hardly feasible: the implementation of a "super comparator" would be expensive, difficult and error-prone; the building of a reference implementation which could match the candidate in very fine detail would be a tremendous task - there are simply too many allowable differences to handle.

A useful compromise is to let configuration of the reference implementation take account of allowable differences in the behaviour of a GKS workstation - i.e. whether coordinates are passed as NDC (normalized device coordinates) or DC (device coordinates), whether linetype is simulated or handled directly, and so on. This ensures that the data streams are at the same logical level. The comparator is left to handle what might be termed device dependent visual differences, such as the actual appearance of a particular linetype (i.e. length of dots, dashes and gaps) or a particular font (i.e. the individual strokes making up a character). These allowable differences essentially form equivalence classes for the comparator. A useful step has already been made in defining the differences to be catered for by the reference implementation, and those to be catered for by the comparator - this work being done at the EEC Certification Workshop held in West Germany (April 1982) [2].

The workshop also specified a preliminary format, or grammar, for the data stream which the comparator will accept. So that the data streams may be compared item-by-item, it is important that each item be self-contained: for example, an item representing a polyline should include all attributes relating to the polyline - the comparator should not be required to maintain a context of attribute values. Some refinement of the grammar is still required, and of course the comparator itself must be constructed, taking account of the equivalence classes mentioned earlier.

A major task will be the construction of a reference implementation that can be configured to mimic the behaviour of any candidate. A useful aid in the design of such a reference implementation is to express the effect of each GKS output function as a pipeline of processes. Figure 4 shows a pipeline for the GKS POLYLINE function. For each box in the pipeline, the process, or transformation, applied and the data set on entry and exit are defined. Different device capabilities correspond to different points in the pipeline. For example, a particular candidate device may take over a polyline with coordinates being in NDC and the polyline bundle index bound to it (P1). Another one might be controlled by polylines in DC and the linetype and colour index of the current polyline bundle bound to it (P2). A third one will take over the polyline after attribute simulation is performed (P3). The configurable reference implementation has to be constructed so that the various pipelines can be realized, and a device interface be isolated at any point in a pipeline.

In practice an implementor would provide the certification agency with details of his candidate implementation. This information would be used to create an appropriate configuration of the reference implementation, and hence produce a data stream at the device interface (or set of device interfaces) suitable for input to the

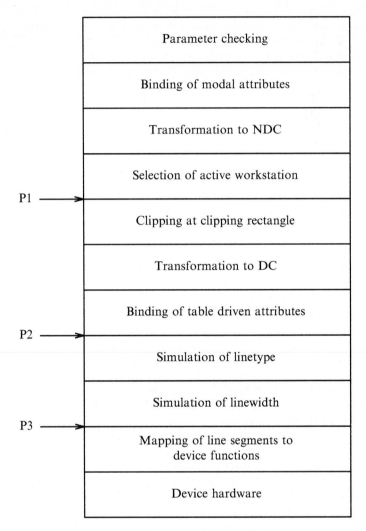

Parameter checking
Binding of modal attributes
Transformation to NDC
Selection of active workstation
Clipping at clipping rectangle
Transformation to DC
Binding of table driven attributes
Simulation of linetype
Simulation of linewidth
Mapping of line segments to device functions
Device hardware

P1 → (at Selection of active workstation / Clipping at clipping rectangle)
P2 → (at Binding of table driven attributes / Simulation of linetype)
P3 → (at Simulation of linewidth / Mapping of line segments)

Figure 4

comparator. It is unlikely that the designers of the reference implementation will be able to conceive initially of all possible configurations, and so in the early stages this dialogue with implementors will be important in improving the scope of the reference implementation.

Operator Interface

No matter how hard one tries to automate the certification process, there are sure to be some features that can only be checked manually. For example, how does one judge automatically that the representation of the letter A by a sequence of straight lines is recognizable to the human eye as the letter A? In any case, the only way to ensure that all the links in the graphical output chain are complete is to view the output on the display surface. The credibility of any certification scheme that did not include any visual checking would surely be low. Similarly complete testing of the graphical input chain requires at least some operator action on physical input devices, even though the bulk of the testing can be done by simulation at the device interface.

It is planned therefore to include a set of specially designed tests that requires operator involvement. The output tests will generate pictures on physical devices, the art in designing the tests being to highlight the appearance of any errors in the picture.

3   Design of Test Suite

3.1   Some Principles and Guidelines

During discussions with experts in compiler validation at the EEC certification meeting in Rixensart, a number of principles and guidelines emerged for the design of a GKS test suite. These have been assembled and developed [7].

A number of the guidelines are concerned with the *technical content* of the suite:

(i)   The test suite should be comprehensive, exercising all GKS functions as thoroughly as possible - this thoroughness being promoted by the following guidelines.

(ii)   GKS functions involving some form of boundary should be subjected to tests within, upon and beyond this boundary (e.g. the appearance of a marker within a viewing window).

(iii)   The order dependency of functions should be checked (e.g. that a workstation cannot be activated before being opened).

(iv)   Error cases may generate undesirable side effects which should be identified (e.g. that setting a window with an invalid transformation number does not cause the window limits to be added to the GKS state list).

Likewise a number of guidelines are concerned with the *administration* of the test suite:

(i)   The suite should consist of many programs, each containing few tests, testing being performed with increasing complexity. This allows errors to be detected both easily and systematically.

(ii)   Test programs should be parameterized with certain implementation specific data. These parameters would include: maximum number of normalization transformations, maximum number of workstations and the valid range of workstation identifiers.

(iii) Checking of test program output should be automated as far as possible.

(iv) The extent to which the suite covers the standard should be monitored (in the simplest case by noting the functions called by each test program).

(v)   The test suite should remain unchanged for a given period (to allow fair comparison between different candidates).

(vi) The test programs should be accompanied by documentation conforming to a prescribed scheme.

With this final guideline in mind, a format for test program documentation has been devised [7]. Each program is classified according to the area of GKS it aims to test. To encourage contributors of test programs to provide documentation (not always an easy task!), an interactive information collection program has been written; this prompts the contributor to enter the details required, and prints the information on file in the necessary format. An example of the documentation generated by this program for a simple test program is included in the appendix.

3.2   Initial Development

The EEC Certification Workshop held in Leicester (February 1982) embarked upon the creation of a test suite for GKS 7.0, for the lowest level - 0a [3]. Effort centred on testing at the application interface and in particular on the checking of GKS data structures and error handling.

3.2.1   Data Structure Testing

Since GKS clearly defines a series of data structures or state lists, it is essential to check that these lists are manipulated correctly in any particular GKS implementation. Data in the state lists are accessible to an application program through GKS inquiry functions. A test program, therefore, can examine values within the state lists and verify their accuracy.

This area of testing is based upon a series of "D-functions", one corresponding to each GKS function (except the inquiry functions). A D-function will test its corresponding GKS function by calling that function and examining state list changes by inquiry. For example, having called ACTIVATE WORKSTATION, the D-function will verify that the list of active workstations has been correctly amended.

The main advantage of this modular approach is that any GKS program can be converted into a data structure validation program by replacing GKS functions with D-functions.

3.2.2   Error Testing

The GKS error handling mechanism is well defined with an explicit list of errors associated with each function (see [6], clause 5 and Annex B). To test this mechanism, a set of "E-functions" has been developed, each function checking all error situations for a particular GKS function. The structure of an E-function is presented below, described in terms of a set of error checking utility functions.

```
        start
        . . .

        repeat for each error situation or test
        INITIALIZE TEST
        SET EXPECTED ERRORS ( < list of expected errors > )
        < call GKS function >
        CHECK ERRORS ( < flag > )
        if  < flag >  indicates test failure
            then: go to  < label >
            else: proceed to next test
        . . .

        REPORT ( < test set passed > )
        stop
< label > :REPORT ( < details of failed test > )
        stop
        end
```

For a particular test to succeed, the following criteria (based upon [6], subclause 4.11) must be satisfied:

(i)   At least one expected error must be reported.

(ii)   If a GKS state error was expected, this must be the first one reported.

(iii)   No unexpected error must be reported.

A number of tests have also been developed for certain error free situations to check that no unexpected errors occur. It is also important to check by inquiry that the GKS data structures are not corrupted when errors occur.

An example E-function for OPEN GKS is shown in the Appendix together with the report produced by a program calling E-functions corresponding to both OPEN GKS and CLOSE GKS.

3.3   Structure of Test Suite

It is important that the testing of an implementation is carried out with increasing complexity. Fundamental features are verified first, so that they can be assumed correct when checking more advanced features of the system. This imposes a certain structure on the test suite. Initial design work has suggested a series of six test classes for graphical output, each set building on its predecessor by introducing essentially a new variable. The test program sets are as follows:

SET	FUNCTION CLASS	FEATURES EXAMINED
1	Simple Control	Fundamental control operations of GKS
2	Output	Appearance of output primitives, on each workstation, under default transformation and attribute settings. Further control function testing (such as clearing the display surface) is included.
3	Primitive Attributes	Appearance of output under different settings.
4	Normalization Transformations and Clipping	Appearance of output under different settings including badly scaled cases.
5	Workstation Attributes	Appearance of output under different settings.
6	Workstation Transformations	Various workstation transformations including cases of the workstation window overlapping the current viewport.

The overall structure of the basic test suite is illustrated in figure 5.

4   Conclusions

This paper has put forward a practical approach to the problem of certifying implementations of GKS. The scale of the task is considerable, and it is clear that many of the ideas put forward here have yet to be thoroughly examined in practice.

However an embryo certification strategy is certainly emerging. One can envisage the validation of a candidate GKS implementation proceeding along the following lines:

(i)   The implementor contacts the test centre to indicate that he wishes to have his implementation certified, and enters full details of his implementation on a special form supplied by the test centre.

(ii)   This information enables the test centre to select an appropriate language version of the test suite and to configure both the test suite and reference implementation appropriately. A set of reference results at the device interface (or group of device interfaces) is generated at the test centre, together with a suitable pictorial output for checking at the operator interface.

(iii) When the implementor indicates he is ready, a representative at the test centre visits him and runs the test suite against the candidate implementation. A certificate is issued listing any errors detected.

The process should be viewed as an aid to implementors as much as a formal examination of their work. Indeed an implementor should contact the test centre at an early stage in the development of his software. The configured test suite, reference results and comparator can then be made available to him and can be used to assist in the debugging of the implementation. A representative of the test centre would still be responsible for the actual test run for which a certificate is issued.

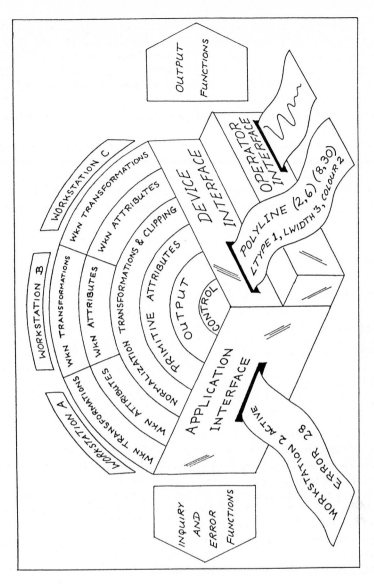

Figure 5

Many implementations of GKS will be designed to be widely distributed, and it would not be feasible to expect that the implementations would be certified with respect to all possible devices. There may be some value, therefore, in nominating a representative set of devices for use in this context. Indeed the reference results for these devices in particular configurations could be made publicly available for use by implementors, end-users and any other interested parties.

It is hoped that setting out a possible scheme at an early stage will encourage debate along technical and political lines. On the technical side, efforts are required to develop a feasible validation scheme that is both a good searching examination of a GKS implementation, and also an economic reality that will attract political support. On the political side, it must be realized that a major investment in manpower and equipment in setting up a test centre is required. But if the intended gains from having an international standard for computer graphics are to be fully realized, can the certification call be ignored?

Acknowledgements

Most of the work reported here has been developed at a series of workshops funded by the EEC. Thanks are due to all those who have participated in the workshops and contributed their ideas to the overall strategy presented in this paper. Particular thanks are due to Martin Goebel, Andre Ducrot, Peter Bono, Jose Encarnacao, David Fisher, Rupert Gnatz, David Rosenthal and Paul ten Hagen.

Postscript

The above paper was written at the outset of a project to establish a validation suite for GKS implementations. Writing this footnote some five years later, it is pleasing to report that a validation suite has indeed been written, and that it will form the basis of a European-wide GKS validation service. Three test centres have been established: GMD in West Germany, NCC in the UK, and a centre in France. The strategy described in this paper has been used as the basis for the validation suite. Testing at the application interface and operator interface is done almost exactly as described; however, testing at the device interface has proved too complicated and has had to be abandoned, at least for the present. This means a greater reliance on the operator interface tests than we would have wished. It will be interesting to see whether device interface testing becomes a feasible proposition one the Computer Graphics Interface (CGI) standard is completed.

References

1.   Anon, "Report on EEC Workshop on Graphics Certification, Rixensart-Brussels," University of Leicester (May 1981). (Copies from Dr K.W. Brodlie, Computer Laboratory, University of Leicester, Leicester, U.K.)

2.   Anon, "Report on EEC Workshop on Graphics Certification - Defining a Device Interface for Certification," Report No. GRIS 82-4, Technische Hochschule Darmstadt, Darmstadt, W. Germany (April 1982).

3.   Anon, "Report on EEC Workshop on Graphics Certification - Leicester," University of Leicester (February 1982). (Copies from Dr K.W. Brodlie, Computer Laboratory, University of Leicester, Leicester, U.K.)

4.   G. N. Baird and L. A. Johnson, "Compiler validation - an assessment," Federal Compiler Testing Centre, Falls Church, Virginia, USA.

5.   CIP Language Group, *Report on a wide spectrum language for program specification and development,* TU Munchen, Munich, W. Germany (May 1981).

6.   ISO, "GKS. Draft International Standard," ISO TC97/SC5/WG2/N117. (January 1982).

7.   M. C. Maguire, "The design of test programs for the certification of graphics standards," Report G3,, Computer Laboratory, University of Leicester, Leicester (November 1981).

Appendix

E-function for OPEN GKS

```
      SUBROUTINE EOPKS
C----------------------------------------------------------------
C   OPEN GKS ERROR TESTING
C   AUTHOR: B. BROWN   FEB 84
C   ERROR TESTED:
C     1. GKS NOT IN PROPER STATE:GKS SHALL BE IN STATE GKCL
C----------------------------------------------------------------
      COMMON /ERR/ GKEF,TYPE,WID,WCON,WTY,FAIL
      INTEGER GKEF,TYPE,WID,WCON,WTY
      LOGICAL FAIL,RESULT
C
C   WRITE TITLE TO REPORT FILE AND INITIALIZE TEST
C
      CALL CTITLE('TEST SET 4101 - OPEN GKS')
C
C   TYPE; STATE ERROR CHECK
C
C     TYPE = 1
C
C   TEST 1 : OPEN GKS IN STATE GKCL - NO ERROR EXPECTED
      CALL CSEXER(0)
      CALL GOPKS(GKEF)
      CALL CHEKER(RESULT)
      IF(RESULT.EQ.FAIL)GOTO 9000
C
C   TEST 2 : OPEN GKS IN STATE GKOP - ERROR 1 EXPECTED
      CALL CSEXER(1)
      CALL GOPKS(GKEF)
      CALL CHEKER(RESULT)
      IF(RESULT.EQ.FAIL)GOTO 9000
C
C   TEST 3 : OPEN GKS IN STATE WSOP - ERROR 1 EXPECTED
      CALL GOPWK(WID,WCON,WTY)
      CALL CSEXER(1)
      CALL GOPKS(GKEF)
      CALL CHEKER(RESULT)
      IF(RESULT.EQ.FAIL)GOTO 9000
C
C   TEST 4 : OPEN GKS IN STATE WSAC - ERROR 1 EXPECTED
      CALL GACWK(WID)
      CALL CSEXER(1)
      CALL GOPKS(GKEF)
      CALL CHEKER(RESULT)
      IF(RESULT.EQ.FAIL)GOTO 9000
C
```

```
C   REPORT TEST SET PASSES OR FAILED
9000  CONTINUE
      CALL CREP(RESULT)
C
      RETURN
      END
```

Report generated by test program calling E-functions for OPEN and CLOSE GKS

****

* TEST PROGRAM E4100 - ERROR REPORTING OF CONTROL FUNCTIONS

****

TEST SET 4101 - OPEN GKS

     ****
        FAILURE IN TEST 3
     ****
     *
     * TYPE: STATE ERROR TEST
     *
     * ERROR 1 EXPECTED
     *
     * ERROR 2 REPORTED
     *
     *   REMAINING TESTS OMITTED
     ****

TEST SET 4102 - CLOSE GKS

     ****
     ALL 4 TESTS SUCCESSFUL
     ****

     ****

SUMMARY OF TEST PROGRAM COVERAGE
     *
     * 6 TESTS PASSED
     * 1 TEST FAILED
     * 1 TEST UNTRIED
     *
     * 0 ERRORS OUTSIDE TESTS
     *
     ****

TEST PROGRAM DOCUMENTATION

1. NAME AND TITLE

E4100
OPEN AND CLOSE GKS error reporting

2. DESCRIPTION

This program checks the correct generation of state errors for OPEN GKS and CLOSE GKS by calling the appropriate E-functions.

3. GKS LEVEL AND VERSION

LEVEL: 0a VERSION: 7.2

4. GKS FUNCTIONS UNDER TEST

OPEN GKS
CLOSE GKS

5. GKS SUPPORT FUNCTIONS

OPEN WORKSTATION
ACTIVATE WORKSTATION

6. GKS ERRORS GENERATED

001 : GKS not in proper state: GKS must be in the state GKCL
002 : GKS not in proper state: GKS must be in the state GKOP

7. REFERENCES TO GKS DOCUMENT

5.2 Control Functions

8. KEYWORDS

CONTROL

9. DATE OF ACCEPTANCE

01 MAR 1984

10. VERSION NUMBER

1

11. ORIGINAL CREATION DETAILS

29 FEB 1984
B. Brown
Leicester University

12. REVISION DETAILS

13. LANGUAGE BINDING

FORTRAN 77
GKS function names based on ISO FORTRAN Language Binding
Report file = unit no. 1
GKS error file = unit no. 3

14. RESOURCES FOR RUNNING

NO. OF PROGRAM LINES (INCLUDING COMMENTS):   148
NO. OF COMMENT LINES: 64
NO. OF INTEGER ARRAY ELEMENTS: 0
NO. OF REAL ARRAY ELEMENTS: 0
ESTIMATED RUN TIME (SECONDS):   2
MACHINE AND OP. SYSTEM ON WHICH ESTIMATE IS BASED:
    PDP 11/44 UNDER RSX/11M
NO. OF GKS WORKSTATIONS REQUIRED: 0
WORKSTATION TYPES: none

15. INPUT DATA FILES

16. INTERACTIVE ACTIONS

17. SOURCE OF RESULTS AND METHOD OF CHECKING

TESTING INTERFACE: APPLICATION PROGRAM

Each E-function checks the results of its own test set and produces a report. If any test fails, the remaining tests in that set are omitted.

18. EXPECTED RESULTS

Each E-function reports either:

ALL < N > TESTS SUCCESSFUL

or:

FAILURE IN TEST < n >

together with details of the failed test.

Configuring Reference Systems for Certifying GKS Implementations

M. Goebel and W. Huebner

1 Introduction

Now that **GKS**, the **Graphical Kernel System**, has become an international standard [7] and a number of implementations have been offered on the market [5], users are looking for criteria for deciding which implementation to buy and use. The most important advantage of a standard in computer graphics is to provide a solid base for the implementation of portable application systems. This will be guaranteed only if each implementation of GKS adheres to the standard. Standardization efforts are really worthless without preserving the goals of **portability** and **uniformity**. Therefore, there is a need for testing strategies to examine whether an implementation conforms with the standard or not. Furthermore, certification tools provide help for both users and implementors. Test programs are made available for use whilst developing an implementation. Reference data flow and results will give assistance to implementors during the life cycle of a GKS implementation.

In the area of software validation two complementary strategies are established, verification and falsification. **Verification** needs a formal means for proving a system correct, **falsification** of software products is an attempt to prove that an implementation is not valid.

2 Falsification Methods for GKS

The complexity, diversity, and semi-formality of the graphical aspects overall are reasons preventing a formal verification of GKS implementations. Therefore checking the functional correctness of GKS implementations relies on a number of test programs where strong efforts are undertaken to detect errors within an implementation [3]. This validation strategy is not able to prove the absence of errors!

The test method in general is to access data from an implementation at a specific level and to compare these data to (so-called) reference data which have been derived from the functional behaviour of the graphics system. The testing of GKS implementations concentrates on

- the system states which are expected to be set or changed;

- errors which are expected to occur;

- the graphical output at the display of a device and

- data exchange (pictures and control functions) between the graphics system and the devices connected to it.

The testing of graphics systems is limited to three interfaces where data can be intercepted:

- The **application interface** which consists of a set of functions used by application programs.

- The **operator interface** which is located between graphical devices and human operators. This interface is represented by visual output of the system and operator input.

- The **device interface** which divides the device-dependent portion from the device-independent part of an implementation. Device drivers of different types can be connected to the system at this interface.

3   Black Box Testing of Graphics Systems

For checking the data accessible either to programmers or to users the strategy of **black box testing** is chosen. This method which is well-known in the area of compiler testing [10] involves calling each function of the system and comparing its output at a specific interface to *'what is expected'*. A graphics system contains functions of different classes, those which have an effect on internal data structures and others which produce graphical output or accept graphical input. The effect of a state setting function can be compared automatically because this data is accessible by corresponding inquiry functions in GKS. Graphical output, however, cannot be compared automatically because there is no 'usable' *readback* facility for pictures. Two different strategies have been set up considering these two function types, the data structures and error tests at the **application interface** and testing of graphical output at the **operator interface**.

All **data structures** in a GKS implementation that maintain the current state of the system (e.g. *GKS state list, workstation state lists*) can be set and accessed at the application interface [4]. The correctness of each data manipulating function in an implementation is tested as follows.

The current states are inquired and stored before invoking the function under test. Next, the state is modified by calling the GKS function. Finally, the states are inquired again and compared with those stored before. State changes which are not expected are erroneous and will be reported by the test program.

This test method is applied to all entries in state lists. The description tables are tested slightly differently as their entries are not settable. The minimal required capabilities and predefined values defined by the document are used as references for testing the description tables.

A similar strategy is applied to the **error handling** mechanism in GKS. Errors which are defined to occur in a specific situation are compared with those which really do occur in that situation.

As mentioned above functions which generate **graphical output** must be tested by another strategy. When programming graphics, a certain picture is expected to appear at the display. If the visual output corresponds to that mental model, the graphics system will be assumed to be correct.

Evaluating the visual effects of GKS functions is left to human operators. For this purpose the operator is asked to compare the graphical output of the test program to a prefabricated reference picture. Although some criteria are given for every reference picture to support the operator in his judgement the review of the suitability of the visual representations is a subjective task. Therefore testing is limited to quite a few simple pictures and test cases the operator is able to handle. For GKS level 0a, for example, the visual effects of output primitive functions and corresponding attribute settings are tested. Furthermore some control functions, like CLEAR WORKSTATION, the transformation functions and clipping facilities are inspected by a human operator [8].

First experiences with running black box tests at the application interface show that most errors are located within the *inquiry* functions because these functions seem to be implemented less carefully than the other functions of an implementation. Most of the errors detected when running the tests at the operator interface are located in the device-specific portion of the implementations (e.g. *colour_mapping*, *area_filling*).

4   Testing the Mapping of GKS Functions onto Device Capabilities

Pictorial reference tests are worthwhile for checking a graphics systems in the whole. Systems like GKS are defined by a set of functions which are allowed to be realized in software and/or in hardware. Visual effects result from invoking some of these function in a specific order. If this output does not conform with a reference picture there is no criterion to judge whether functions of the device-independent part of the implementation or the device software or hardware failed.

In most device-independent GKS implementations graphics devices are connected to the device-independent portion using an internal interface. At this interface the function set for one device usually corresponds to the device capabilities. For instance, if a device is able to transform objects, the function SET SEGMENT TRANSFORMATION should be sent to it. Functions which cannot be interpreted by the device will not be sent to it.

The device interface is suitable for gathering data for testing a GKS implementation. It provides an acceptable base for certifying GKS implementations even if a special graphic device does not work as expected. Therefore the examination of the device interface is very useful and really necessary for testing graphical output. The idea for testing the correct functional mapping of GKS functions onto device functions is as follows (see figure 1).

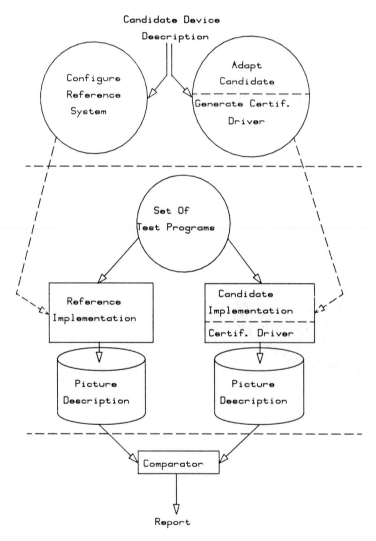

Figure 1 The Model for Testing at the Device Interface

While a test program is running on a GKS implementation (called the candidate) the data passing the device interface is intercepted by a specific certification driver and stored on a file in some uniform format. The same program is executed a second time, using a so-called **reference implementation** which has been constructed according to the functional level of the candidate's device. It is assumed that the output of the candidate implementation at the device interface is functionally equivalent to the results produced by the reference implementation. The comparison of both sets of output can be done automatically if the same data structures and types are used for describing visual effects of each. Comparing a functional description of a picture against a reference description even allows testing of more complex and precise pictures than a human operator is able to do.

A problem is seen in the diversity of graphics devices and therefore in the wide **range of device interfaces** supported by different GKS implementations or even by one implementation. There exist no rules for mapping GKS functions onto device functions and there are quite a lot of mappings that are reasonable for one GKS function. The mapping chosen by an implementation should correspond to the capabilities of the device because GKS is meant to serve each device according to its facilities.

For example, the GKS function POLYLINE is mapped onto a corresponding device function *polyline* for those devices which perform at least a static polyline attribute binding. Furthermore, *polylines* could be mapped onto *vector_sets* or *move_and_draw* sequences or even onto *pixel* output for raster devices. Table 1 shows the realization of the GKS POLYLINE function for very low level devices.

Consider another device which is able to perform for instance *clipping* or *transformation*. In this case there will be a separate function within the device interface and it will no longer be resolved in the workstation function *polyline* as in the example above.

POLYLINE:	*GKS function*	
	parameter checking binding of attributes from GSL normalization transformation selection of active workstations	
POLYLINE:	*workstation function*	
	clipping workstation transformations binding of workstation attributes attribute emulation : <device dependent coding>	| range | of | device | interfaces
POLYLINE:	*device function*	
	vectors / move_and_draw / pixels	

Table 1 The Range of Device Interfaces for *Polyline*

Of course, the certification approach does not support all particular physical device interfaces. A reasonable range of logical device interfaces is defined by the workstation interface of GKS [1] as the 'highest' interface and a few (minimal required) functions (e.g. *open_device, clear_display, draw_vector*) building the 'lowest' device interface.

As mentioned above, the idea of testing is to construct reference results at **one particular** device interface and to compare these reference data with those gathered from the candidate implementation when running the same test. There is no limitation for test programs, i.e. every GKS program can be transformed into a test program. Reference data is obtained by running programs on a reference system.

The reference system has to perform the same transformation steps as the candidate implementation does to serve the same device interface. There were two initial ideas for the realization of the reference system [9]

(1) a general purpose implementation of GKS which selects a specific device interface by resolving runtime conditions and

(2) a fixed, tailor-made implementation for a particular device interface.

The disadvantage of a general purpose implementation is its complexity. It would take very strong efforts to ensure the correctness and completeness of such an implementation.

By using prefabricated modules and program construction techniques to generate **one device-specific reference implementation** for each interface under test it is a lot easier to control the matching of the candidate's transformation steps by the reference implementation.

For these reasons the realization of a **separate** reference implementation for **each** device interface of the candidate was chosen. A large number of complex test programs will then be executed to test the candidate's functional mapping.

5 Constructing a GKS Reference Implementation

The configuration process for reference implementations is divided into single tasks which perform a stepwise translation of the functional specification of GKS to a device-specific implementation. The modularity of the reference specification and the well-defined interfaces between the modules guarantee that changes in the standard will affect only some internal tables. Moreover the structure of the overall process allows validation of each transformation step and thus, of the correctness of each generated reference system.

No	Phase	Tool	Result
0	*Specification*	Specification Language	Reference Specification
1	*Description*	Editor	Device Interface Descr.
2	*Configuration*	Configurator	-
3	*Program Generation*	Interpreter	Reference Implementation
4	*Testing*	Comparator	Test Report

Table 2 The five Phases of the Test Process at the Device Interface

In an initial step a functional specification of GKS is defined. This describes the effects of each GKS functions at the device interface more formally than the GKS document. In phases 1 to 3, a reference implementation is created for each device supported by the candidate implementation. In phase 4, test programs are run on both candidate and reference, producing results at the same logical level and in the same format. Output at the device interface is collected in picture element descriptions (PED) which are created for each graphical output function or control function. Finally, a comparator checks whether the picture element descriptions of the same test program are identical for candidate and reference system. The process of constructing a reference system is shown in figure 2. The particular phases are detailed in the following sections.

5.1   The Reference Specification

Prerequisite for the testing at the device interface is a device-independent valid specification of GKS (phase 0) as a reference which describes the effects of GKS functions on device interfaces of various logical levels. GKS functions that pass data to devices are mainly output, segmentation and input functions and attribute setting functions with retroactive effects. Within these functions the transformation steps from the GKS application interface to the respective device interface are specified, e.g. *attribute binding, normalization transformation, clipping* etc. For each step which can be seen as an entity that should not be divided into smaller parts, a function is defined describing the effect on the current picture element description, which is the functional pictorial reference. The specification contains several different implementation decisions, e.g. type and data of transformation modules, varying device facilities. The specified functions are available in a module library in different realizations.

A functional specification language [6] was developed to describe effects in the reference implementation by methods which are seen as abstract data types. Those methods are taken to be black boxes communicating via their parameters and manipulating the current picture element description. The specification is based on system states, modules and communication functions.

(1)   The system states are represented by structured data types. Four different classes are defined in the reference specification:

The Configuration Process

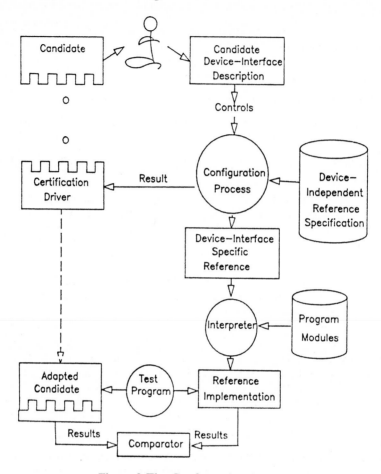

Figure 2 The Configuration Process

- the GKS state vector consisting of the GKS data structures, such as the GKS state list and workstation description tables and state lists,

- parameters of GKS functions like positions in world coordinates or text strings,

- data types which are used in the specification, i.e. the current picture description,

- candidate specific data like data type used to realize the clipping rectangle or the linetype (e.g. integer, indexed, enumeration) which are collected in an internal device description table.

(2) Basic modules that are implemented and available in a source code library of a higher level programming language. If these modules are specified in the specification language an interpreter will generate source code of a higher level programming language. These modules cover

- *fundamental algorithms* like coordinate transformation or clipping,

- *specification-dependent modules* like adding or removing parts of the current picture element description,

- *candidate specific modules*, i.e. converting logical attribute values to device attributes.

(3) Communication modules using basic modules, assignments, and control structures. These modules describe the transformation steps of a GKS function from the application program to the device (e.g. *wk_polyline* in Table 3 and figure 3).

The current picture element description (CPED) as a part of the system state vector, represents the appearance of the picture (primitive or segment) or parts of it. The CPED is defined to include most candidate specific parameter types for output primitives and the corresponding static and/or dynamic attributes. In Table 3 a specification of those entries of the picture element description (PED) is shown which are relevant for polylines. Each step specified in the reference (figure 3, Table 1) affects the current PED. For example, if a device is able to perform the workstation transformation the transformation matrix will be added to the CPED. Otherwise this step (transformation) will be resolved by the reference implementation and the NDC-points and the transformation matrix will be removed from the CPED. The entry *valid_entries* defines the current states and data types of the CPED-entries.

Note, that various entries in the device-independent specification are configurable, for instance the data types used within the picture element record (e.g. linetype_type) and especially the device-specific *wk_polyline* function which has to be filled out following a decision tree (figure 3). The device-independent reference specification is set up, once a device-specific specification is configured for each candidate device under test.

5.2   The Candidate Device Description

In phase 1, the description phase, the device interface for the tests is specified by the implementor of the candidate system. The information needed for the configuration process is requested by an editor that guides the implementor and generates a candidate device interface description. This interface description is used to create an internal device description table for the reference specification and to define the data types of the reference (e.g. linetype_type).

Reference Specification
RECORDS
WK_DESCR_TBL_TYPE   : RECORD   < record specification >   END

PED_TYPE   : RECORD
 	
                         valid_entries   : SET OF STRING (21,);
                         points   : LIST OF POINT_TYPE ();
                         list_of_asfs   : LIST OF STRING
                                                     (13;'bundled','individual');
                         wk_transf_matrix   : LIST OF REAL (6,);
                         clipping_rectangle : RECTANGLE_TYPE ();
                         polyline_index   : INTEGER (1,);
                         polyline_bundle   : POLYLINE_BUNDLE_TYPE ();
                         linetype   : LINETYPE_TYPE ();
                         linewidth   : LINEWIDTH_TYPE ();
                         colour   : COLOUR_TYPE();
                         < other entries >
                         END
  < other data types >

DECLARATIONS

cped   : PED_TYPE ();
    wk_dt   : WK_DESCR_TBL_TYPE ();
    wk_sl   : WK_STATE_LST_TYPE ();
  < other data declarations >

METHODS

split_pl_to_vector_set   (LIST OF POINT_TYPE) (VECTOR_SET_TYPE);
    add_to_cped   (SET OF STRING,STRING) (SET OF STRING);
    remove_from_cped   (SET OF STRING,STRING) (SET OF STRING);
  < other method declarations >

NAME   *wk_polyline*
    TYPE INPUT   points   : LIST OF POINT_TYPE (2,)
    EFFECT
      collect_polyline_index (points);
      calculate_pl_vector_set ();
      add_picture_element_to_device ()
    END

All available methods for the *wk_polyline* function are specified in this format. As an example the function *calculate_pl_vector_set* is specified.

NAME   *calculate_pl_vector_set*
    TYPE
    EFFECT
      split_pl_to_vector_set (cped.points) (cped.vector_set);
      remove_from_cped (cped.valid_entries,'points') (cped.valid_entries);
      add_to_cped (cped.valid_entries,'vector_set') (cped.valid_entries)
    END

NAME < next specification >

Table 3 Configurable Specification of the Reference System

WK_POLYLINE

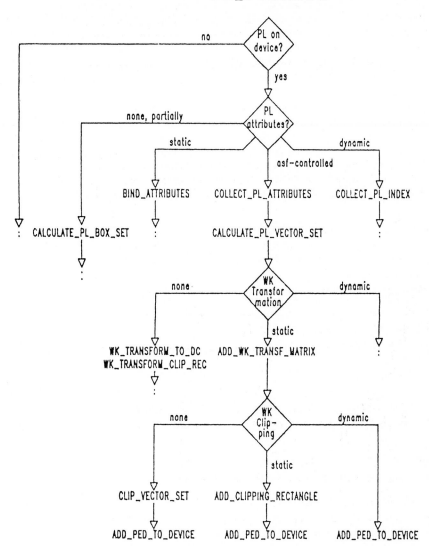

Figure 3 Decision Tree for *wk polyline*

The editor generates a series of questions controlled by decision trees. In cases of positive answers the corresponding data types and valid ranges of data values, too, are inquired. The information needed for the configuration process is collected using the same branch mechanisms as the configurator does in a later phase. Device-specific information is gathered for all those GKS functions that have an effect on the device interface (e.g. output primitives, representation settings, etc.).

5.3   The Configuration Process

In the next phase a tailor-made reference system is configured from the device-independent reference specification. The configuration of each reference function with an effect at the device interface is controlled by a decision tree (as shown in figure 3). The entities represent single transformation steps which correspond to modules. These modules describe the effects of one step. Modules referred to are realized either in the specification language or directly in source code of a programming language. Each decision tree represents various device interfaces for one workstation function. The diamonds stand for device facilities considered at the device interface, for instance, whether a device performs clipping or not. The method names represent module calls which are selected to fill the device-independent specification of the communication modules (e.g. *wk_polyline*). The configuration of one communication module stops when the method *add_picture_element_to_device* is reached. All methods passed create the device-dependent reference specification of the function.

A second task of the configurator is to declare the device-dependent data types and to choose parameter types for the methods included, e.g. whether coordinates are accepted in DC or NDC and whether the DC type means raster units (integer) or metres (real).

Finally, the configured reference specification consists of:

- device-dependent and -independent records like system state vector, picture element description etc.;

- the specification of all variables and methods needed;

- complete specification of communication modules.

A third main task of the configurator is to generate a certification driver which is an adapter between the candidate implementation and the test mechanism (figure 2) and formats. A candidate device-specific certification driver is made from a skeleton driver which realizes only those device functions described in phase 1.

5.4   Generating Reference Implementations

The device-dependent reference is specified in an abstract specification language and must be transferred into a programming language for running tests. In phase 3, an interpreter converts the specification constructs into programming language constructs. Complex data structures such as the system state vector are mapped onto data types of the target language. In a first version this interpreter generates FORTRAN 77 output, others will certainly follow.

Only the device-dependent parts of the reference implementation are processed by the tools of phases 1 to 3. The device-independent parts which are fixed for each workstation type and device interface (e.g. *inquiries*, mapping of GKS functions onto workstation functions) are specified in the form of non-configurable modules which only have to be transferred into a programming language by the interpreter.

5.5   Testing and Comparison

When a reference implementation and a certification driver are generated for a specific candidate device interface both systems are installed for testing. The candidate implementor replaces the device driver by the certification driver which collects output within picture element descriptions and handles file output. Both systems have to be compiled and linked with test programs. The test programs access GKS functions via a test layer that brackets the output at the device interface by the GKS function's name. This block structure is necessary in order to identify the different formats of picture element descriptions during comparison. The reference implementation uses the module *add_picture_element_to_device* to write the contents of the CPED onto a comparator file.

In the last phase of this testing procedure a comparator inspects the candidate output file and compares it to the reference output. Comparison is done on the basis of picture element descriptions which have been collected at the device interface in a certain sequence assuming that no picture redrawing occurred. The contents of corresponding candidate and reference PEDs are compared entry by entry. Varying representations of the same data type are accepted by the comparator (e.g. clockwise and counter clockwise orientation of area definitions). The comparison of software simulation output (e.g. linetype by a number of strokes) is limited to a test whether the objects are located inside a surrounding box. The same applies to the redrawing facility for segments. In this case the graphics objects are expected to be placed inside the union of all clipping rectangles. The comparator creates a report that contains a list of all errors detected during the comparison of the test results.

6   Conclusions

Graphics systems need means for testing the correctness of graphical output on and to graphics devices. A method for testing graphics output with high data rates and complex picture structures is applied in addition to human judgement. For that purpose a tailor-made reference system is configured which serves the same level of device interface as the GKS implementation under test does. Although it takes a lot of effort to generate one reference system for each interface it is worthwhile for establishing the testing of device interfaces of various logical levels. Standardization efforts, too, concentrate on defining an interface to graphics devices (CGI) [2]. If a standard is established in this area the test procedures may be applied to the functional mapping of GKS functions to Computer Graphics Interface functions.

The reference specification and the implementation of basic graphics modules are completed for GKS level 0a (already in a revised version). The first reference system with a high level device interface (a workstation interface) has been configured. By the end of 1985 testing of device interfaces will cover GKS level 1a.

Acknowledgements

We would like to express our gratitude to a number of experts involved in the design and realization of the certification model for GKS. Especially, we would like to thank K. Brodlie, G. Pfaff, A. Ducrot, M. Maguire and J. Encarnacao. Moreover we owe thanks to F. Gessert who was heavily involved in realizing the 'configurable reference implementation' for GKS.

References

1. Anon, "Workstation Interface (DIN Proposal)," Working Document ISO/TC97/SC5/WG2-N238 (June 1984).

2. ANSI, "Computer Graphics Interface, Working Draft," ANSI Document number X3H33/84-10R1 (1984).

3. K. W. Brodlie, M. C. Maguire, and G. E. Pfaff, "A practical strategy for certifying GKS implementations," in *Eurographics '82*, ed. D. S. Greenaway and E. A. Warman, North-Holland, Amsterdam (1982). (Reproduced in this Volume.)

4. K. W. Brodlie, "GKS Certification - An Overview," *Computers and Graphics* **8**(1), pp.13-17 (1984).

5. G. Enderle, "GKS Implementations Overview - Second Edition," *Computer Graphics Forum* **3**(2), pp.181-189 (1984).

6. W. Huebner, "Entwurf und Implementierung eines Codegenerators zur funktionalen Spezifikation graphischer Systeme," Diploma Thesis, TH Darmstadt, FB 20, FG GRIS (1983). (In German.)

7. ISO, "Information Processing - Graphical Kernel System (GKS); Functional Description," Draft International Standard ISO/DIS 7942.

8. M. C. Maguire, "Visual testing of GKS at the human interface," *Computers and Graphics* **8**(1), pp.19-27 (1984).

9. G. E. Pfaff, "Functional conformance testing of graphics software," *Computers and Graphics* **8**(1), pp.29-37 (1984).

10. R. S. Scowen, "Conformance Testing of Software," *Computers and Graphics* **8**(1), pp.5-12 (1984).

An Algebraic Approach to the Standardization and the Certification of Graphics Software

R. Gnatz

1 Introduction

During the last decade most advances in programming languages as well as in programming methodology resulted from a consequent use of sound mathematical tools: the most impressive indicator of such a trend is the use of *abstract data types* which relate immediately to algebra, model theory and mathematical logic.

In connection with the standardization of software the certification problem has grown to be of interest. It deals with the problem of how to make sure that an implementation (i.e. the candidate to be certified) satisfies a given standard.

The certification of graphics software (in particular of the draft international standard GKS [11]) is currently the topic of a series of workshops (for example [1, 2]). It has been pointed out that there should be two kinds of certification procedures (i.e. two ways to make sure that an implementation of a software standard is a correct implementation). One way relies heavily on testing methods. This approach is called "certification by testing" and will basically consist of a comparison of a candidate implementation against a reference implementation of the standard.

The other approach is the "certification by verification". It should be based on formal methods for program construction or correctness proofs. The last approach, in particular, needs a formal specification of the standard.

The purpose of this paper is to identify a formal framework for such specifications and to exhibit at the same time the methodological environment of such a framework. It revolves around a wide spectrum language for program specification and development [10] and the associated programming methodology.

First of all it may be useful to give a short summary of the fundamental concepts of abstract data types. Then, they are discussed as a tool for the specification of graphics software i.e. as a tool for the standardization and verification of graphics software.

The main part of our algebraic approach is an abstract data type IMAGE$_1$. By a technique, which informally may be called "lifting", the semantics of a graphics metafile is unambiguously based on the type IMAGE$_1$.

2   Fundamental Concepts of Abstract Data Types

2.1   The Nature of Abstract Data Types

The shortest description of our approach to abstract data types can be given by means of the following two statements:

1. An abstract data type is an (abstract) mathematical structure (like a group, a semigroup, a ring, a field) as known from modern algebra.

2. Looking at a mathematical structure as an abstract data type means that only those models of the structure are considered which are finitely generated. (This means in particular, that an induction principle, the so-called data type induction, is always available for the proof of theorems.)

A reader familiar with these concepts may step forward immediately to section 3 of this paper.

2.2   The Signature

An (abstract) mathematical structure (and consequently an *abstract data type*) T consists of a set Σ and a set E : T = (Σ,E).

Σ is called the *signature* of T. It is a family of sorts i.e. identifiers s_i (i = 1, 2, ..., m) for carrier sets, and a family of identifiers f_j (j = 1, 2, ..., n) for functions ("operations") on these sets. Each function symbol f_j is associated with its *functionality*

$$s_{i_1}.....s_{j_k} \rightarrow s_{i_{k+1}}$$

or in a notation of the programming language CIP-L [10]

$$\mathbf{funct}(s_{i_1}, \cdots , s_{i_k})\ s_{i_{k+1}}$$

with k > 0 and $i_n \in [1:m]$, $n \in [1:k+1]$. k=0 also may hold. Then f_j denotes a nullary function i.e. a constant value of some set s_{i_1} (and the keyword **funct** may be omitted).

Σ defines a *language* L_Σ, which is the set of all *well-formed formulas* (the "terms", for short) built from the function identifiers of Σ. If in addition to the identifiers of Σ free variables for objects of the carrier sets $s_1, \cdots ,s_m$ are used to build the well-formed formulas we get a language L_Σ^* with $L_\Sigma^* \supset L_\Sigma$. (Note, that we only consider terms of finite lengths.)

2.3   The Axioms

The set E is a set of boolean expressions i.e. the *system of axioms* of T. These boolean expressions are formed from terms of L_Σ^* by means of the equality symbol $=$, the boolean operations $\wedge, \vee, \neg, \Rightarrow, \Leftrightarrow$, and the quantifiers $\forall$ "for all ...", $\exists$ "there is ...".

2.4   Extensions

It should be mentioned that we may have functions which are *partial functions* on $s_{i_1} \times \cdots \times s_{i_k}$. The functionalities of such functions are expressed in the following way

$$\{(x_1, \cdots, x_k): x_1 \in s_{i_1} \wedge \cdots \wedge x_k \in s_{i_k} \wedge p(x_1, \cdots, x_k)\} \to s_{i_{k+1}}$$

or

$$\mathbf{funct}(s_{i_1}\, x_1, \cdots, s_{i_k}\, x_k : p(x_1, \cdots, x_k))s_{i_{k+1}}$$

where p denotes a boolean expression restricting the domain of the function.

Moreover, it should be mentioned that a structure (data type) may be based on some other structures, i.e. the so-called *primary structures*. In this way a *hierarchy* of structures may be built. Each structure is implicitly based on the (universal) structure BOOLEAN of the truth values.

In addition, the structures may be *parameterized* in such a way that constituents of other structures can be brought in.

2.5   The Stack Example

A well-known example of a data type is the type STACK which we give in the notation of CIP-L.

type STACK $\equiv$ (**sort m**) **stack**, empty, isempty, append, top, rest:
    sort stack,
    stack empty,
    funct (stack) bool isempty,
    funct (stack, m) stack append,
    funct (stack s: $\neg$ isempty(s)) **m** top,
    funct (stack s: $\neg$ isempty(s)) **stack** rest
laws
    isempty(empty) = **true**,
    $\forall$ **stack** s, **m** x : isempty(append(s, x)) = **false**,
    $\forall$ **stack** s, **m** x : rest(append(s, x)) = s,
    $\forall$ **stack** s, **m** x : top(append(s, x)) = x
end of type

STACK is the identifier for the whole type whereas **stack** identifies its carrier set. The sort **m** is the parameter of the type STACK. Note that top and rest are partial functions on **stack**. By an *instantiation* we may get a special kind of stack e.g. a stack of integers or a stack of characters or even a stack of stacks of integers. Due to the fact that there could be several instantiations of the same type, side by side, the instantiation mechanism provides for renaming the constituents of the types e.g.

type (**intstack**, intempty, intisempty, intappend, inttop, intrest) ≡ STACK (**int**),

type (**intstackstack**, intstackempty, intstackisempty, intstackappend,

intstacktop, intstackrest) ≡ STACK(**intstack**)

where **intstackstack** denotes the set of stacks of stacks of integers.

intstackappend (intstackempty, intappend(intempty, 17))

may serve as an example of a well-formed formula.

The identifiers (i.e. the "constituents") which are made available by instantiation can be used to write programs "on top of" the type e.g.:

funct intstacklength ≡ (**intstackstack** iss) **int**:

if intstackisempty (iss) **then** 0 **else**

1 + intstacklength (intstackrest (iss))

fi

Note that such a recursive function terminates iff iss is finitely generated (see below).

2.6   "Concrete" Algebras

The type (and the corresponding mathematical structure) are called *abstract* because they deal only with identifiers for sets and functions and not with "concrete" sets and functions.

A family of (concrete) sets S_i (i = 1,2, $\cdots$,m) and a family of (concrete) functions F_j (j = 1,2, $\cdots$,n) operating on these sets are said to be an *algebra* A = $<S_i, F_j>$.

2.7   Interpretations

Let $\bar{\phi}_A$ be a mapping of Σ onto A such that $\bar{\phi}_A(s_i) = S_i$, $\bar{\phi}_A(f_j) = F_j$ and the functionality of f_j corresponds (with respect to $\bar{\phi}_A$) to the functionality of F_j. If there exists such a mapping $\bar{\phi}_A$ the algebra A together with $\bar{\phi}_A$ is said to be a Σ-algebra, and $\bar{\phi}_A$ defines a mapping ϕ_A of the terms $t \in L_\Sigma$ onto the elements of A:

$$\phi_A: L_\Sigma \rightarrow A$$

in the following way. ϕ_A substitutes each identifier f_j of a term t by the corresponding operation $\bar{\phi}_A(f_j) = F_j$. The resulting expression is then evaluated and yields an element of a carrier set of A.

ϕ_A is called an *interpretation* of L_Σ in A.

2.8   The Term Algebra

For each signature there exists the *term algebra* W_Σ having L_Σ as its carrier set. The operation F_j of W_Σ yields those terms which are formed by the corresponding symbol f_j.

2.9   Finitely Generated Models

If for a given type $T = (\Sigma,E)$ and a given Σ-algebra A there exists an interpretation ϕ_A of T in A such that the axioms of E are mapped on valid propositions of A, then A is said to be a *model* of T.

Each signature Σ trivially corresponds to a type $T_\Sigma = (\Sigma,\emptyset)$ the set of axioms of which is empty. W_Σ is always a (finitely generated) model of T_Σ.

A Σ-algebra A (and consequently a model A of a type T) is said to be *finitely generated* iff there exists the interpretation ϕ_A such that for each element x of the carrier sets of A there is a term t of L_Σ with

$$x = \phi_A(t)$$

This means that we can get each element by the interpretation of some term of L_Σ. (Keep in mind, that these terms are of finite length.) We take the class of finitely generated models of T as the semantics of the *abstract data type* T.

2.10 Σ-homomorphisms

Let A, B be two Σ-algebras, and ϕ be a partial mapping of A onto B such that

$$\phi(f(t_1, \cdots ,t_k)) \text{ defined} \Leftrightarrow f_\phi(\phi(t_1), \cdots ,\phi(t_k)) \text{ defined}$$

and

$$f_\phi(\phi(t_1), \cdots ,\phi(t_k)) \text{ defined} \Rightarrow \phi(f(t_1, \cdots ,t_k)) = f_\phi(\phi(t_1), \cdots ,\phi(t_k))$$

for each operation f of A and its corresponding operation f_ϕ of B. Then ϕ is said to be a (weak) Σ-*homomorphism* of A onto B.

Note, that each finitely generated Σ-algebra A is a homomorphic image of the term algebra W_Σ. Moreover A is a homomorphic image of itself.

For a Σ-homomorphism $\phi: A \rightarrow B$ it may happen that different elements of a carrier set of A are mapped onto the same element in B. Elements of A which are mapped onto the same element in B are said to be *equivalent* with respect to ϕ. This leads to an *equivalence relation* $\equiv_\phi$ which is compatible with the operations of Σ, and we find that B is isomorphic to the algebra of the equivalence classes of A with respect to $\equiv_\phi$ i.e. to the *quotient structure* $A/\equiv_\phi$. Hence, $B \cong A/\equiv_\phi$. Consequently each finitely generated Σ-algebra A is isomorphic to some quotient algebra $W_\Sigma/\equiv_\phi$ of the term algebra W_Σ. In other words, the quotient structures $W_\Sigma/\equiv_\phi$ form a system of representations of the (finitely generated) Σ-algebras, and the class of (finitely generated) models of some type $T = (\Sigma,E)$ is a subsystem. The class of finitely generated models of T is denoted by MOD(T).

2.11   The Ordering of the Σ-algebras

Due to the fact that each Σ-algebra is a homomorphic image of W_Σ there exists at most one Σ-homomorphism $\phi: A \to B$ for any two Σ-algebras A, B, and we say that B *is rougher than* A (A⊃B). Two algebras A, B, with A⊃B ∧ B⊃A are isomorphic (A ≅ B), and, based on this equivalence relation, the ⊃-relation forms a partial ordering within the class of Σ-algebras. It may happen that neither A⊃B nor B⊃A hold. Moreover, for two classes of Σ-algebras U, V we write again $U \supset V$ iff for all algebras B in V there is an algebra A in U such that A⊃B.

Given two abstract data types $T_1 = (\Sigma, E_1)$, $T_2 = (\Sigma, E_2)$ having the same signature Σ we write $T_1 \supset T_2$ iff $MOD(T_1) \supset MOD(T_2)$, and T_2 is said to be a (strong) *implementation* of T_1 or T_2 is *more concrete than* T_1.

A more detailed presentation of the fundamentals of abstract data types is given in [4].

By a transition from A to B with A⊃B information is lost. Such transitions may occur in computer graphics if we have, for example, only ten pixels per inch instead of a hundred pixels (see figure 1). Such a loss of information is one of the problems with pictorial testing of graphics systems. On the other hand some symbolic testing could be done on the level of L_Σ, and the algebraic framework should provide for a sound foundation for the discussion of such questions.

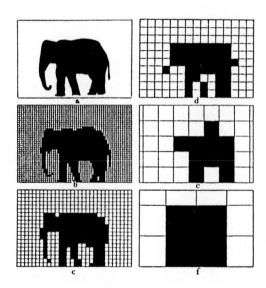

Figure 1

3 An Abstract Data Type Approach to Computer Graphics

3.1 The Need for Phenomenological Studies

The central problem of an algebraic approach to computer graphics is to explicate of what kind the types are which are considered to be typical for graphics. Such an explication needs, in principle, a careful phenomenological discussion of graphics. Reference [6] contains such a discussion leading to a type BASISGRAPHIC, but it is too extensive to be repeated in this paper. Nevertheless, to give at least a rough idea, we can rely on the following model (which is oversimplified for reasons of brevity). We deal with a function view which maps a display element (graphic primitive, output primitive; c.f. definitions in [11]) and its attributes onto a viewgraph ("grapheme") on a transparent foil. Then the appearance of a display image (i.e. a collection of graphic primitives; c.f. definitions of [11]) may result from a superimposition of such transparent foils. The idea is that the display surface (i.e. in a display device, the medium on which display images may appear; c.f. definitions of [11]) *is* a pile of superimposed foils. Formally, the superimposition may be described by means of a function combine. Note that, with respect to the functional behaviour, the oversimplification mainly results from the restriction to only one such function combine.

Generally speaking we say that the aspect of a display image which appears on a display surface is an "image" (a view) of the display image. Images are considered to be the (abstract) contents of a display surface. In the following paragraphs we try to give an algebraic explication of such a notion of image. We assume that the images (which may appear on the display surface of a given display device) form a carrier set of an abstract data type.

3.2 A Rough Notion of Image

Following this line, we deal with images which are finitely generated. Thus, as a first approach we will define the following type:

type IMAGE ≡ (**sort graphicprimitive, sort attribute**)
          image, emptyimage, combine, view:
    sort image,
    image emptyimage,
    funct(image, image) image combine,
    funct(graphicprimitive, attribute) image view
laws
    ∀ **image** a, b, c:
    combine(a, emptyimage) = combine(emptyimage, a) = a,
    combine(combine(a,b),c) = combine(a,combine(b,c))
end of type

If we deleted the function view from the signature of IMAGE we would get the abstract data type of semigroups containing emptyimage as the null element.

Each image (i.e. the elements of **image**) can be defined by a term of the following kind:

emptyimage,

view(p_1, a_1),

combine(view(p_1, a_1) view(p_2, a_2)),

combine(view(p_1, a_1),combine(view(p_2, a_2), view(p_3, a_3))),

$\cdots$

Due to the laws of type IMAGE the terms can be transformed into a normal form e.g.

$$combine(emptyimage, view(p_1, a_1)) = view(p_1, a_1)$$

3.3   A Graphics System

On top of (an instantiation of) IMAGE a graphics system may be defined as a module. Such a module contains mainly a local variable displaysurface which carries a value of sort **image**. It contains, moreover, a set of procedure declarations which manipulate the contents of displaysurface. Thus, we may find the module definition given in figure 2.

It should be mentioned that the mathematical meaning of the comprehensive choice (**some** $\cdots$) within the procedure identify is given in [10]. The use of such non-deterministic constructs for the precise specification of input operations is discussed in [6, 7].

```
module GK₀ ≡ (sort graphicprimitive,sort attribute) draw, identify, clear:
     type (image, emptyimage, combine, view) ≡
          IMAGE(graphicprimitive, attribute);
     var image displaysurface : = emptyimage;
     proc draw ≡ (graphicprimitive p, attribute a):
          displaysurface : = combine(displaysurface, view(p, a));
     proc identify ≡ (var graphicprimitive vp, var bool ve):
     begin
          ve : = (displaysurface ≠ emptyimage);
          if ve then
               vp : = some graphicprimitive p: ∃ image i, j, attribute a:
                    displaysurface = combine(i, combine(view(p, a), j));
          fi
     end;
     proc clear ≡ : displaysurface : = emptyimage
end of module
```

Figure 2

Note, that GK_0 specifies a class of modules. For each model of IMAGE we get a (concrete) module for GK_0 provided that the parameters **graphicprimitive** and **attribute** are instantiated by (concrete) sets. Technically, we get such a more concrete module from GK_0 if we substitute IMAGE by some IMAGE′ which is a (strong) implementation of IMAGE i.e. IMAGE $\supset$ IMAGE′.

An application program on top of GK_0 is defined for each model of type IMAGE(**graphicprimitive**, **attribute**). Thus, the application program is completely portable from one implementation of GK_0 to another one. Nevertheless, the images which are generated by the application program may look quite different if one implementation is rougher than the other one or, in particular, if they are even not comparable with respect to the $\supset$-relation.

In order to describe the situation more generally and more precisely the following definitions are useful. To express that some module GK is hierarchically based on (an instantiation of) a type I we write GK^I. GK^I may be considered as a family of classes of modules and we write again

$$GK^{I_1} \supset GK^{I_2} \text{ iff } I_1 \supset I_2$$

i.e. GK^{I_2} is more concrete than (or is an implementation of) GK^{I_1}, and if $MOD(I_2)$ contains only isomorphic algebras GK^{I_2} is a most concrete implementation of GK^{I_1}.

Moreover, each module GK^I is associated with the class $TRANS(GK^I)$ of all modules which may be mapped onto GK^I by equivalence preserving program transformations, see [10]. These modules are equivalent with respect to the mathematical semantics, but they may be different with respect to algorithmic details, efficiency, language style etc. If G_1, G_2 are two modules in $TRANS(GK^I)$ we write $G_1 \Leftrightarrow G_2$, and we say that G_1 is another *version* of G_2 and vice versa. All versions of GK^I possess the same external interface.

Consequently, each application program written on top of GK^I is *portable* to any version of a strong implementation of GK^I.

3.4 System Architecture

The module GK_0 defines a certain "architecture" and we may call $TRANS(GK_0)$ its abstract (functional) architecture. It is very easy to specify a module GK_1 having another architecture. It may happen that the attribute a doesn't change very frequently during a drawing process, and a procedure setattribute which is independent from the procedure draw could be useful. Nevertheless GK_1 is based on the same type IMAGE (see figure 3).

3.5 System Adaptation

Application programs written on top of GK_0 are not portable to GK_1 or vice versa. To achieve portability, for example, of GK_0-programs to GK_1 it is necessary to implement a GK_1-driver GK_0ONGK_1 for the GK_0-interface. GK_0ONGK_1 is a module, too. It contains an instantiation of GK_1 (see figure 4).

```
module GK₁ ≡ (sort graphicprimitive, sort attribute, attribute defaultattribute)
            draw, identify, clear, setattribute, inform:
        type (image, emptyimage, combine, view) ≡
            IMAGE (graphicprimitive, attribute);
        var image displaysurface : = emptyimage;
        var attribute a : = defaultattribute;
        proc draw ≡ (graphicprimitive p):
                displaysurface : = combine (displaysurface, view(p, a));
        proc identify ≡ · · · ;
        proc clear ≡ · · · ;
        proc setattribute ≡ (attribute t):  a : = t;
        proc inform ≡ (var attribute vt):  vt : = a;
end of module
```

Figure 3

```
module GK₀ONGK₁ ≡ (sort graphicprimitive, sort attribute)
                draw, identify, clear:
        module (dr, identify, clear, se, in) ≡
            GK₁(graphicprimitive, attribute, defaultattribute);
        proc draw ≡ (graphicprimitive p, attribute a):
                begin call se(a); call dr(p) end;
end of module
```

Figure 4

It is possible to give a formal proof that GK_0 and GK_0ONGK_1 specify the same class of graphics systems i.e. $GK_0ONGK_1 \in TRANS(GK_0)$. This proof is done by a textual expansion of the instantiation of GK_1 and by straightforward simplification.

Note that, for the portability of GK_0-programs to a GK_1-system, it is sufficient that GK_0ONGK_1 is a version of a strong implementation of GK_0.

3.6 A More Detailed Notion of Image

The type IMAGE is obviously a very rough formalization of the notion "image" because the class of models of IMAGE may be too large. A more detailed approach describes an image as a function on pixels. Such an approach may support the relationship between computer graphics and picture processing. It leads to a heterogeneous type $IMAGE_1$ with three carrier sets **image**, **pixel**, and **colour** (see figure 5).

The list of identifiers in the heading of the type contains those identifiers which can be seen from outside the type. The other identifiers of the signature are hidden.

The predicate "in" is meant to describe the set of pixels which belong to the display surface. With respect to a given image, the function value yields the colour of some pixel inside the display surface. Two images are said to be equal iff the

```
type IMAGE₁ ≡ (( sort graphicprimitive, sort attribute)
                 image, emptyimage, combine, view:
      sort image,
      sort pixel,
      sort colour,
      image emptyimage,
      funct(image, image) image combine,
      funct(graphicprimitive, attribute) image view,
      colour background,
      funct(image, pixel) colour value,
      funct(pixel) bool in
laws
      ∃ pixel p: in(p),
      ∃ colour c: ≠ background,
      ∀ pixel p: in(p) ⇒ (value(emptyimage, p) = background)
      ∀ image a, b:
          (a = b) = (∀ pixel p: in(p) ⇒ (value(a, p) = value(b, p)))
      ∀ image b:
          combine(emptyimage, b) = combine(b, emptyimage) = b
      ∀ image a, b, c:
          combine(combine(a, b), c) = combine(a, combine(b, c))
end of type
```

Figure 5

corresponding pixels inside the display surface carry the same colour. Moreover, at least two different colours are necessary. It is obvious that IMAGE₁ is a model of IMAGE.

3.7 Trivial Models of IMAGE₁

The class of models of IMAGE₁ includes still very small models. Let **pixel** contain only one element, let **colour** contain only two values e.g. black and white with black as the background colour. Then **image** also may contain only one element i.e. the empty image associating the background colour with the single pixel. The view function maps each graphic primitive onto the empty image. We denote by ZERO the class of all algebras which are isomorphic to that model. Then, for all models A of type IMAGE₁ we get the proposition A ⊃ ZERO i.e. ZERO contains the most rough models of IMAGE₁. A ZERO-image doesn't give any information on the graphic primitives which were used to produce that image.

Let **image** now contain two elements i.e. the empty image as above and that image which associates white with the single pixel. In this case it is possible to have view functions which extract from the graphic primitives a one-bit-information. A hardware realization of such a graphic system might be built with an incandescent bulb which can be switched on or off ("one-bit-graphics").

3.8   A Non-trivial Model of IMAGE$_1$

Of course, there are much richer models of the type IMAGE$_1$. One of the most important classes of models relates to a class of plotters. They may still have a binary set of colours corresponding to pen up and pen down. The set of pixels should be given in the following way. Let point(i, j) denote a point with the coordinates i, j and let line(p$_1$, p$_2$) denote a straight line connecting the points p$_1$, p$_2$ then **pixel** should be the following set

$$\bigcup_{0 \leq i,k \leq n} \bigcup_{0 \leq j,l \leq m} \{line(point(i,j), point(k,l)): |i-k| \leq 1 \wedge |j-l| \leq 1\}$$

with integral numbers i,j,k,l. Such pixels are typical for the incremental plotters moving, at a time, at most one unit in each direction of the coordinate system as shown in figure 6.

Figure 6

The set **image** may contain the "full" image which associates each pixel of the display surface with the non-background colour. If we choose n = m = 7 this full image may appear as shown in figure 7.

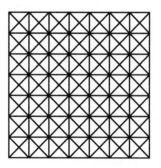

Figure 7

Here the unit has been scaled by 0.5cm. Note that in this class of models the function combine is commutative. This means that the resulting image is independent from a particular sequencing of the graphic primitives.

The function combine is usually not commutative in those models where the colour of a pixel is substituted by another colour if two images are combined. This occurs mainly in connection with raster devices.

Of course it would be a nice exercise to give a taxonomy of graphics hardware which is governed by an abstract data type like IMAGE$_1$.

3.9   A Powerful Class of Graphic Primitives

Let us turn over now to graphic primitives. They can be described by abstract data types as well. But there is again a very large variety which has engendered the generalized drawing primitive in GKS. The type POLYNOM, given in figure 8, is only one example contained in that variety. POLYNOM is based on a type REAL, on a type POINT, and on some type TRANSFORMATION. REAL and POINT provide for the usual arithmetic operations which are, in the case of POINT, the operations of a vector space. The transformations map points onto points. The application of a transformation f to a point x is denoted by apply(f, x).

The function line used above could now be specified in the following way

funct line $\equiv$ (**point** x, **point** y) **polynom**: add(rise(const(x − y)), const(y))

according to $l(t) = (x-y) \times t + y$ and $t \in R$. Let f be a linear transformation and let x, y be two different points, then

$$\text{mult}(f, \text{line}(x, y)) \qquad\qquad (*)$$

yields again a line. In general, this is not true. It depends on the actual model of the type TRANSFORMATION what curve, as a parametric function, is described by (*).

The models GK_0, GK_1 and GK_0ONGK_1 can be instantiated with the type POLYNOM and with some type ATTRIBUTE e.g.

module (drawpolynom, pickpolynom, clear) $\equiv GK_0$(**polynom, attribute**)

We keep in mind, that this instantiation still stands for a class of graphic systems. They have all the same system architecture but they may produce different pictorial appearances of the same primitive.

---

type POLYNOM $\equiv$ **polynom**, val, const, add, mult, rise:
\>\> POLYNOM is based on REAL, POINT, TRANSFORMATION \<\<
     sort polynom,
     funct (polynom, real) point val,
     funct (point) polynom const,
     funct (polynom, polynom) polynom add,
     funct (transformation, polynom) polynom mult,
     funct (polynom) polynom rise
laws
     $\forall$ **real** t, **point** x, **transformation** f, **polynom** p, p_1, p_2:
     val(const(x), t) = x,
     val(add(p_1, p_2), t) = val(p_1, t) + val(p_2, t),
     val(rise(p), t) = t$\times$val(p, t),
     val(mult(f, p),t) = apply(f, val(p, t))
end of type

Figure 8

3.10   On the Semantics of the VIRTUAL DEVICE METAFILE

An algebraic approach appears to be very helpful for the definition of the semantics of a graphics metafile [9] and of related concepts. This approach is very attractive because it relies on an algebraic process which informally may be called "lifting", and which can be used to switch over to a functional style of programming (c.f. also [5]).

Lifting is a method for specifying the delay of the evaluation of a term by introducing an evaluation function which has to be applied explicitly (c.f. function val of type POLYNOM in 3.9). ("Lifting" is a process, the result of which is not uniquely determined, at least in general. The basic idea is well-known in mathematical logic and relates to "currying".)

In the case of graphics systems the lifting technique can be applied to the type $IMAGE_1$. This yields, as an example, a type DELAYIMAGE shown in figure 9.

Technically, the type DELAYIMAGE is an enrichment of type $IMAGE_1$. Based on type DELAYIMAGE a module GK_2 may be defined as shown in figure 10.

For reasons of simplicity, GK_2 is only capable of doing output. metafile identifies the storage for objects of type **delayimage**. An application program on top of GK_2 may file a sequence of graphic primitives together with their attributes. Then by calling update, the image defined by metafile is combined with the image on the displaysurface. Note, in addition, that "**call** frame" is equivalent to

$$\big|\,\textbf{call } \text{clear; } \textbf{call } \text{update}\,\big|$$

```
type DELAYIMAGE ≡ (sort graphicprimitive, sort attribute)
                   image, emptyimage, combine, view,
                   delayimage, emptydelayimage, delayview,
                             composition, eval:
     type (image, emptyimage, combine, view)
                        ≡ IMAGE₁(graphicprimitive, attribute);
     sort delayimage,
     delayimage emptydelayimage,
     funct (graphicprimitive, attribute) delayimage delayview,
     funct (delayimage, delayimage) delayimage composition,
     funct (image, delayimage) image eval
laws
     ∀ image p, graphicprimitive g, attribute a, delayimage u, v:
     eval(p, emptydelayimage) = p,
     eval(p, delayview(g, a)) = combine(p, view(g, a)),
     eval(p, composition(u, v)) = eval(eval(p, u), v)
end of type
```

Figure 9

---

module GK_2 ≡ (**sort graphicprimitive, sort attribute**)
      draw, clear, clearfile, file, update, frame:
  type (**image**, emptyimage, combine, view,
      delayimage, emptydelayimage, delayview, composition, eval)
        ≡ DELAYIMAGE(**graphicprimitive, attribute**);
  var image displaysurface : = emptyimage;
  var delayimage metafile : = emptydelayimage;
  proc clear ≡: displaysurface : = emptyimage;
  proc draw ≡ (**graphicprimitive** g, **attribute** a):
    displaysurface : = combine(displaysurface, view(g, a));
  proc clearfile ≡: metafile : = emptydelayimage;
  proc file ≡ (**graphicprimitive** g, **attribute** a):
    metafile : = composition(metafile, delayview(g, a));
  proc update ≡: displaysurface : = eval(displaysurface, metafile);
  proc frame ≡: displaysurface : = eval(emptyimage, metafile)
end of type

Figure 10

representation of the objects of type **delayimage**.

Of course, for certain purposes e.g. for the exchange of pictures between different modules or for multiple access to the same picture a metafile must be able to exist outside GK_2. This obviously would need a more sophisticated systems architecture. There has to be a program (or a module) on top of the graphics system which provides for variables capable of storing metafiles. It should be mentioned that the terms of sort **delayimage** can be mapped onto strings of characters. Such mappings may be used for the exchange of data via tape, network or the like. Such a mapping establishes a certain encoding of a metafile [8]. Moreover, the example exhibits that lifting can be used in a similar way for the definition of a segment concept [11].

The effect of delaying the display of an image may be illustrated by an example. The following sequences of procedure calls on top of GK_2 are equivalent with respect to the contents of the display surface:

   begin call clearfile;
    call file(g_1, a_1);
    . . .
    call file(g_n, a_n);
    call draw(g_{n+1}, a_{n+1});
    call update **end**

and

   begin call draw(g_{n+1}, a_{n+1});
    call draw(g_1, a_1);
    . . .
    call draw(g_n, a_n) **end**

The second sequence is obviously equivalent to an assignment statement of the following form:

displaysurface : =
  combine($\cdots$ combine(combine(displaysurface,
  $$view(g_{n+1}, a_{n+1})),$$
  $$view(g_1, a_1)),$$
  $$\cdots,$$
  $$view(g_n, a_n))$$

The first sequence yields as an intermediate state just before calling update:

begin
  metafile : = composition($\cdots$
    composition(emptydelayimage,
      delayview(g_1, a_1)),
      $\cdots$,
      delayview(g_n, a_n));
  displaysurface : = combine(displaysurface,
      view(g_{n+1}, a_{n+1}))
end

Then, by calling update, we get

displaysurface : = eval(combine(displaysurface, view(g_{n+1}, a_{n+1})),
      composition($\cdots$
      composition(emptydelayimage, delayview(g_1, a_1))
      $\cdots$,
      delayview(g_n, a_n)))

Now, using the algebraic laws of type DELAYIMAGE the term can be simplified by eliminating eval. This leads to the same term which was derived for the second sequence of procedure calls. Consequently, both sequences are equivalent.

The above example exhibits how to use the declarations of some module GK_2 and the laws of some type DELAYIMAGE in order to prove that two sequences of procedure calls are equivalent. Obviously, the proof was done by means of correctness preserving program transformations [10].

Following [1] the approach to certification by testing will be heavily based on the comparison of sequences of procedure calls of a virtual device interface (see 5.2). Hence it is quite clear that even "certification by testing" may gain advantage from an algebraic approach to computer graphics.

4 Remarks on Graphics Software Standards

4.1 The Need for Further Detailization

Consider the class of all finitely generated models of $IMAGE_1$. It should be mentioned that for the purpose of standardization this class, on one hand, may be too large because the type $IMAGE_1$ doesn't pay regard to coordinates, colour models, attributes etc. But it is always possible to adjunct further properties to the axioms of $IMAGE_1$ in order to distinguish special concepts.

4.2   A Standard as a Collection of Modules

On the other hand, with respect to the systems architecture the class may be too small because GK_0 represents only one special architecture. It contains at the same time an output procedure draw and an input procedure identify. But a standard like GKS has to comprise the typical capabilities of devices for output only and for input only, as well. For this reason, GKS has introduced the level concept.

Embedding the level concept into our formal framework means that a graphics software standard has to be a (finite) collection of modules which should have the following properties (only to make a hypothesis for further discussion):

(1)   Each module of such a collection is based on the same common image-type (e.g. $IMAGE_1$).

(2)   The parameterization of the image-type and of all the modules is the same.

(3)   There is a partial ordering within the collection of modules. A module GK_i is said to be *below* a module GK_j (or GK_j *above* GK_i) iff each procedure p which is made available to an application program by GK_i is made available by GK_j too. To be explicit, this means that such a procedure p has the same semantic meaning in GK_i and GK_j for all the finitely generated models of the common image-type. The abstract architectures of GK_i and GK_j are different, but by deletion of appropriate procedure declarations of the module GK_j it can always be restricted to a version of GK_i.

It is quite clear that property (3) is the most serious demand which is imposed on the different modules of a standard. But it is such a partial ordering which enables the portability of an application program written for some module GK to some other module *above* GK.

With respect to (2) a standard prescribes a certain instantiation of the parameters (see also 5.3).

5   On Implementations of Graphics Software Standards

5.1   Functional Description of Graphics Hardware Devices

Finally a remark should be made with respect to the implementation of a graphics system. (The special definitions of GK_0, GK_1 given above are no longer relevant. They may only support the reader's imagination.)

The *functioning* of a graphics hardware device G always can be specified by the formal tools introduced so far, i.e. as a module which is based on some special image-type.

The description of G should be given by means of an instantiation of some module GK_0

$$\textbf{module } (p_1, \cdots, p_n) \equiv GK_0^J(\textbf{gp}_0, \textbf{attr}_0)$$

such that G has the same functional architecture as GK_0 and

$$\text{IMAGE}_1(\mathbf{gp}_0, \mathbf{attr}_0) \supset I(\mathbf{gp}_0, \mathbf{attr}_0).$$

$p_1, \cdots, p_n$ are the identifiers of the procedures which are available to an application program on top of G.

$\mathbf{gp}_0$ denotes a certain set of graphic primitives and $\mathbf{attr}_0$ denotes a set of attributes (c.f. for example, 3.8).

Note that this is a very special way to give a functional description of a given hardware device, and, so far, it is only an hypothesis that it is possible to maintain the assumption $\text{IMAGE}_1 \supset I$. Nevertheless, the phenomenological studies provide for a high degree of certainty.

5.2   Intentional Vagueness of a Formal Description

It may happen that there is only one model of I, then the instantiation

$$\text{GK}_0^I(\mathbf{gp}_0, \mathbf{attr}_0)$$

gives the most precise functional description. But sometimes the hardware description may be intentionally left vague by only formalizing, say, the most typical properties of G. In this case there can be more than one model of type I (c.f. also [3]).

5.3   On Certification by Verification

Now let us assume that $\text{GK}_1^{\text{IMAGE}_1}(\mathbf{gp}_1, \mathbf{attr}_1)$ specifies a standard which has to be implemented for the device G. This means that we have to look at a type $I^*(\mathbf{gp}_1, \mathbf{attr}_1)$ such that

type $I^* \equiv$ (sort gp_1, sort $attr_1$) image, emptyimage, combine, view:
        type (image, emtpyimage, combine, w) $\equiv I(\mathbf{gp}_0, \mathbf{attr}_0)$,
        funct $(gp_1, attr_1)$ image view
end of type

Note that the function w has the functionality $\mathbf{gp}_0 \times \mathbf{attr}_0 \to \mathbf{image}$, whereas view has the functionality $\mathbf{gp}_1 \times \mathbf{attr}_1 \to \mathbf{image}$. Due to the finite generatability of the elements of **image** (c.f. 3.2) the function view always yields an approximation of $(g^1, a^1) \in \mathbf{gp}_1 \times \mathbf{attr}_1$ in the set $\mathbf{gp}_0 \times \mathbf{attr}_0$, at least implicitly. It holds that

$$\forall \mathbf{gp}_1\, g^1,\, \mathbf{attr}_1\, a^1: \text{view}(g^1, a^1) = \text{emptyimage}$$

$$\vee\, \exists\, \mathbf{gp}_0\, g_1^0,....,g_n^0,\, \mathbf{attr}_0\, a_1^0, \cdots, a_n^0:$$

$$\text{view}(g^1, a^1) = \text{combine}(\cdots \text{combine}(\text{emptyimage}, w(g_1^0, a_1^0)) \cdots, w(g_n^0, a_n^0))$$

Obviously, $\text{IMAGE}_1(\mathbf{gp}_1, \mathbf{attr}_1) \supset I\,(\mathbf{gp}_1, \mathbf{attr}_1)$ holds, and consequently

$$\text{GK}_1^{\text{IMAGE}_1}(\mathbf{gp}_1, \mathbf{attr}_1) \supset \text{GK}_1^I(\mathbf{gp}_1, \mathbf{attr}_1)$$

Thus the class $\text{TRANS}(\text{GK}_1^{I^*}(\mathbf{gp}_1, \mathbf{attr}_1))$ contains all versions of strong implementations of the standard for the image-type I of the device G. We say that the standard is implementable on top of G if this class contains a version which is hierarchically based on an instantiation of I only via an instantiation of $\text{GK}_0^I(\mathbf{gp}_0, \mathbf{attr}_0)$

completely encasing this instantiation of I.

Such a version may possess a hierarchical structure which is similar to GK_0ONGK_1. Due to architectural incompatibilities, it may happen that the standard is not implementable on top of G. An output system cannot be implemented, for example, on a system which is capable of only doing input.

Hence, given a standard $GK_1^{IMAGE_1}(gp_1, attr_1)$ and given a description of G (a version of) a (strong) implementation may be derived in a similar way as in [7]. If such a derivation is done by correctness preserving program transformations the implementation is *a priori* correct. The "certification by verification" (in addition to "certification by testing", see [2]) can be based on an appropriate documentation of the derivation. Note, that such an approach does not depend on pictorial testing or on operational testing. It is a constructive approach to the certification of standards.

If, on the other hand, an implementation C of a standard should be certified by verification then *a posteriori* verification needs to establish a chain of proofs which can be similar to the chain of correctness preserving program transformations if in both cases the same formal framework is used. But experience shows that *a posteriori* program verification will be drowned by the algorithmic complexity of bit-oriented software. Consequently, the constructive approach should be advocated.

6   Final Remark

The intention of this paper is to give a theoretical framework for the formal specification of a graphics software standard, and to exhibit some algebraic background to the certification problem. The theoretical framework is in line with the programming methodology which has been developed since 1974 within the project CIP of the Technical University of Munich (c.f. [10]). The methods for the formal description of a graphics standard appear to be quite well developed. Nevertheless, the design of an appropriate hierarchy of types and of a collection of modules still needs further work and discussions.

Acknowledgements

This research was carried out within the Sonderforschungsbereich 49, Programmiertechnik, at the Technical University of Munich.

The first draft of this paper was presented to K.W. Brodlie (UK), S. Carson (USA), G. Dettori (Italy), D. Duce (UK), P. ten Hagen (The Netherlands), W. Herzner (Austria), G. Pfaff (Germany), F.C. de Witte (The Netherlands), who participated in the workshop on the Certification of Graphics Standards at Steensel, The Netherlands.

I gratefully acknowledge valuable discussions with my colleagues from the project CIP in particular R. Berghammer, A. Laut, P. Pepper, and M. Wirsing.

References

1. Anon, "Report on the EEC Workshop on Graphics Certification, Defining a Device Interface for Certification, Miltenberg/ Darmstadt, FRG, 25/28 April 1982," Research and Development Report, Fachgebiet Graphisch-Interaktive Systeme, Nr. GRIS 82-4, Technische Hochschule Darmstadt (1982).

2. Anon, "Report on the EEC Workshop on Graphics Certification, Formal Specification of Graphics Standards, Steensel (near Eindhoven), NL, 8/9 June 1982," Technical University of Munich (1982).

3. F. L. Bauer, "Programming a fulfilment of a contract," *Infotech State of the Art Report, Series 9, Number 6*, Pergamon Infotech Limited (1981).

4. M. Broy, W. Dosch, H. Partsch, P. Pepper, and M. Wirsing, "Existential quantifiers in abstract data types," in *Proc. of the Sixth Colloquium on Automata, Languages and Programming, Graz, Lecture Notes in Computer Science, 71*, ed. H. M. Maurer, Springer-Verlag (1979).

5. W. Dosch, G. F. Mascari, and M. Wirsing, "On the algebraic specification of data bases," *1982 International Conference on Very Large Data Bases*, Mexico City (September 1982).

6. R. Gnatz, "Referenzmodell fuer graphische Systeme, Versuch einer Axiomatik," in *Geraeteunabhaengige graphische Systeme, Drittes Darmstaedter Kolloquium*, ed. J. Encarnacao and W. Strasser, Muenchen-Wien: Oldenbourg (1981). (In German.)

7. R. Gnatz, "Funktionelle Spezifikation interaktiver Systeme und ihre Zerlegung in Teilsysteme," in *Programmiersprachen und Programmentwickhung*, ed. H. Woessner, 7. Fachtagung Muenchen, Informatik-Fachberichte 53, Springer-Verlag (1982). (In German.)

8. R. Gnatz, "Specification of Interfaces: A Case Study of Data Exchange Languages," in *Product Data Interfaces in CAD/CAM Applications*, ed. J. Encarnacao, R. Schuster and E. Voege, Symbolic Computation, Springer-Verlag (1986).

9. ANSI X3H33 Virtual Device Interface Task Group, "Draft Proposed American National Standard for the Virtual Device Metafile," X3H33 81-15 R1, X3H33 82-33 R1, ANSI (1982).

10. The CIP-Language Group, "The Munich Project CIP, Volume I: The Wide Spectrum Language CIP-L," Lecture Notes in Computer Science, Volume 183, Springer-Verlag (1985).

11. ISO, "Information Processing - Graphical Kernel System (GKS), Functional Description," ISO TC97/SC5/WG2 N117 (January 1982).

Towards a Formal Specification of the GKS Output Primitives

D. A. Duce and E. V. C. Fielding

1 Introduction

The literature contains a number of papers which look at the application of formal specification techniques to the specification of computer graphics systems [3, 5, 6, 7, 8, 10, 14]. A landmark in computer graphics was reached on 15 August 1985, with the publication of the Graphical Kernel System (GKS) as the first ISO standard for computer graphics programming [13]. This paper extends some of the ideas for defining graphics data types contained in [3] and [14] and applies them to GKS. Of particular interest, is a more formal definition of the geometry of the GKS output primitives than that given in the GKS document.

Leaving aside the parts of GKS concerned with graphical input, the functions defined in GKS may be divided into two classes: those directly concerned with the generation of graphical output, and those concerned with controlling graphical output (for example defining transformations). Our earlier papers on formal specification of GKS concentrated on the control mechanisms in GKS, and did not describe the geometry of the output primitives beyond indicating what geometrical data are present in each form taken on by a primitive as it is processed by GKS. This paper redresses the balance, and gives formal definitions which describe the geometry of the GKS output primitives and which capture the binding of attributes and aspects to the geometry.

The view of graphical primitives given here integrates into the framework given in earlier papers. Previous specifications have shown the mechanisms by which the parameters with which primitives are to be created and displayed are determined. Now, we give a meaning to the primitives themselves.

2   Background

Mallgren [14, 15] gives definitions for four general graphics concepts, *region*, *picture*, *graphical transformations* and *hierarchic picture structure*. The first three are relevant to the discussion of the GKS primitives in this paper. A *region* corresponds to an area in two dimensions, and is defined as a set of points in some universe U, typically the real plane for a two-dimensional area. A *picture* is modelled by a partial function P whose domain (the points contained in the picture) is a subset of the universe, and the values in the range represent, for example, grey levels or colours. Graphical transformations, such as translation of a picture, are defined as functions operating on the domain of a picture. Clipping is defined by a function which restricts the domain of a picture to a specified region.

With these definitions, Mallgren then defines a simple graphics language for line drawings and gives the outline of a correctness proof for a small programming language example.

Carson [3] and Carson and Post [2] used similar ideas to specify pictures in their specification of the PMIG graphics system. The graphic data type ideas can be extended to enable data types for the GKS output primitives to be defined.

3   GKS

GKS is a 2D graphics system which aims to provide an interface between applications programs and a wide variety of graphics devices. It is defined independently of programming languages, though standard bindings to common languages (for example, FORTRAN and Pascal) are being developed. GKS caters for both graphical output and graphical input; full descriptions are to be found in [11, 13]. Device independence in GKS is achieved through the concepts of abstract output, abstract input and abstract workstations. The input capabilities of GKS are not considered here.

Pictures in GKS are constructed from a number of basic building blocks, called *output primitives*, which are abstractions of the basic actions that a graphical output device can perform (for example, drawing a line). There are six output primitives in GKS:

(1)   *polyline*: which generates a sequence of connected line segments;

(2)   *polymarker*: which generates a sequence of points marked with the same symbol;

(3)   *fill area*: which generates a specified polygonal area;

(4)   *text*: which generates a string of characters;

(5)   *cell array*: which generates an image composed of a variety of colours or grey scales;

(6)   *generalized drawing primitive*: which addresses special output capabilities of a particular workstation.

In this paper, formal definitions are given for the primitives: polyline, polymarker, fill area and cell array and a definition for text is sketched out in Appendix 3, which draws on the description of the text primitive given by Brodlie and Pfaff [1].

There are three coordinate systems in GKS:

(1) *world coordinates* (WC): Cartesian coordinate systems used by the application program to specify geometric data;

(2) *normalized device coordinates* (NDC): a uniform coordinate system for all workstations;

(3) *device coordinates* (DC): each workstation has its own device coordinate system which represents its display space coordinates.

Each output primitive has an associated set of *parameters* which defines a particular instance of the primitive. For example, the parameter of a polyline is a list of the coordinates of its vertices. Coordinate data in the parameters of an output primitive are specified in world coordinates. The transformation of the world coordinates in which primitives are defined, to the device coordinate system in which they are displayed, is accomplished in two stages. The *normalization transformation*, a window to viewport mapping, maps WC to NDC. A second window to viewport mapping, the *workstation transformation*, maps NDC to DC.

The parameters of a primitive enable its form to be specified, but additional data, termed *primitive attributes* are necessary to describe the appearance (or *aspects*) of a primitive. GKS distinguishes two types of aspects, workstation independent aspects, which have the same value on all workstations on which the primitive is displayed, and workstation dependent aspects which may have different values on different workstations.

For workstation independent aspects, there is one attribute per aspect. These attributes are termed *geometric attributes*. For workstation dependent aspects, two methods of specification are possible, *bundled specification* and *individual specification*. In the former method there is one attribute for each type of primitive which determines the values of all the workstation dependent aspects. In the latter method, there is one attribute per aspect. Only bundled specification is considered here, as the extension to individual specification is straightforward [5]. The attributes which control the values of the workstation dependent aspects are termed *non-geometric attributes*.

When a primitive is created, the current values of the primitive attributes are bound to the primitive and cannot subsequently be changed.

The non-geometric attributes used in bundled specification are indices into tables called *bundle tables*. Each table entry is termed a *bundle* or *representation* and specifies values for each of the aspects. Each workstation has its own bundle tables, one for each class of output primitive. Thus primitives with the same attribute value may have different representations on different workstations.

The colour aspects of primitives are specified indirectly. Each workstation has its own colour table and associated with each primitive is a colour index aspect, which defines a position in the colour table. The colour table entry gives the colour (as an RGB triple) with which the primitive is to be displayed.

It is clear from the above description that there are three distinct stages in the transformation and attribute/aspect binding process, known as the viewing pipeline, through which primitives pass. Firstly the application program constructs pictures in world coordinates and here only the geometric data defining the primitives are known. Secondly primitives are *created* when their coordinate data (transformed to NDC coordinates) and the values of the primitive attributes are bound together. The application program is, in effect, building a conceptual NDC picture composed of parts (in turn composed of primitives), which may have been defined in different world coordinate systems. Thirdly, primitives are *displayed* when their coordinate data (transformed to DC coordinates) and the values of their aspects are bound together. The application is building a conceptual DC picture on each workstation. The DC picture is an abstraction of the picture actually displayed on the display surface of a workstation, and is defined over a region of the real plane. The representation of this abstract picture on a physical display surface (which in general is discrete) is a rendering issue which is not discussed here. These ideas are illustrated in figure 1.

Previous papers specifying the mechanisms in GKS by which transformations, and attribute and aspect values are determined, have given descriptions of the components of NDC and DC level primitives and of the NDC and DC pictures that are formed. This paper gives specifications of the primitives themselves, and it can be seen that combining functions could be given which create the NDC and DC pictures from these primitives.

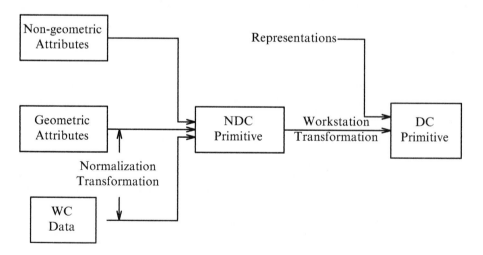

Figure 1

4   Specification of World Coordinate Output

4.1   Introduction

At the start of the viewing pipeline, primitives are described by their parameters which define their geometric data in WC space (the real plane $\mathbb{R}^2$). The specifications of the primitives at this stage define the geometry of the objects represented by these data. These geometric objects in the real plane are character-ized by the set of points they cover.

4.2   Polyline

The parameter associated with the polyline primitive is a list of points. The GKS document [13] states that the POLYLINE function generates a sequence of con-nected straight lines, starting from the first point and ending at the last (see figure 2).

In order to define a polyline primitive formally, firstly, a formal definition of a line segment between points with position vectors **p** and **q** respectively is given. The equation of a line through **p** and **q** is:

$$\mathbf{r} = \mathbf{p} + t(\mathbf{q} - \mathbf{p}) \quad \textbf{where} \quad t \in \mathbb{R}$$

Throughout this paper, vectors are represented by symbols in bold type (**p**, **q**, etc.) and scalars by symbols in italic type. A point is denoted either by a position vector from the origin or an ordered pair of x, y coordinates. The coordinate pair corresponding to the position vector **p** is (p_x, p_y). These two representations are used interchangeably, to permit the most concise descriptions.

The set of all points lying on the line segment between points **p** and **q** is given by:

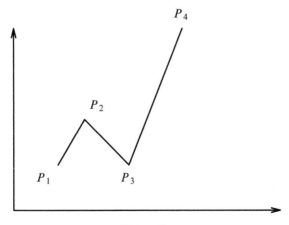

Figure 2

$$\{ \mathbf{p} + t(\mathbf{q}-\mathbf{p}) \mid 0 \le t \le 1 \}$$

This specification of a line segment is incorporated in the function:

lineseg : *Point* × *Point* → **set of** *Point*
lineseg(**p, q**) $\triangleq$ { **p** + t(**q**−**p**) | $0 \le t \le 1$ }

The first line of the function definition is its signature, which gives the types of its arguments and result.

A polyline (type *Polyline*) at the WC level is then represented by the set of points in all the line segments comprising the polyline:

Polyline = **set of** *Point*
mk_Polyline : **list of** *Point* → *Polyline*
pre *mk_Polyline*(*l*) $\triangleq$ *len l* ≥ 2
mk_Polyline(*l*) $\triangleq \bigcup\limits_{i \in 1..(len\ l)-1} lineseg\ (\mathbf{l}_i, \mathbf{l}_{i+1})$

where $\mathbf{l}_i$ denotes the ith element of the list l, and *len l* denotes the length of l. Formal definitions of data types such as **list** are given in the algebraic specification language OBJ [9] in Appendix 2. The symbol $\bigcup$ denotes distributed union and combines into one set the sets of points comprising the individual line segments making up the polyline. A glossary of such symbols is given in Appendix 1. The function *mk_Polyline* is a partial function, that is a function which is not defined on all values in its domain. The pre-condition (**pre**) is a predicate over the parameters which must be satisfied for the function to be defined.

4.3   Polymarker

The polymarker primitive draws a sequence of points marked with the same symbol. The parameter associated with the primitive is a list of points. The world coordinate object is represented as the set of points to be marked.

Polymarker = **set of** *Point*
mk_Polymarker: **list of** *Point* → *Polymarker*
pre *mk_Polymarker*(*l*) $\triangleq$ *len l* ≥ 1
mk_Polymarker(*l*) $\triangleq$ *vertices*(*l*)
vertices: **list of** *Point* → **set of** *Point*
vertices(*l*) $\triangleq$ { $\mathbf{l}_i$ | $i \in 1..len\ l$ }

4.4 Fill Area

The parameter associated with the fill area primitive is again a list of points, which are the vertices of a polygonal region. If the region defined by the parameter is not closed, it will be closed by joining the last point to the first. This is defined by the function *close*:

---

close: **list of** *Point* → **list of** *Point*
pre *close*(*l*) $\triangleq$ *len l* > 2
close(*l*) $\triangleq$ **if** $l_{len\ l} = l_1$ **then** *l*
        else *l* || (l_1 :: *empty_list*)

The operator '::' is the list construction operator which adds a new element to the head of a list and '||' is the append operator which concatenates two lists.

Given a list of points defining a closed region, the boundary of the region is just the polyline whose vertices are these points:

---

boundary: **list of** *Point* → **set of** *Point*
pre *boundary*(*l*) $\triangleq$ *close*(*l*) = *l*
boundary(*l*) $\triangleq$ *mk_Polyline*(*l*)

The GKS document [13] defines the interior of a polygon in the following way (see figure 3). For a given point, create a straight line starting at that point and going to infinity. If the number of intersections between the straight line and the polygon is odd, the point is within the polygon; otherwise it is outside. If the straight line passes through a polygon vertex tangentially, the intersection count is not affected. Dickman [4] has pointed out that this description does not cater for the case where the straight line is coincident with an edge of the polygon, for then the number of intersections is infinite. The definition given here is an adaptation of that given by Dickman.

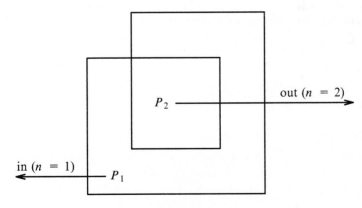

Figure 3

The interior of a polygon is defined in the following way (see figure 3). For any point not on the boundary of the polygon, if the number of intersections between any ray (not passing through a vertex) from the point to infinity, and the boundary of the polygon is odd, the point is within the polygon, otherwise it is outside. The formal definition follows.

A ray is defined by a starting point **p** and another point **q** (distinct from **p**) which defines the direction of the ray.

$ray : Point \times Point \rightarrow$ **set of** $Point$
pre $ray(\mathbf{p}, \mathbf{q}) \triangleq \mathbf{p} \neq \mathbf{q}$
$ray(\mathbf{p}, \mathbf{q}) \triangleq \{\mathbf{p} + t(\mathbf{q} - \mathbf{p}) \mid t \geq 0\}$

The function *intersects* defined below, can be applied to a ray and a line segment to determine whether they have a point in common and thus intersect. It returns the value 1 if the two sets of points given as arguments intersect, and the value 0 otherwise.

$intersects$: **set of** $Point \times$ **set of** $Point \rightarrow \mathbb{N}$
$intersects(s_1, s_2) \triangleq$ **if** $s_1 \cap s_2 = \emptyset$ **then** 0 **else** 1

The function *interior* can now be defined:

$interior$: **list of** $Point \rightarrow$ **set of** $Point$
pre $interior(l) \triangleq close(l) = l$
$interior(l) \triangleq \{\mathbf{p} \mid \mathbf{p} \notin boundary(l) \land$
$\qquad for\ any\ point\ \mathbf{q} \neq \mathbf{p}\ s.t.\ ray(\mathbf{p}, \mathbf{q}) \cap vertices(l) = \emptyset$
$\qquad \exists n \in \mathbb{N}\ s.t.\ \sum_{i=1}^{(len\ l)-1} intersects(ray(\mathbf{p}, \mathbf{q}), lineseg(l_i, l_{i+1})) = 2n + 1\}$

A fill area at the WC level can be represented by the sets of points contained in the interior and on the boundary of the polygonal region defined by its parameter. Thus:

$Fill\_Area =$ **set of** $Point \times$ **set of** $Point$

mk_Fill_Area: **list of** $Point \rightarrow Fill\_Area$
pre $mk\_Fill\_Area(l) \triangleq len\ l > 2$
$mk\_Fill\_Area(l) \triangleq (interior(close(l)), boundary(close(l)))$

4.5   Cell Array

A cell array is defined by three parameters: two distinct points, P and Q, defining two opposing corner points of a rectangle, and a colour index array. The GKS document defines the cell array primitive in the following way. A rectangle, which is taken to be aligned with the world coordinate axes, is defined by the points P and Q. This rectangle is conceptually divided into a grid of $n \times m$ cells. Each cell has a width of $|P_x - Q_x|/m$ and a height of $|P_y - Q_y|/n$, where (P_x, P_y) are the coordinates of the corner point P and (Q_x, Q_y) are the coordinates of the corner point Q. The colour index array is oriented with respect to the rectangle by associating the four corners as follows: the $(1, 1)$ element is associated with the cell having P at one corner; the (n, m) element with the cell having Q at one corner; the $(n, 1)$ element with the cell having the point (P_x, Q_y) at one corner; the $(1, m)$ element with the cell having the point (Q_x, P_y) at one corner. The colour of each cell is specified by the index of the corresponding element of the colour index array (see figure 4).

A rectangle determined by corner points **p** and **q** is defined as follows:

$$
\begin{aligned}
&rectangle: Point \times Point \rightarrow \textbf{set of } Point \\
&\textbf{pre } rectangle(\textbf{p}, \textbf{q}) \triangleq \textbf{p} \neq \textbf{q} \\
&rectangle(\textbf{p}, \textbf{q}) \triangleq \{\textbf{p} + a\textbf{w} + b\textbf{h} \mid 0 \leq a, b \leq 1 \wedge \textbf{w}.\textbf{h} = 0 \wedge \textbf{p} + \textbf{w} + \textbf{h} = \textbf{q} \\
&\qquad\qquad\qquad\qquad \wedge \textbf{w}.\textbf{j} = 0 \wedge \textbf{h}.\textbf{i} = 0 \}
\end{aligned}
$$

where **i** and **j** are unit vectors along the x and y axes respectively. The rectangle is then divided into a grid of $n \times m$ rectangular cells, where $n = rows(ca)$ and $m = cols(ca)$ are the number of rows and columns in the colour index array ca, respectively. The geometry of each cell can be represented by a set of points, and the grid of cells by a set of sets of points. The association of a colour index with each cell is achieved by modelling the cell array as a function from **set of** $Point$ to $Colour\_Index$.

$$Cell\_Array = \textbf{set of } Point \rightarrow Colour\_Index$$

The complete definition of the cell array at the WC level, determined by the points **p**, **q** and colour index array ca, is thus:

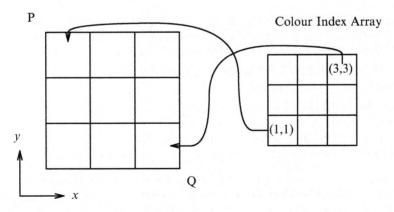

Figure 4

$Cell\_Array$ = **set of** $Point \rightarrow Colour\_Index$

mk_Cell_Array: $Point \times Point \times 2Darray$ **of** $Colour\_Index \rightarrow Cell\_Array$
$mk\_Cell\_Array(\mathbf{p}, \mathbf{q}, ca) \triangleq \{ rectangle(\mathbf{r}, \mathbf{s}) \mapsto ca_{ij} \mid$
$$\mathbf{r} = \mathbf{p} + (i-1)\mathbf{dx} + (j-1)\mathbf{dy} \wedge$$
$$\mathbf{s} = \mathbf{r} + \mathbf{dx} + \mathbf{dy} \wedge$$
$$i \in 1..cols(ca) \wedge j \in 1..rows(ca) \wedge$$
$$\mathbf{dx} = \mathbf{w}/cols(ca) \wedge \mathbf{dy} = \mathbf{h}/rows(ca)$$
$$\textbf{where } \mathbf{w.h} = 0 \wedge \mathbf{p} + \mathbf{w} + \mathbf{h} = \mathbf{q} \wedge$$
$$\mathbf{w.j} = 0 \wedge \mathbf{h.i} = 0 \}$$

5   Normalized Device Coordinate Primitives

5.1   Introduction

At this second stage in the pipeline, world coordinate objects are transformed to normalized device coordinate space and their primitive attributes and a clipping rectangle are bound to them. Primitives at this stage are modelled as functions, whose domains represent the geometry of the primitives and whose ranges represent the clipping rectangle and primitive attributes.

Normalized Device Coordinate space is also the real plane, but the maximum region which is visible on a workstation is the unit square. GKS requires that an implementation support coordinate values in the range $[-7, 7]$, though this restriction will not be described here.

Points in world coordinates are transformed to normalized device coordinates by the normalization transformation. It is a linear transformation which maps a rectangular window in WC onto a rectangular viewport in NDC. The normalization transformation T_N can be described as the composition of three transformations: a translation of the window to the origin, a scaling of the window to be the same size as the viewport, and a translation of the scaled window to the position occupied by the viewport. Functions defining translation T_T and scaling T_S are defined below in Curried form using lambda notation as described in [16].

T_T: $Point \rightarrow (Point \rightarrow Point)$
$T_T(\mathbf{t}) \triangleq \lambda\mathbf{p} \,.\, \mathbf{p} + \mathbf{t}$

T_S: $\mathbb{R} \times \mathbb{R} \rightarrow (Point \rightarrow Point)$
$T_S(s_x, s_y) \triangleq \lambda\mathbf{p} \,.\, (s_x p_x, s_y p_y)$

Windows and viewports are described by the data types *Window* and *Viewport* defined in Appendix 2. If the window is defined by points $\mathbf{w}_{min}$, $\mathbf{w}_{max}$, (lower left hand and upper right hand corners respectively), and similarly the viewport by points $\mathbf{v}_{min}$, $\mathbf{v}_{max}$, then the normalization transformation T_N is given by:

$$T_N: Window \times Viewport \rightarrow (Point \rightarrow Point)$$
$$T_N(w, v) \triangleq T_T(\mathbf{v}_{min}) \circ T_S(\Delta v_x/\Delta w_x, \Delta v_y/\Delta w_y) \circ T_T(-\mathbf{w}_{min})$$
$$\text{where } w = (\mathbf{w}_{min}, \mathbf{w}_{max})$$
$$\text{and } \quad v = (\mathbf{v}_{min}, \mathbf{v}_{max})$$
$$\text{and } \quad \Delta \mathbf{w} = \mathbf{w}_{max} - \mathbf{w}_{min}$$
$$\text{and } \quad \Delta \mathbf{v} = \mathbf{v}_{max} - \mathbf{v}_{min}$$

In GKS only transformations which satisfy $\Delta w_x, \Delta w_y, \Delta v_x, \Delta v_y > 0$ can be defined.

The function *normalize* applies the normalization transformation to a set of points:

$$normalize: Window \times Viewport \times \textbf{set of } Point \rightarrow \textbf{set of } Point$$
$$normalize(w, v, s) \triangleq \{ T_N(w, v)(\mathbf{p}) \mid \mathbf{p} \in s \}$$

The viewport of the normalization transformation also serves as a clipping rectangle when clipping is enabled. Clipping is actually delayed until primitives are displayed, and hence a clipping rectangle is associated with each primitive in the NDC picture. A clipping rectangle is represented as the set of points that it covers.

Also associated with each primitive at the NDC level are its primitive attributes. These are required to allow its appearance to be determined at the display stage. The attributes applying to each type of primitive are listed below. Geometric attributes are transformed to NDC space before being bound to primitives.

Primitive	Primitive Attributes	
	Non-geometric	Geometric
Polyline	POLYLINE INDEX	None
Polymarker	POLYMARKER INDEX	None
Fill Area	FILL AREA INDEX	PATTERN REFERENCE POINT PATTERN WIDTH VECTOR PATTERN HEIGHT VECTOR
Cell Array	None	None

5.2 Polyline

The polyline primitive at the NDC level is modelled as a tuple consisting of the set of points representing the line segments comprising it, the clipping rectangle and the polyline index.

$$NDC\_Polyline = \textbf{set of } Point \times Clip\_Rectangle \times Polyline\_Index$$

$$mk\_NDC\_Polyline: Polyline \times Window \times Viewport$$
$$\times Clip\_Rectangle \times Polyline\_Index \rightarrow NDC\_Polyline$$
$$mk\_NDC\_Polyline(pl, w, v, cr, pi) \triangleq (normalize(w, v, pl), cr, pi)$$

5.3   Polymarker

The primitive at the NDC level is modelled as a tuple consisting of the set of points, the clipping rectangle and polymarker index associated with the primitive.

$NDC\_Polymarker$ = **set of** $Point \times Clip\_Rectangle \times Polymarker\_Index$

$mk\_NDC\_Polymarker$: $Polymarker \times Window \times Viewport$
$\qquad\qquad\qquad \times Clip\_Rectangle \times Polymarker\_Index \rightarrow NDC\_Polymarker$
$mk\_NDC\_Polymarker(pm, w, v, cr, pmi) \triangleq (normalize(w, v, pm), cr, pmi)$

5.4   Fill Area

The fill area primitive at the NDC level is modelled in a similar way to the polyline primitive, as a tuple consisting of the set of points representing the interior of the fill area, the set of points representing its boundary, the clipping rectangle and primitive attributes associated with the primitive. The pattern reference point, and pattern width and height vectors are defined in world coordinates, and are transformed to normalized device coordinates before being bound to the primitive.

NDC_Fill_Area = **set of** $Point \times$ **set of** $Point \times Clip\_Rectangle \times Fill\_Area\_Index$
$\qquad\qquad\qquad \times Pattern\_Reference\_Point \times Pattern\_Width\_Vector$
$\qquad\qquad\qquad \times Pattern\_Height\_Vector$

$mk\_NDC\_Fill\_Area$: $Fill\_Area \times Window \times Viewport \times Clip\_Rectangle$
$\qquad\qquad\qquad \times Fill\_Area\_Index$
$\qquad\qquad\qquad \times Pattern\_Reference\_Point \times Pattern\_Width\_Vector$
$\qquad\qquad\qquad \times Pattern\_Height\_Vector \rightarrow NDC\_Fill\_Area$
$mk\_NDC\_Fill\_Area(fa, w, v, cr, fi, \mathbf{prp}, \mathbf{pw}, \mathbf{ph}) \triangleq$
$\qquad\quad$ **let** $fa = (i, b)$ **in**
$\qquad\qquad\quad (normalize(w, v, i), normalize(w, v, b), cr, fi, T_N(w, v)(\mathbf{prp}),$
$\qquad\qquad\qquad\qquad\qquad\qquad\qquad\qquad\quad T_N(w, v)(\mathbf{pw}),$
$\qquad\qquad\qquad\qquad\qquad\qquad\qquad\qquad\quad T_N(w, v)(\mathbf{ph}))$

5.4.1   Cell Array

The cell array primitive at the NDC level is a tuple, the first component of which is modelled in a similar way to the world coordinate object, and the second component of which is a clipping rectangle.

NDC_Cell_Array = (**set of** $Point \to Colour\_Index$) $\times$ $Clip\_Rectangle$

$mk\_NDC\_Cell\_Array$: $Cell\_Array \times Window \times Viewport \times Clip\_Rectangle$
$$\to NDC\_Cell\_Array$$
$mk\_NDC\_Cell\_Array(cfn, w, v, cr) \triangleq$
$$(\{ normalize(w, v, s) \mapsto cfn(s) \mid s \in dom\ cfn \}, cr)$$

6 Display Primitives

6.1 Introduction

At this final stage of the pipeline, normalized device coordinate primitives are transformed to device coordinate space, the clipping operators are applied, and the values of the aspects corresponding to the primitive attribute values are bound. The resulting DC primitives can be modelled as relations, whose domains (points) represent their geometry and whose range is the colour index with which the geometry is to be displayed. Relations, rather than functions, are necessary because more than one colour index may be associated with any particular point by the fill area and cell array primitives.

The mapping from NDC space to DC space is accomplished by the workstation transformation. There is one important difference between the normalization transformation and the workstation transformation. The window and viewport in the normalization transformation may have different aspect ratios and still the whole of the window is mapped to the whole of the viewport. The workstation transformation on the other hand preserves aspect ratio; the workstation window is mapped onto the largest rectangle that can fit within the workstation viewport such that the aspect ratio of the workstation window is preserved and the lower left-hand corner of the workstation window is mapped to the lower left-hand corner of the workstation viewport. The function $wstrans$ accomplishes this, and is defined in terms of the transformation functions T_T and T_S defined earlier. There is a compulsory clip to the window of the workstation transformation that cannot be disabled.

T_{WS}: $Window \times Viewport \to (Point \to Point)$
$T_{WS}(w, v) \triangleq T_T(\mathbf{v}_{min}) \circ T_S(s, s) \circ T_T(-\mathbf{w}_{min})$
   where $w = (\mathbf{w}_{min}, \mathbf{w}_{max})$
   and $v = (\mathbf{v}_{min}, \mathbf{v}_{max})$
   and $\Delta\mathbf{w} = \mathbf{w}_{max} - \mathbf{w}_{min}$
   and $\Delta\mathbf{v} = \mathbf{v}_{max} - \mathbf{v}_{min}$
   and $\Delta w_y / \Delta w_x \geq \Delta v_y / \Delta v_x \Rightarrow s = \Delta v_y / \Delta w_y \wedge$
       $\Delta w_y / \Delta w_x < \Delta v_y / \Delta v_x \Rightarrow s = \Delta v_x / \Delta w_x$

$wstrans$: $Window \times Viewport \times$ **set of** $Point \to$ **set of** $Point$
$wstrans(w, v, s) \triangleq \{ T_{WS}(w, v)(\mathbf{p}) \mid \mathbf{p} \in s \}$

The aspects whose values are bound to each primitive are listed below.

Primitive	Aspects	
	Workstation Dependent	Workstation Independent
Polyline	Linetype Linewidth Scale Factor Polyline Colour Index	None
Polymarker	Marker Type Marker Size Scale Factor Polymarker Colour Index	None
Fill Area	Fill Area Interior Style Fill Area Style Index Fill Area Colour Index	Pattern Reference Point Pattern Width Vector Pattern Height Vector
Cell Array	None	None

The values of the workstation independent aspects are taken from the corresponding primitive attributes. The values of the workstation dependent aspects are obtained by indexing into a workstation dependent bundle table for the class of primitive with the index that was bound to the primitive when it was created.

6.2   Polyline

A display polyline will be modelled as a relation from a point to a colour index. (In fact this actually reduces to a function in the case of a display polyline.) The meaning of this is that a point is to be displayed with the colour corresponding to the associated colour index.

$$DC\_Polyline \; = \; Point \leftrightarrow Colour\_Index$$

The display primitive is specified by the function $mk\_DC\_Polyline$, which applies the workstation transformation and clipping to the coordinates of the corresponding NDC polyline and associates the polyline colour index with each point in the resulting set of coordinates. The clipping operation is modelled as the intersection of the set of points representing the primitive and the set of points representing the clipping region (which is the intersection of the clipping rectangle and workstation window). Only those points in the primitive which lie within the clipping region appear in the resulting set of points. This may represent a disjoint set of line segments.

The type $Polyline\_Bundle$ models the aspects of a polyline:

$$Polyline\_Bundle \; = \; Linetype \times Linewidth\_Scale\_Factor \times Colour\_Index$$

The precise effects of the aspects linetype and linewidth scale factor are implementation dependent, but may be encapsulated in a function $linestyle$, which given a linetype and linewidth scale factor as arguments, delivers a function from a set of points to a set of points. This function when applied to a set of points produces a new set of points which represent the effect of the application of the linetype and linewidth scale factor aspects.

$mk\_DC\_Polyline$: $NDC\_Polyline \times Window \times Viewport$
$\qquad\qquad \times Polyline\_Bundle \to DC\_Polyline$
$mk\_DC\_Polyline(ndcpl, w, v, b) \triangleq$
    let $ndcpl = (ndcpts, cr, pi)$
    and $b = (lt, lw, pci)$
    and $w = (\mathbf{w}_{min}, \mathbf{w}_{max})$
    and $wr = rectangle(\mathbf{w}_{min}, \mathbf{w}_{max})$
    in $\{ (\mathbf{p}, pci) \mid \mathbf{p} \in wstrans(w, v, linestyle(lt, lw)(ndcpts \cap cr \cap wr)) \}$

Note that in this definition clipping takes place before linestyle is applied. GKS does not define whether clipping takes place before or after the linestyle has been computed; clearly different effects are achievable by each alternative. The following definition is also allowed:

    in $\{ (\mathbf{p}, pci) \mid \mathbf{p} \in wstrans(w, v, linestyle(lt, lw)(ndcpts) \cap cr \cap wr) \}$

These specifications indicate that linestyle is applied before the workstation transformation. It is worth noting that there are alternative formulations in which linestyle is applied after the workstation transformation. For example:

    in $\{ (\mathbf{p}, pci) \mid \mathbf{p} \in linestyle\_dc(lt, lw)(wstrans(w, v, ndcpts \cap cr \cap wr)) \}$

where $linestyle\_dc$ is a function which operates on DC points, is equivalent to the first formulation given if

$$wstrans(w, v, linestyle(lt, lw)(s)) = linestyle\_dc(lt, lw)(wstrans(w, v, s))$$

Implementations would obviously make use of such equivalences.

6.3   Polymarker

The display level primitive is modelled as a relation (which again reduces to a function) from a point to a colour index. The set of points constituting a positioned marker symbol is given by the function *marker*, which places the marker specified by the marker type and marker size scale factor arguments at a specified position. A marker is visible if, and only if, the marker position is within the clipping rectangle. It is workstation dependent how partially visible markers are clipped, and this is indicated by the operator $\cap_{wd}$.

$Polymarker\_Bundle = Marker\_Type \times Marker\_Size\_Scale\_Factor \times Colour\_Index$
$DC\_Polymarker = Point \leftrightarrow Colour\_Index$

$marker: Point \times Marker\_Type \times Marker\_Size\_Scale\_Factor \rightarrow \textbf{set of } Point$

$mk\_DC\_Polymarker: NDC\_Polymarker \times Window \times Viewport \times Polymarker\_Bundle$
$\rightarrow DC\_Polymarker$
$mk\_DC\_Polymarker(ndcpm, w, v, b) \triangleq$
   let $ndcpm = (ndcpts, cr, pmi)$
   and $b = (mt, msf, mci)$
   and $s = \bigcup\limits_{\mathbf{p} \,\in\, cr \,\cap\, ndcpts} (marker(\mathbf{p}, mt, msf) \cap_{wd} wr)$
   in $\{ (\mathbf{p}, mci) \mid \mathbf{p} \in wstrans(w, v, s) \}$

6.4 Fill Area

A display fill area primitive is again modelled as a relation from a point to a colour index.

$$DC\_Fill\_Area = Point \leftrightarrow Colour\_Index$$

Clipping a polygon may result in new boundaries being formed and may divide it into a number of disjoint regions.

The workstation dependent aspects of the fill area primitive are modelled by the type *Fill_Area_Bundle*:

$$Fill\_Area\_Bundle = Fill\_Area\_Interior\_Style$$
$$\times Fill\_Area\_Style\_Index \times Colour\_Index$$

The appearance of a fill area primitive depends on the value of the fill area interior style aspect in the following way:

(1)   *HOLLOW*: only the boundary of the clipped polygon is drawn using the colour associated with the fill area colour index. The linestyle with which the boundary is drawn is implementation dependent.

(2)   *SOLID*: The interior of the clipped polygon is filled with the colour associated with the fill area colour index.

(3)   *PATTERN*: The interior of the clipped polygon is filled using fill area style index. This is an index into a workstation dependent pattern table, each entry of which specifies a pattern as an array of colour indices. The pattern is replicated as a grid of cells emanating from the pattern reference point. Patterns are modelled by the type *Pattern*:

$Pattern = 2Darray \textbf{ of } Colour\_Index$

(4)   *HATCH*: The interior of the clipped polygon is filled in a hatch style selected by the fill area style index from one of those available on the workstation, and in a colour determined by the colour index.

These cases will be defined in turn.

Fill Area Style **HOLLOW**

The display fill area is modelled as a relation (which reduces to a function) from a point to a colour index where the points in the domain represent the boundary of the clipped fill area. The function *perimeter* returns the boundary (or boundaries) of the (possibly disjoint) region(s) represented by a set of points. A point is on the boundary of a region if there is at least one open line segment (a line segment which does not include its starting point) from the point, which does not intersect any region. In the function definition below, the *perimeter* function is used to obtain the boundary of the clipping rectangle. The definition of clipping handles reentrant and concave polygons, including polygons with regions which share a common edge.

The linetype and linewidth scale factor with which the boundary is drawn are implementation dependent. These values are denoted by *id_lt* and *id_lsf* respectively.

$$
\begin{aligned}
&perimeter\text{: }\textbf{set of } Point \rightarrow \textbf{set of } Point \\
&perimeter(a) \triangleq \{ \, \mathbf{p} \mid \mathbf{p} \in a \, \wedge \, \exists \, \mathbf{q} \neq \mathbf{p} \ s.t. \ (lineseg(\mathbf{p}, \mathbf{q}) - \{\mathbf{p}\}) \cap a = \varnothing \, \} \\[2mm]
&mk\_DC\_Fill\_Area\text{: } NDC\_Fill\_Area \times Window \times Viewport \\
&\qquad\qquad\qquad\quad \times Fill\_Area\_Bundle \times Pattern \rightarrow DC\_Fill\_Area \\
&mk\_DC\_Fill\_Area(f, w, v, b, pa) \triangleq \\
&\qquad \textbf{let } f = (\, i, b, cr, \mathit{fi}, \mathbf{prp}, \mathbf{pw}, \mathbf{ph} \,) \\
&\qquad \textbf{and } b = (style, si, fci) \\
&\qquad \textbf{and } w = (\mathbf{w}_{min}, \mathbf{w}_{max}) \\
&\qquad \textbf{and } wr = rectangle(\mathbf{w}_{min}, \mathbf{w}_{max}) \\
&\qquad \textbf{and } r = cr \cap wr \\
&\qquad \textbf{in }\ \ style = HOLLOW \Rightarrow \\
&\qquad\qquad \{ \, (\mathbf{p}, fci) \mid \mathbf{p} \in wstrans(w, v, linestyle(id\_lt, id\_lsf) \\
&\qquad\qquad\qquad\qquad\qquad ((b \cap r) \cup (perimeter(r) \cap (i \cup b)))) \, \}
\end{aligned}
$$

Fill Area Style **SOLID**

The display fill area is modelled as a relation (which again reduces to a function) from a point to a colour index. The domain of this function represents the boundary and interior of the clipped fill area.

$mk\_DC\_Fill\_Area(f, w, v, b, pa) \triangleq$
    let $f = (i, b, cr, fi, \textbf{prp}, \textbf{pw}, \textbf{ph})$
    and $b = (style, si, fci)$
    and $w = (\textbf{w}_{min}, \textbf{w}_{max})$
    and $wr = rectangle(\textbf{w}_{min}, \textbf{w}_{max})$
    in $style = SOLID \Rightarrow \{ (\textbf{p}, fci) \mid \textbf{p} \in wstrans(w, v, i \cap cr \cap wr) \}$

Fill Area Style **PATTERN**

The display fill area is modelled as a relation from a point to the colour index with which it is displayed.

The first stage in the specification of fill area style PATTERN is to describe how the pattern box is constructed. The pattern box is a parallelogram, located at the pattern reference point, whose sides are defined by the pattern width vector and pattern height vector. Let **prp** denote the pattern reference point, **pw** the pattern width vector and **ph** the pattern height vector. Then the set of points in the pattern box is given by:

$parallelogram$: $Point \times Point \times Point \to$ **set of** $Point$
$parallelogram(\textbf{prp}, \textbf{pw}, \textbf{ph}) \triangleq \{ \textbf{prp} + a\,\textbf{pw} + b\,\textbf{ph} \mid 0 \le a \le 1 \wedge 0 \le b \le 1 \}$

The pattern box is divided into a grid of $rows(pa) \times cols(pa)$ cells where $rows(pa)$ and $cols(pa)$ are the number of rows and columns in the pattern array, pa, respectively. Colour indices are associated with the grid cells in a manner analogous to cell array. The pattern box whose origin is at **prp** is given by:

box: $Point \times Point \times Point \times Pattern \to (\textbf{set of } Point \to Colour\_Index)$
$box(\textbf{prp}, \textbf{pw}, \textbf{ph}, pa) \triangleq \{ parallelogram(\textbf{q}, \textbf{dw}, \textbf{dh}) \mapsto pa_{ij}$
                        $\mid \textbf{q} = \textbf{prp} + (i - 1)\textbf{dw} + (j - 1)\textbf{dh} \wedge$
                        $i \in 1..cols(pa) \wedge$
                        $j \in 1..rows(pa) \wedge$
                        $\textbf{dh} = \textbf{ph}/rows(pa) \wedge \textbf{dw} = \textbf{pw}/cols(pa) \}$

A pattern is now defined by replicating the pattern box throughout the real plane from the pattern reference point (see figure 5).

$pattern$: $Point \times Point \times Point \times Pattern \to (\textbf{set of } Point \to Colour\_Index)$
$pattern(\textbf{prp}, \textbf{pw}, \textbf{ph}, pa) \triangleq \bigcup \{ box(\textbf{q}, \textbf{pw}, \textbf{ph}, pa) \mid \textbf{q} = \textbf{prp} + (k - 1)\textbf{pw} + (l - 1)\textbf{ph} \wedge$
                                            $k, l \in \mathbb{Z} \}$

The distributed union operator '$\bigcup$' has the effect of combining the functions representing individual pattern boxes into one function which maps each cell in the grid to an associated colour index. The display fill area is modelled as a relation from a point to a colour index, where the domain of the relation is just that region of the pattern which is within the fill area. Clipping is defined as before.

$mk\_DC\_Fill\_Area(f, w, v, b, pa) \triangleq$
  let $f = (i, b, cr, fi, \textbf{prp}, \textbf{pw}, \textbf{ph})$
  and $b = (style, si, fci)$
  and $w = (\textbf{w}_{min}, \textbf{w}_{max})$
  and $wr = rectangle(\textbf{w}_{min}, \textbf{w}_{max})$
  in $style = PATTERN \Rightarrow$
    $\{ (\textbf{p}, ci) \mid \textbf{p} \in wstrans(w, v, i \cap cr \cap wr \cap ppts)$
      $\wedge \; ppts \mapsto ci \in pattern(\textbf{p}, \textbf{pw}, \textbf{ph}, pa) \}$

Points on the boundaries of cells are common to neighbouring cells, and hence the colour of a boundary point can be any of the colours of the neighbouring cells. This many-to-one mapping is captured by defining the primitive as a relation rather than a function. The rules given in GKS which determine the colour allocated to a pixel when the primitive is mapped to the pixels of a raster display contain an ambiguity. The pixel is assigned the colour of the cell that contains the pixel's centre point. However, since each boundary line in the cell grid is contained in the neighbouring cells on each side of the boundary, the colour will not be uniquely determined if the pixel's centre point lies on a cell boundary. Similar considerations apply to the cell array primitive.

Fill Area Style **HATCH**

A hatch style is represented as a function from a point to a set of points. The notation $hatch(i)$ is used to denote the function corresponding to fill area style index i.

The displayed fill area is then:

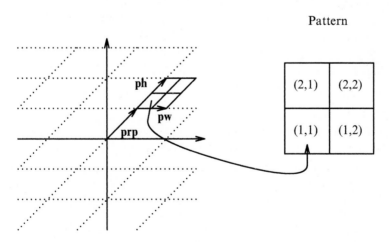

Figure 5

$mk\_DC\_Fill\_Area(f, w, v, b, pa) \triangleq$
  let $f = (i, b, cr, fi, \mathbf{prp}, \mathbf{pw}, \mathbf{ph})$
  and $b = (style, si, fci)$
  and $w = (\mathbf{w}_{min}, \mathbf{w}_{max})$
  and $wr = rectangle(\mathbf{w}_{min}, \mathbf{w}_{max})$
  in $style = HATCH \Rightarrow$
    $\{ (\mathbf{p}, fci) \mid \mathbf{p} \in wstrans(w, v, hatch(si)(i \cap cr \cap wr)) \}$

6.5   Cell Array

The cell array primitive is modelled as a relation from a point to a colour index.

$DC\_Cell\_Array = Point \leftrightarrow Colour\_Index$

$mk\_DC\_Cell\_Array: NDC\_Cell\_Array \times Window \times Viewport \rightarrow DC\_Cell\_Array$
$mk\_DC\_Cell\_Array(ndcca, w, v) \triangleq$
  let $w = (\mathbf{w}_{min}, \mathbf{w}_{max})$
  and $wr = rectangle(\mathbf{w}_{min}, \mathbf{w}_{max})$
  and $(f, cr) = ndcca$
  in $\{ (\mathbf{p}, ci) \mid \mathbf{p} \in wstrans(w, v, ndcpts \cap cr \cap wr)$
     $\wedge (ndcpts \mapsto ci \in f) \}$

7   Conclusions

This paper has shown how formal definitions can be given for the output primitives
in GKS. A model of the viewing pipeline has been presented which shows the precise state of a primitive at each stage of the pipeline, and explains the attribute and
aspect binding models of GKS. The description of the pipeline shows how information is added to primitives at each stage, until display is possible. A common model
for the displayed primitives has been found in terms of relations from points to
colour index values. Primitives can be combined to form pictures by taking the
union of the relations that represent them. This is a reasonable description of pictures in GKS, because, in general, GKS does not describe how to resolve the
conflicts which arise when different primitives or parts of primitives overlap. This
use of relations rather than functions to describe pictures is an extension of the concept of pictures as functions as defined by Mallgren [14].

There are two important applications of this work. The first is that a framework
such as that presented here can be used for the formal definition of attribute binding
and the effects of transformations in a computer graphics reference model, such as
that under development within the ISO working group on computer graphics. The
second application is related to this, namely describing the relationship between
GKS and GKS-3D, an extension of GKS to 3D graphics, currently under development within ISO [12]. The functions in GKS-3D and GKS generate instances of the
same output primitives, hence the effects of the GKS-3D functions should be

expressible in terms of the relations given here, in suitable coordinate systems.

These definitions also allow different binding models to be investigated, for example the implications of computing the cell array grid in NDC space rather than WC space, or clipping a polyline after the linestyle transformation.

This paper, together with the control framework in our earlier papers, now gives the basis of a specification of the output side of GKS.

References

1. K. W. Brodlie and G. Pfaff, "An Algorithmic Interpretation of the GKS TEXT Primitive," *Computer Graphics Forum* **2**(4), pp.233-241 (1983). (Reproduced in this Volume.)

2. G. S. Carson and E. Post, "The Formal Specification of a Computer Graphics System," TR 83-6, GSC Associates (1983).

3. G. S. Carson, "The Specification of Computer Graphics Systems," *IEEE Computer Graphics and Applications*, pp.27-41 (September 1983).

4. P. Dickman, "Definition of Interior Points in CGI, CGM, GKS-3D and PHIGS," Laser Scan Ltd (June 1985).

5. D. A. Duce and E. V. C. Fielding, "Better Understanding through Formal Specification," RAL-84-128, Rutherford Appleton Laboratory, Chilton, Didcot, OXON OX11 0QX, U.K. (1984).

6. D. A. Duce, E. V. C. Fielding, and L. S. Marshall, "Formal Specification and Graphics Software," RAL-84-068, Rutherford Appleton Laboratory, Chilton, Didcot, OXON OX11 0QX, U.K. (1984).

7. D. A. Duce and E. V. C. Fielding, "Formal Specification - A Comparison of Two Techniques," RAL-85-051, Rutherford Appleton Laboratory, Chilton, Didcot, OXON OX11 0QX, U.K. (1985).

8. D. A. Duce and E. V. C. Fielding, "Formal Specification - A Simple Example," *ICL Technical Journal*, pp.96-111 (May 1986).

9. K. Futatsugi, J. A. Goguen, J.-P. Jouannaud, and J. Meseguer, "Principles of OBJ2," *Proceedings of the 1985 Symposium on Principles of Programming Languages* (1985).

10. R. Gnatz, "An Algebraic Approach to the Standardization and the Certification of Graphics Software," *Computer Graphics Forum* **2**(2/3) (1983). (Reproduced in this Volume.)

11. F. R. A. Hopgood, D. A. Duce, J. R. Gallop, and D. C. Sutcliffe, *Introduction to the Graphical Kernel System (GKS)*, Academic Press (1986). (Second Edition.)

12. ISO, "Information processing systems - Computer graphics - Graphical Kernel System (GKS) for three dimensions (GKS-3D) functional description," ISO/DP 8805 (1985).

13. ISO, "Information processing systems - Computer graphics - Graphical Kernel System (GKS) functional description," ISO 7942, ISO Central Secretariat (August 1985).

14. W. R. Mallgren, "Formal Specification of Graphic Data Types," *ACM Transactions on Programming Languages and Systems* **4**(4), pp.687-710 (October 1982).

15. W. R. Mallgren, "Formal Specification of Interactive Graphics Programming Languages," Technical Report 81-09-01, PhD Dissertation (also published by ACM-MIT Press Distinguished Dissertation Series in June 1983), Department of Computer Science, University of Washington, Seattle.

16. J. E. Stoy, *Denotational Semantics,* The MIT Press (1977).

Appendix 1 - Glossary of Symbols

$\triangleq$	"is defined to be".
$\mathbb{N}$	The set of natural numbers (the non-negative integers).
$\mathbb{Z}$	The set of integers.
$\mathbb{R}$	The set of real numbers.
$\{x \mid P\}$	The set of all x such that P is true.
$m..n$	The set of natural numbers between m and n inclusive: $\{i \mid m \leq i \leq n \land i \in \mathbb{N}\}$.
$\emptyset$	The empty set.
$\in$	Set membership.
$\notin$	Not a member of.
$\cap$	Set intersection.
$\cup$	Set union.
$\bigcup$	Distributed set union.
$f(x)$	The function f applied to x.
$dom\ f$	The domain of the relation or function f.
$a \mapsto b$	The element of a function which maps a to b.
(a, b)	The ordered pair of elements a and b.
$\circ$	Functional composition: $(f \circ g)(x) = f(g(x))$.
$\land$	Logical conjunction.
$\lor$	Logical disjunction.
$\Rightarrow$	Logical implication.
$\exists$	Existential quantifier. There exists a ...
$\mathbf{w.h}$	The inner (dot) product of the vectors $\mathbf{w}$ and $\mathbf{h}$.
$\mathbf{i, j}$	Unit vectors along x and y axes respectively.

Appendix 2 - Additional Data Types

This appendix gives definitions of the data types *Point*, **list of** α (where α is any type), 2Darray **of** α, *Window* and *Viewport*. The definitions are given in the algebraic specification language OBJ [9].

```
obj   POINT / ℝ
sorts Point
ops   mk_Point : ℝ × ℝ → Point
      _x : Point → ℝ
      _y : Point → ℝ
vars  x, y : ℝ
eqns  ( mk_Point(x, y)_x = x )
      ( mk_Point(x, y)_y = y )
jbo
```

```
obj   LIST / α, ℕ
sorts list of α
ops   empty_list : → list of α
      _::_ : α × list of α → list of α
      _‖_ : list of α × list of α → list of α
      _ : list of α ℕ → α
      len : list of α → ℕ
vars  p : α
      l, l₁, l₂ : list of α
      i : ℕ
eqns  ( empty_list ‖ l = l )
      ( l ‖ empty_list = l )
      ( (p :: l₁) ‖ l₂ = p :: (l₁ ‖ l₂) )
      ( len(empty_list) = 0 )
      ( len(p::l) = 1 + len(l) )
      ( (p::l)ᵢ = p if (i = 1 + len(l)) )
      ( (p::l)ᵢ = lᵢ if (1 < i < 1 + len(l)) )
      ( (p::l)ᵢ = UNDEFINED if (i < 1 ∨ i > 1 + len(l)) )
jbo
```

obj *Array* **of** α / $\mathbb{N}$
sorts *Array* **of** α
ops *mk_Array* : *array* **of** $\alpha \times \mathbb{N} \times \mathbb{N} \times \mathbb{N} \rightarrow$ *array* **of** α
     empty_Array : $\rightarrow$ *array* **of** α
     access : *array* **of** $\alpha \times \mathbb{N} \times \mathbb{N} \rightarrow \mathbb{N}$
     assign : *array* **of** $\alpha \times \mathbb{N} \times \mathbb{N} \times \mathbb{N} \rightarrow$ *array* **of** $\mathbb{N}$
vars *i, j, k, l* : $\mathbb{N}$
     v, w : α
     a : *array* **of** α
eqns (*access(empty_array, i, j)* = *UNDEFINED*)
     (*access(mk_array(a, k, l, v), i, j)* = *v* **if** $(i == k \wedge j == l)$)
     (*access(mk_array(a, k, l, v), i, j)* = *access(a, i, j)* **if** $(i \neq k \vee j \neq l)$)
     (*assign(empty_array, i, j, v)* = *mk_array(empty_array, i, j, v)*)
     (*assign(mk_array(a, k, l, w), i, j, v)* = *mk_array(assign(a, i, j, v), k, l, w)*
                                if $(i \neq k \wedge j \neq l)$)
     (*assign(mk_array(a, k, l, w), i, j, v)* = *mk_array(a, i, j, v)*
                                if $(i = k \wedge j = l)$)
jbo

---

obj *2DArray* / α, *array* **of** α
sorts *2Darray* **of** α
ops *mk_2Darray* : $\mathbb{N} \times \mathbb{N} \times$ *array* **of** $\alpha \rightarrow$ *2Darray*
     declare_2Darray : $\mathbb{N} \times \mathbb{N} \rightarrow$ *2Darray*
     rows : *2Darray* $\rightarrow \mathbb{N}$
     cols : *2Darray* $\rightarrow \mathbb{N}$
     _ _ _ : *2Darray* $\times \mathbb{N} \times \mathbb{N} \rightarrow \mathbb{N}$
     _ _ _ := _ : *2Darray* $\times \mathbb{N} \times \mathbb{N} \times \mathbb{N} \rightarrow$ *2Darray*
vars *i, j, k, m, n* : $\mathbb{N}$
     v : α
     a : *array* **of** α
eqns (*declare_2Darray(m, n)* = *mk_2Darray(m, n, empty_array)*)
     (*rows(mk_2Darray(m, n, a))* = *m*)
     (*cols(mk_2Darray(m, n, a))* = *n*)
     (*mk_2Darray(m, n, a)*$_{ij}$ = *access(a, i, j)* **if** $(1 \leq i \leq m \wedge 1 \leq j \leq n)$)
     (*mk_2Darray(m, n, a)*$_{ij}$ = *UNDEFINED* **if** $(i < 1 \vee i > m \vee j < 1 \vee j > n)$)
     (*mk_2Darray(m, n, a)*$_{ij}$:= *v* = *assign(a, i, j, v)* **if** $(1 \leq i \leq m \wedge 1 \leq j \leq n)$)
     (*mk_2Darray(m, n, a)*$_{ij}$:= *v* = *UNDEFINED* **if** $(i < 1 \vee i > m \vee j < 1 \vee j > n)$)
jbo

obj   *WINDOW | POINT*
sorts *Window*
ops   *mk_Window* : *Point* × *Point* → *Window*
jbo

obj   *VIEWPORT | POINT*
sorts *Viewport*
ops   *mk_Viewport* : *Point* × *Point* → *Window*
jbo

Appendix 3 - The Text Primitive

This appendix sketches a specification of the text primitive, in the same style as the definitions given for the other GKS primitives in the main body of the paper.

Text is the most complex of the GKS output primitives. The world coordinate object is represented as a point (the text starting position) and a string (list of characters).

$$Text = Point \times \text{list of } Char$$

$$mk\_Text: Point \times \text{list of } Char \to Text$$
$$mk\_Text(\mathbf{p}, s) \triangleq (\mathbf{p}, s)$$

The primitive at the NDC level is modelled as a tuple whose components are the transformed text starting point, the character string, the clipping rectangle and text attributes associated with the primitive. The meaning of these attributes is explained in [13]. The character height and character up vector attributes have been combined into an up vector, whose direction is that of the character up vector and magnitude is equal to the character height. The character width and character base vector are similarly combined into a single base vector.

$$NDC\_Text = Point \times \text{list of } Char \times Clip\_Rectangle \times Text\_Index$$
$$\times Up\_Vector \times Base\_Vector \times Text\_Path \times Text\_Alignment$$

$$mk\_NDC\_Text: Text \times Window \times Viewport \times Clip\_Rectangle \times Text\_Index$$
$$\times Up\_Vector \times Base\_Vector$$
$$\times Text\_Path \times Text\_Alignment \to NDC\_Text$$
$$mk\_NDC\_Text(t, w, v, cr, ti, \mathbf{uv}, \mathbf{bv}, tp, ta) \triangleq$$
$$\textbf{let } t = (\mathbf{p}, s)$$
$$\textbf{in } (T_N(w, v)(\mathbf{p}), s, cr, ti, T_N(w, v)(\mathbf{uv}), T_N(w, v)(\mathbf{bv}), tp, ta)$$

The primitive at the DC level is represented as a relation (which reduces to a function) from a point to a colour index. The text bundle indexed by the text index defines the following aspects:

      Text font and precision
      Character expansion factor
      Character spacing
      Text colour index

Characters are represented as sets of points. The geometry of a displayed character is determined by the aspects:

Text font and precision
Character height
Character up vector
Character width
Character base vector
Character expansion factor

The function *character* generates the set of points (in NDC space) for a given character at a given position, with given values of the aspects listed above:

character: *Font_and_Precision* × *Up_Vector* × *Base_Vector* × *Expansion_Factor*
        × *Char* × *Point* → **set of** *Point*

The positions of the starting points of each character in the string are determined from the aspects and primitive data, by the function *at*. This function needs knowledge of the widths of the characters in the font, which are supplied through the function *width*:

width: *Font_and_Precision* → (*Char* → $\mathbb{R}$)

at: *Point* × **list of** *Char* × *Up_Vector* × *Base_Vector*
        × *Expansion_Factor* × *Text_Path* × *Text_Alignment*
        × (*Char* → $\mathbb{R}$) → **list of** *Point*

The definition of such a function has been given by Brodlie and Pfaff [1].

The rendering of the text aspects is complicated because there are three precisions of text in GKS: STROKE, CHAR and STRING. For STROKE precision text, the aspects must be rendered precisely. For the lower precisions, there are some relaxations on this, though we only describe STROKE precision here. The definition of *mk_DC_Text* closely follows that of *mk_DC_Polymarker*.

DC_Text = *Point* ↔ *Colour_Index*

mk_DC_Text: *NDC_Text* × *Window* × *Viewport* × *Text_Bundle* → *DC_Text*

mk_DC_Text(*t*, *w*, *v*, *b*) $\triangleq$
    let *t* = (**p**, *s*, *cr*, *ti*, **uv**, **bv**, *tp*, *ta*)
    and *b* = (*tfp*, *expf*, *csp*, *ci*)
    and *pts* = $\bigcup_{i=1..len\ s}$ (*character*(*tfp*, **uv**, **bv**, *expf*, s_i,
                        at(**p**, *s*, **uv**, **bv**, *expf*, *csp*, *tp*, *ta*, *width*(*tfp*))$_i$) ∩ *cr* ∩ *wr*)
    in { (**p**, *ci*) | **p** ∈ *wstrans*(*w*, *v*, *pts*) }

Part IV: Programming Language Interfaces

In addition to the standardization of GKS itself as a functional description, major work has also been done within the ISO Computer Graphics Working Group (ISO/TC97/SC21/WG2) to create standardized language bindings to GKS. However, this work can be done only for languages that are already an ISO standard (FORTRAN, Pascal, and Ada) or that are being standardized (C). As we have already suggested in the preface, major contributions, published within the framework of the Eurographics Association, have helped to resolve some technical problems that arose, but these papers are mainly of a historical interest today. There are, however, programming languages where the question of how to produce a GKS language binding is still open. In this section, we have gathered three papers which present interesting proposals in this context. Two of them are concerned with PRO-LOG (**Sykes et al; Huebner et al.**), while the third deals with ALGOL 68 (**Martin et al.**).

GKS Inquiry Functions within PROLOG

P. Sykes and R. Krishnamurti

1 Introduction

GKS, the international standard for 2D graphics software, provides a set of functionalities which are specified in a language independent manner. However, for GKS to be used, a binding must be defined for some host programming language. To date a FORTRAN binding [1] has been accepted, and proposals for bindings in Pascal [8] and Ada are under consideration in ISO. Possible bindings for C [7] and ALGOL 68 [5] have also been proposed.

A language binding for the PROLOG programming language is currently under development [9], and a draft version is being implemented within an enhanced version of the C-PROLOG interpreter [6] running on UNIX. GKS is designed to be implemented in the natural programming language of the host system and to have a language dependent layer as an interface to each of the other programming languages on the system. Our PROLOG implementation, therefore, forms an interface to a library of GKS functions written in the C programming language.

Different PROLOG implementations may have different syntactical rules for differentiating between variables and atoms. The convention adopted in this binding document is that adopted by the C-PROLOG interpreter. Variables start with an upper case letter or an underscore, atoms start with a lower case letter or may be any string enclosed within single quotes.

The draft ANSI standard GKS document [1, 3] specifies guidelines for language bindings. These essentially constrain a binding, in effect, to provide a one-to-one mapping of GKS abstract functions to atomic language functions, and to specify data types corresponding to the GKS abstract data types. The rules also require the binding to observe good software engineering principles, a requirement which we have taken to mean that the functions names be mnemonic and that the parameter lists be kept to manageable proportions. Within a PROLOG environment it is possible for the programmer to define multiple predicates having the same name but with differing argument lists. That is, the arguments may differ in length and/or type. This feature has been utilized to provide the binding with a degree of flexibility. This is illustrated in this paper in one area, namely that of the GKS inquiry functions.

In their paper on a C binding, Rosenthal and ten Hagen [7] added two more rules to the list, namely,

(a)   The GKS specification should not be interpreted literally as to prevent the application programmer making use of the full range of the host language's facilities.

This rule is particularly relevant to a PROLOG graphics binding. Prolog is a declarative language. Any binding in PROLOG must either be declarative or must at least look declarative. A PROLOG binding that forces procedural programming techniques on the applications programmer will not find widespread acceptance by the PROLOG community.

(b)   The GKS document should not be interpreted literally as to force inefficient techniques on the implementor.

PROLOG provides a flexible environment for programming that may be attributed to many factors among which are the following. First, arguments to a PROLOG predicate are not strongly data typed. That is, for example, some clauses of a PROLOG predicate may have arguments that are instanced to simple constants or atoms whilst others may have the same arguments instanced to compound terms or structures. Second, arguments to a predicate do not have fixed scope in that they may, in general, serve as either input or output. Third, PROLOG permits definitions for predicates with the same name that differ in parameter lengths. In other words, a predicate is uniquely specified only by both its name and its parameter length (arity). A consequence of this is that GKS functions may be used in ways which were not foreseen in the original standard specifications.

Most PROLOG implementations whether they are compilers or interpreters are written partially in some host language and partially in PROLOG. The simplest way to implement a PROLOG binding is to write it essentially in PROLOG rather than in the host language of the Prolog compiler/interpreter. This ensures that the binding is specified in a manner that makes it more natural to use within a PROLOG environment.

2   The PROLOG Binding

The PROLOG under development at EdCAAD provides for this mapping of GKS functions to PROLOG predicates. We have adopted a naming convention for the predicates that does not err on the side of being too terse, yet is still reasonably compact. All the GKS predicates have the prefix **gk_** and all GKS inquiry predicates have the prefix **gk_q_**. Wherever possible and without ambiguity as to the intended functionality, the predicate names are abbreviated. The naming convention is given in the document describing the suggested binding [9].

The data types in the standard are merely tools for describing the semantics of the standard. They should be replaced by actual data types conforming to the host language. PROLOG has no context independent notion of data typing. Also PROLOG has no context independent semantics for operators, though the operator syntax must be strictly obeyed in a PROLOG term. For example, $<$ is a PROLOG infix operator. Any expression involving $<$ must be of the form LHS $<$ RHS where LHS and RHS are valid PROLOG terms. However, PROLOG will not interpret this expression as the conditional

> LHS "less than" RHS

unless it is stated as a PROLOG goal. Moreover, PROLOG permits overloading of operator type. Thus, for example, the operator $+$ is both prefix and infix. There is no reason why it can't be declared postfix as well.

We have found it convenient to employ some PROLOG operators, for instance, $X:Y$ to describe coordinate pairs, and *Attribute = Value* to name parameters in lengthy argument lists. In many cases we have parameters that are structures; for example, the polyline representation is denoted by the PROLOG functor *line(Id, Type, Width, Colour)*. In fact, the structured parameters may themselves have arguments which need not be atomic, for example, data record items.

Lastly, it should be noted that PROLOG clauses are logical implications that either *succeed* (when **true**) or *fail* (when **false**) and take one of the two following forms:

/★ 1 ★/

    Goal.

/★ 2 ★/

    Goal :- $condition_1$
           $condition_2$
           .
           .
           .
           $condition_n$

In the first case, 'Goal' is treated as a fact which succeeds whenever its arguments, if any, are matched. In the second case, 'Goal' succeeds only if each condition 1 through n succeeds and fails otherwise. Each condition, in turn, is a PROLOG goal.

3 Inquiry Functions

The GKS inquiry functions return information about the current state of GKS. In a conventional von Neumann language the value of the return parameter would be tested and the program would continue as required. The PROLOG equivalent of this may be described as

```
gk_q_function (Var),     /★ get value of Var ★/
test (Var, value),       /★ succeeds if Var is value ★/
    .
    .
    .
etc                      /★ carry on only if test succeeds ★/
```

A more natural implementation would require the inquiry and the test to work in one go. Thus, we have

```
gk_q_function (value),     /★ succeeds if the inquired function matches value ★/
```

This is the preferred form where the returned value is usually one in a set of enumeration types. A typical PROLOG application would then have several clauses of the form:

```
inquire_and_do :-
                gk_q_function (value₁),
                !,
                do_action_1.

inquire_and_do :-
                gk_q_function (value₂),
                !,
                do_action_2.
                  .
                  .

inquire_and_do :-
                gk_q_function (valueₙ),
                !,
                do_action_n.
```

The effect of this is that PROLOG would first determine if the result of the inquiry was $value_1$ and if so then it would 'do_action_1'. The goal can fail in two ways. Either if the inquiry failed in which case the next 'inquire_and_do' clause is tried, or the 'do_action' clause fails in which case the goal fails. The cut (!) operator acts as a *barrier* to prevent PROLOG from backtracking and trying other 'inquire_and_do' clauses in the event of a successful inquiry. PROLOG would repeat this process with each of the 'inquire_and_do' clauses in the given order until either one succeeds or the entire goal fails.

Many GKS inquiry functions return several values. In a conventional von Neumann language each of these parameters is specified by its position in the parameter list which has a predetermined length. In PROLOG it is possible to allow the programmer to state which of the parameters he is interested in and in a similar manner to the example above to state what he expects it to be. Furthermore the parameter may be specified by name and not by position.

The general format of an inquiry function is

gk_q_GKS_FUNCTION (*Attribute* = *Value*)

or

gk_q_GKS_FUNCTION ([List of *Attribute* = *Value* terms])

The list may contain as many different attributes as required.

4   Examples

Consider the function INQUIRE WORKSTATION NUMBERS. This returns three small integers corresponding to the maximum number of workstations that are simultaneously open, active or have associated segments. The FORTRAN binding implements this as

SUBROUTINE GQWKM (ERR, MXOPWK, MXACWK, MXASWK)

which returns in the four arguments an error indicator and the three maximums. (In the PROLOG binding an error situation corresponds to a failure of the inquiry goal.)

The obvious equivalent PROLOG predicate is:

gk_q_ws_max ([open = *Mxop*, active = *Mxac*, assoc = *Mxas*]),

However, if all the parameters are not required the PROLOG binding allows the applications programmer to use this inquiry function in the following ways:

gk_q_ws_max (open = *Mxop*),

to ask the maximum number of open workstations;

gk_q_ws_max (open = 3),

will succeed only if the maximum number of open workstations is 3;

gk_q_ws_max (*M* = 3),

will instantiate *M*, in turn via 'backtracking', to each one of open, active or assoc provided the corresponding maximum number of workstations equals 3, and fails otherwise;

gk_q_ws_max ([open = 3, active = *Mxac*]),

succeeds only if the maximum number of open workstations is 3 and instantiates *Mxac* to the maximum number of active workstations.

The last case is:

gk_q_ws_max (*L*),

instantiates *L* to a list with the three members of the form *Attribute* = *Value*.

Combinations of the above cases are also permitted. For instance,

gk_q_ws_max ([open = 3 | *L*]),

will succeed if the maximum number of open workstations is 3 and instantiates *L* to a list of the other parameters. The order of the arguments is not important. Thus, the inquiry

> gk_q_ws_max ([open = *Mxop*, active = *Mxac*])

is the same as

> gk_q_ws_max ([active = *Mxac*, open = *Mxop*])

The above mechanism works equally well with enumerated data types. For instance, consider the GKS functionality INQUIRE SEGMENT ATTRIBUTES which returns for a given segment name, its transformation matrix, relative priority, and three enumerated types which correspond to the visibility, highlighting and detectability of the segment. The PROLOG implementation allows the programmer to form the query in such a way that his code is not cluttered with unwanted variables. For instance, the goal

> gk_q_seg (*SEG*, [norm = *MAT*, detect = yes]),

will return the transformation matrix in *MAT* for segment *SEG* only if it is detectable.

Some of the GKS inquiry functions return so many arguments that even this implementation would be unwieldy. For instance, the functionalities INQUIRE CURRENT PRIMITIVE ATTRIBUTE VALUES and INQUIRE CURRENT INDIVIDUAL ATTRIBUTE VALUES have 11 and 13 arguments respectively. The arguments relate to the various graphics primitives - for example, polyline, text etc - and their attributes.

It is possible to implement these as single predicates each with a list of ten or more arguments, some of which are points, some integers, some names, some enum types and some lists; or as in the FORTRAN binding and indeed as suggested in other bindings, to implement these as separate inquiry functions, one for each attribute. The method chosen for the PROLOG binding is to allow the application to specify which attribute of some primitive is required. As in the previously considered inquiry function, it is desirable to have the goal succeed if the return value matches what is expected. Therefore in this example, the PROLOG goal

> gk_q_line (index = *LI*)

will succeed with the variable *LI* instantiated to the current polyline index. Similar goals can be specified for the other primitives. The general form of the primitive attribute inquiry function takes the form:

> gk_q_ < primitive > (List of one or more *Attribute* = *Value* terms)

where < primitive > is one of the GKS output primitives. The attribute(s) depends on the primitive.

In the example above, the attributes are atomic constants. It is possible to have attributes which are structures. For instance, to inquire the line type aspect source flag we can invoke the predicate:

> gk_q_asf (line(type) = *Flag*).

This form allows the application programmer to program goals such as:

/★ Gather 'in a bag' the primitives and their indices whose asf's are bundled
'bag' has three arguments (Element, Condition, Bag)
=.. is a PROLOG operator that takes *Prim* with *Index* to form
the term *Prim(Index)* ★/

inquire_bundled_asf(*Bag*):-
        bag((*Prim*, *Index*),
            (gk_q_asf(*Attribute* = bundled),
            Attribute =.. [*Prim, Index*]),
            Bag).

The last example we consider also deals with structured parameters. Consider the
function INQUIRE PREDEFINED PRIMITIVE REPRESENTATION. For each
primitive, namely, polyline, polymarker, text etc most GKS implementations hold in
the workstation description table a structure representing the primitive representation. For a polyline, this representation has four attributes, namely, the polyline
index, the line type, the line width scale factor and polyline colour index. While the
applications programmer may wish to query a particular attribute, from an implementation standpoint this would require accessing the internal GKS tables once for
each attribute queried. In general it is faster for our implementation for the C-GKS
internal structures to be accessed once and for the applications programmer to
extract the particular attributes of interest. This is easily done in PROLOG with the
use of the don't care variable '_'. Thus, the call,

      gk_q_rep(*WS, line(ID, _, _, Colour)*)

will instantiate *Colour* to the polyline colour index only if polyline index equals *ID*
on workstation *WS*. Other variations can easily be described.

5 Concluding Remarks

In this paper we have attempted to show that it is possible to define a PROLOG
binding for GKS in a manner that makes declarative graphics programming a viable
proposition yet at same time conforming to the guidelines laid down by the GKS
standards specifications. The few examples presented in this paper highlight some of
the potential flexibility that PROLOG achieves through the use of named attributes
and structured arguments. Moreover, this flexibility is achieved without sacrificing
both the readability and conciseness of the application programmers code.

Since we have only barely hinted at implementation details, it should be remarked
that the interface to the GKS functions as illustrated by the examples above can be
written entirely in PROLOG though at the present time this is likely to result in an
unreasonably slow implementation. Our particular implementation is written in
PROLOG and calls GKS routines written in C. (A full implementation [4] of C-
PROLOG/ GKS is now available.) The C-GKS system [2] on which our implementation is based utilizes macros for the inquiry functions which in turn take as arguments pointers to the various GKS tables. It is a relatively straightforward matter to
translate PROLOG attribute names to the C table pointers.

Acknowledgements

This work has been carried out as part of the ACORD project supported by the ESPRIT programme.

References

1.   Anon, "Special GKS Issue," *Computer Graphics* (1984).

2.   M. Bakker (ed.), *The GKS Reference Manual,* Stichting Mathematisch Centrum, Stichting Computer Grafiek, Systeem Experts b.v. (1986).

3.   G. Enderle, K. Kansy, and G. Pfaff, *Computer Graphics Programming: GKS - The Graphics Standard,* Springer-Verlag (1984).

4.   R. Krishnamurti (ed.), "Prolog/ GKS Reference Manual," Technical Report, EdCAAD, University of Edinburgh (1987).

5.   R. R. Martin and C. Anderson, "A proposal for an ALGOL 68 Binding of GKS," *Computer Graphics Forum* **4**(1), pp.43-57 (1985). (Reproduced in this Volume.)

6.   F. C. N. Pereira, "C-Prolog User's Manual," Technical Report, EdCAAD, University of Edinburgh (revised 1984).

7.   D. S. H. Rosenthal and P. J. W. ten Hagen, "GKS in C," pp. 359-370 in *Eurographics '82*, ed. D. S. Greenaway and E. A. Warman, North-Holland (1982).

8.   M. Slater, "Pascal Interface for GKS 7.2," BSI OIS/5/WG5/207, BSI Working Group on Computer Graphics (1984).

9.   P. Sykes and R. Krishnamurti, "A Proposal for a Prolog binding to GKS," Technical Report, EdCAAD, University of Edinburgh (revised 1985).

GKS Based Graphics Programming in PROLOG

W. Huebner and Z. I. Markov

1 Introduction

It is evident that every computer language needs a graphics extension for the same reason as it needs input and output functions. Graphics may be seen as a powerful extension of the input and output facilities. This is even more evident for interactive languages like PROLOG. PROLOG is a computer language widely accepted for the purpose of symbolic computation. It is gaining popularity because of its simplicity and the new descriptive way of programming. A PROLOG program is a description of a problem in the form of some assertions and rules about how the solution may be inferred from the facts. It also provides some powerful data processing mechanisms, mainly relational data base facilities, tree searching with backtracking, and pattern matching. All these advantages make PROLOG suitable for many applications such as relational data bases, architectural design, natural language understanding and other AI fields. Most of the applications mentioned above also need computer graphics. Thus, integration of graphics into PROLOG can be seen as a step towards providing a more intelligent environment for these applications. The design of the graphics extension described in this paper is based on the principles and concepts of the Graphical Kernel System (GKS) [8]. GKS provides all capabilities required by most of the PROLOG applications that produce computer generated pictures. It provides a suitable methodological framework for the creation of computer graphics programs because of its consistency, completeness, and compactness. The Graphical Kernel System supports the whole range of graphics devices, guarantees the portability of applications between different installations and is defined independently of any programming language. Moreover, GKS has become the first International Standard in computer graphics and is widely accepted in practice. This paper describes some approaches to integration of graphics and PROLOG. The "core PROLOG" syntax [1] is being used in the consideration of PROLOG predicates.

2 Graphics in PROLOG - Problems and Approaches

From its beginning computer graphics has been connected to algorithmic languages. There are many applications for full graphical interaction with computers, mostly at a lower level than PROLOG. The graphical interaction is usually embedded in an algorithmic language by some graphics extensions. Therefore, since most algorithmic languages are procedural (the algorithm is a procedure), computer graphics is also procedurally orientated. In other words, in each implementation a set of graphics procedures (subroutines, etc.) exists, representing the basic graphics functions.

Some attempts have been made to find a general set of graphics functions suitable for a wide range of applications and not connected to a particular algorithmic language. GKS is a good example for such a language-independent system. However, the structure of graphics packages is strongly influenced by the procedural structure of the algorithmic languages even if they are language-independent.

Considering GKS, it is a set of functions for the manipulation of graphics data structures and for the management of graphics devices. For several programming languages (e.g. FORTRAN, Pascal) GKS language bindings are standardized. These block-oriented languages of the third generation realize the abstract GKS functions as subroutines or procedures, available in libraries. The GKS data types are based on the data types generally used by most of the algorithmic languages.

PROLOG on the other hand differs from the other algorithmic languages in its basic concept. It is a descriptive language belonging to the group of non-procedural programming languages of the fourth generation such as LISP, META-IV or SQL.

Procedural languages are based upon the idea of specifying the problem solution algorithm by sequential steps. The programmer describes how the problem is solved using basic operations that can be executed by the classical von Neumann machine.

In PROLOG the programmer only describes what problem has to be solved. He is not concerned with how the specification is executed by a machine. The problem-specific knowledge (i.e. the logic) is separated from the control components which are left to the machine. This paradigm of separation between logic and control (Kowalski [10]) is realized in PROLOG.

Programming in PROLOG is based upon Horn clauses. A logic program consists of facts and rules about relationships among values. Facts describe relationships which are unconditionally true like

$$father(X,Y)$$

This means that X is the father of Y. Rules are relationships with conditions and are described in the following way:

$$parent(X,Y) :- father(X,Y).$$

This clause says that if X is the father of Y, then X is a parent of Y. A PROLOG program consists of a list of clauses building a data base.

Then the user can ask questions to the data base:

? − father (adam ,cain).

The PROLOG interpreter searchs the data base and answers the question using inference rules. So the programmer is free from any control specification.

A brief tutorial about logic programming and PROLOG is given in [2]. For defining the PROLOG-graphics interface the requirements of both the procedure-oriented graphics applications and the description-oriented host language PROLOG have to be satisfied. There are two approaches to integrating graphics into PRO-LOG:

(1)   the implementation of graphical functions especially designed for PROLOG, taking into account the PROLOG features;

(2)   the connection of PROLOG with an existing graphical package like GKS.

The first approach is appropriate for small graphics packages which support simple PROLOG applications. The visualization of the PROLOG execution tree (depth-first and left-to-right strategy) or the use of graphics for debugging PROLOG programs are examples of such applications. This approach is also suitable for Personal Computer-implementations, taking into account some performance and memory restrictions. Graphics in Micro-PROLOG [9] is a good example for this approach.

For more complex graphics applications a powerful graphics package is required. By following the second approach, the problems of integrating a standardized graphics package in the description-oriented language PROLOG have to be solved.

We integrated GKS while not strictly following only a single approach. We combined both approaches by embedding GKS as a basic graphics package in a PROLOG-specific environment. Several additional description-oriented functions are implemented on a higher level. This approach is illustrated in figure 1.

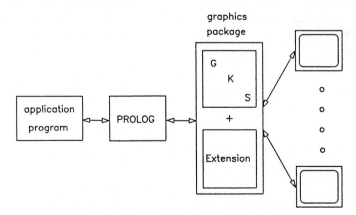

Figure 1 The Graphics-PROLOG Interface

We would like to emphasize the integration of the procedural graphics package like GKS into PROLOG for the following reasons:

- GKS is the result of long practice and experience in the area of computer graphics applications. Thus, it contains a full set of graphics functions and provides very useful concepts, such as device independency.

- The transfer of these functions and concepts into PROLOG guarantees the coverage of existing GKS applications as well as the combination of PROLOG and GKS applications, like expert systems and intelligent CAD systems.

- PROLOG is not a pure logic interpreter. The logic programming in PROLOG is based on a procedural approach for the interpretation of logic. Some procedural extensions (built-in predicates) are also available in PROLOG.

Thus, we can add GKS functions at a PROLOG procedural level using built-in predicates. Procedural graphics in PROLOG provides an environment which is the basis for further work towards the ultimate goal of graphics programming in PRO-LOG: the integration of graphics and logic (see also section 6).

The implementation of GKS functions as PROLOG predicates provides a basic graphics interface. In the layer model of GKS (see figure 2) it represents the language-dependent layer.

As mentioned above it is essential to specify a complete graphics interface in PROLOG in order to define an application-oriented layer on top of the GKS language layer. It has the following features we consider necessary for graphics programming in PROLOG:

- The real numbers widely used in graphics applications are not available in the core PROLOG. Therefore, some additional structures and predicates have to be realized to represent real numbers and to simulate real arithmetic. The description of this PROLOG extension is given in section 3.

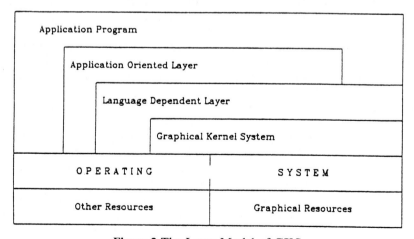

Figure 2 The Layer Model of GKS

- The lack of mathematical functions in PROLOG can be overcome by providing some additional graphics functions. For this reason we define built-in predicates for geometric transformations (see section 4). Obviously additional functions can be added whenever required by particular applications.

- Finally, a set up of predicates for picture generation and manipulation has been developed. It defines graphics data structures in PROLOG based on the GKS built-in predicates. As shown in figure 1, these extensions are independent of GKS. They are described in section 4.

In view of the purpose of our efforts, the approach proposed here towards integrating graphics and PROLOG may be seen as a fusion of both ideas:

- combining the procedural graphics suitable for a wide range of applications with the powerful PROLOG data processing mechanism, thus defining a new tool for many applications.

- providing the necessary environment for future work towards non-procedural graphics programming, i.e. connecting graphics to the basic concepts of PROLOG.

3   The Integration of GKS Functions

The basis of the graphics-PROLOG interface consists of a set of direct built-in predicates which correspond exactly to the abstract functions defined by the Graphical Kernel System. These functions producing computer generated pictures satisfy the majority of applications in this special domain.

In the area of PROLOG graphics applications the field of generative computer graphics is most evident. We do not consider PROLOG applications for picture processing and picture analysis. For this reason the basic graphics package is restricted to functions for generation and representation of pictures, workstation control and normalization and workstation transformation. This means, we exactly provide the full GKS level 0a as a procedural graphics system.

This approach does not support input handling from workstations. In this highly interactive host language the graphics described here will be used in parallel to the PROLOG dialog. Nevertheless, expanding the basic graphics package to input facilities (i.e. GKS level 0b) is not a problem.

The requirements for picture structuring, manipulation and long-time storage are satisfied by the descriptive graphics extensions closer to PROLOG.

The GKS functions are mapped one-to-one to PROLOG predicates. Note that it is not our final aim to define a GKS language binding for PROLOG but we consider the mapping of GKS level 0a functions and data types as a basis for the PROLOG graphics interface. Nevertheless, we followed the rules given in Annex C of the ISO Standard on GKS [8] for language bindings whenever possible. An interesting proposal for a PROLOG binding to GKS is described by Sykes and Krishnamurti [11].

The GKS data types are mapped to a small number of PROLOG data types. PROLOG provides, amongst other types, integers, characters, lists, and structures. The GKS data type String is mapped to a list of characters, Name and Enumeration Type are copied to integers. As real numbers do not exist in several PROLOG implementations, a special structure is used for this purpose. The GKS Data Record is not specified by the Standard but is left open as implementation and language dependent. In our approach it is employed only for ESCAPE and the GENERAL-IZED DRAWING PRIMITIVE (GDP). For ESCAPE, we chose a list of characters as appropriate data type, for GDP a list of reals and a list of integers, as is suggested in Annex E of the Standard for storing a GDP item in a metafile. For structured data types like points or matrices the PROLOG terms are used to define suitable structures consisting of PROLOG data type components.

For the specification of real numbers as parameters in the following predicates a double quotation mark is used. In PROLOG syntax this means a real number is represented as a list of ASCII codes of its digits including the decimal point. The following built-in predicates are provided for the basic mathematical operations:

$$add(X,Y,Z)$$
$$sub(X,Y,Z)$$
$$mul(X,Y,Z)$$
$$div(X,Y,Z)$$

The corresponding mathematical operations are performed between the first and the second argument of these predicates and the result is unified with the third argument. All arguments are lists of ASCII codes (reals have to be typed in double quotes). PROLOG integers can also be specified as arguments in places where reals are required. In this case they are automatically converted to whole real numbers.

The following designations are used for the arguments of the GKS built-in predicates:

< int >	a PROLOG integer or an instantiated to integer variable;
< real >	the PROLOG structure for reals described above or < int >;
< string >	a PROLOG string (single quoted characters);
< point >	a pair of two < real >s representing the point coordinates;
< list of points >	a PROLOG list of < point >s;
< list of reals >	a PROLOG list of < real >s;
< list of integers >	a PROLOG list of < integer >s.

The effect of the following predicates is specified in the Standard Document (for further details see Enderle et al [5]).

Basic Control Predicates

open gks	g_open (< int >, < int >)
close gks	g_close
open workstation	g_open_wk (< int >, < int >, < int >)
close workstation	g_close_wk (< int >)
active workstation	g_act_wk (< int >)
deactivate workstation	g_deact_wk (< int >)
clear workstation	g_clear_wk (< int >, < int >)

update workstation	g_upd_wk (<int> , <int>)
escape	g_escape (<int> , <string>)

Output Primitives

polyline	g_pl (<list of points>)
polymarker	g_pm (<list of points>)
text	g_tx (<point> , <string>)
fill area	g_fa (<list of points>)
cell array	g_ca (<point> , <point> , <int> , <int> , <int matrix>)
generalized drawing primitive	g_gdp (<list of points> , <int> , <list of int> , <list of real>)

Note that GKS provides the GDP to support special capabilities of a workstation like circle or spline interpolation. In the PROLOG environment this is the only possibility to describe curves because of the lack of mathematical functions.

Output Attributes

set polyline index	g_set_plx (<int>)
set linetype	g_set_lt (<int>)
set linewidth scale factor	g_set_lwscal (<int>)
set polyline colour index	g_set_plcolx (<int>)
set polymarker index	g_set_pmx (<int>)
set marker type	g_set_mt (<int>)
set marker size scale factor	g_set_mszscal (<real>)
set polymarker colour index	g_set_pmcolx (<int>)
set text index	g_set_txtx (<int>)
set text font and precision	g_set_txtfp (<int> , <int>)
set character expansion factor	g_set_charex (<real>)
set character spacing	g_set_charsp (<real>)
set text colour index	g_set_txtcolx (<int>)
set character height	g_set_charht (<real>)
set character up vector	g_set_charup (<real> , <real>)
set text path	g_set_txtpth (<int>)
set text alignment	g_set_txtalg (<int> , <int>)
set fill area index	g_set_fax (<int>)
set fill area interior style	g_set_fainst (<int>)
set fill area style index	g_set_fastx (<int>)
set fill area colour index	g_set_facolx (<int>)
set pattern size	g_set_patsz (<real> , <real>)
set pattern reference point	g_set_patrefp (<real> , <real>)
set aspect source flags	g_set_asf (<list of int>)
set colour representation	g_set_colrep (<int> , <int> , <real> , <real> , <real>)

Transformation Predicates

set window	g_set_wn (<int> , <point> , <point>)
set viewport	g_set_vp (<int> , <point> , <point>)
select normalization transformation	g_selnt (<int>)
select clipping indicator	g_selclipind (<int>)
set workstation window	g_set_wkwn (<int> , <point> , <point>)
set workstation viewport	g_set_wkvp (<int> , <point> , <point>)

Error Handling

emergency close gks	g_emclose
error handling	g_errhand (<int> , <int> , <int>)
error logging	g_errlog (<int> , <int> , <int>)

4   Graphical Data Structures in PROLOG

PROLOG provides sophisticated and flexible data structures which are defined entirely by the programmer. This advantage and the availability of graphics built-in predicates (GKS functions) on the other hand gives the user various opportunities to create his own graphical data structures. Section 4.1 describes this approach.

The second approach presented here is an implementation of higher level built-in predicates in PROLOG supporting special graphical data structures. These predicates form an intermediate level between the GKS functions and user programs and provide a more convenient graphics interface in PROLOG. We prefer the second approach, which is described in detail in section 4.2.

4.1   Using Graphical Functions as Ordinary Predicates

This approach is simpler than constructing special graphics structures and gives the user many possibilities to organize graphics in PROLOG. However, some problems concerning the scope of geometric transformations and attribute settings arise in this case. There are two ways to avoid them:

● The use of a special built-in predicate, which denies the current transformation and attributes and restores the parameters of the previous ones. In other words, the transformations and attribute settings can be used as opening and closing parentheses.

● The definition of the scope of geometric transformations and attributes as the scope of PROLOG variables, i.e. the transformations are valid only in the current clause. This means, the transformations and attributes hold until the clause in which they appear is active (it is in the stack of active goals). This approach is natural for PROLOG and is convenient, when the graphics primitives are mixed with other predicates causing backtracking. However, the implementation of such "intelligent" geometric transformations is difficult, since the PROLOG interpreter algorithm (stack mechanism) has to be taken into account.

4.2   Special Graphical Data Structures in PROLOG

A way to reach the aim presented in the previous section without going into the PROLOG implementation details is to organize special graphical data structures and to implement an interpreter controlled by built-in predicates for these structures. It will manage the geometric transformation, attribute setting parameters, and will ensure their locality. Our implementation is based on this approach.

For the purpose of building graphical data structures in PROLOG, we introduce the term picture as a basic element. The formal definition of a picture is as follows:

< picture > ::= < graphics primitives > | < picture > < graphics primitives > |
        < picture > < geometric transformations > | < picture > < attributes >
< graphics primitives > ::= < GKS polyline > | < GKS polymarker > |
        < GKS fill area > | < GKS text > | < GKS cell array > |
        < GKS GDP >
< geometric transformations > ::= < translation > | < rotation > | < scaling >
< attributes > ::= < GKS polyline attributes > | < GKS polymarker attributes > |
        < GKS fill area attributes > | < GKS text attributes > |
        < GKS cell array attributes >

We consider the above mentioned terms as picture components. The graphics primitives and attribute setting functions are the direct built-in predicates which correspond to the GKS functions.

In addition a set of predicates is defined on the PROLOG level. They are based on the picture concept and do not correspond to the GKS functions. The following geometric transformations belong to this set of extensions:

translate (Tx,Ty)

translates the origin of the current coordinate system to the point (Tx,Ty).

rotate (R)

rotates the current coordinate system about its origin. R is specified in degrees.

scale (Sx,Sy)

scales the current coordinate system.

The above named predicates define a set of PROLOG reals Tx,Ty,R,Sx,Sy, which in turn define the current transformation matrix. This matrix is applied to each of the graphics primitives. This means that each point, which is a parameter in a drawing predicate is transformed before the corresponding GKS primitive is executed.

The semantics of the geometric transformations are closely related to the concept of the picture. Therefore, their main feature is that they are local, i.e. their effect is limited to the logical frame of the picture, in which they appear. More details about geometric transformations are given below in connection with the picture manipulating predicates.

The PROLOG structure, which is used to describe a picture is the following predicate:

picture (Name,List)

Name is the picture name and List is a PROLOG list of the picture components given as executable goals. The picture name can take the form of a PROLOG clause head. The aim is to facilitate the use of parameters (variables) in the picture definition, which can be used as parameters in some predicates from the list of picture components by means of the PROLOG mechanism of sharing variables.

This representation of the picture is very close to the representation of the ordinary PROLOG clause. The reason for using a special representation instead of the PROLOG clauses is the necessity of managing the parameters of the geometric transformations and attribute setting functions, which have to be local for each picture.

Predicates may have different meanings and therefore may describe different graphical objects depending on the type of its execution (with or without backtracking). For this purpose not only picture components, but also the cut and fail predicates affecting backtracking can be included in the picture definition list.

Moreover, recursive descriptions of pictures are possible. For example, the following picture called with $X = 4$ is a rhombus, its size depends on the second parameter Y:

> picture (rom(0,Y),[!]).
> picture (rom(X,Y), [g_pl([Y,0,0,Y]),
> rotate(90), Z is X-1, rom(Z,Y)]).

The following built-in predicates are provided to support the management of the described PROLOG graphical picture:

define_picture(Name,List)

With this predicate the picture description given by the predicate picture is added to the PROLOG LOG data base.

delete_picture(Name)

This predicate removes the specified picture from the data base (only the matched picture clause, not the whole picture predicate). It is analogous to the PROLOG predicate "retract" and is based on it.

save_picture(File_name)

The predicates save_picture and load_picture are used for long time storage of pictures. All defined pictures which exist in the PROLOG data base are saved with this command onto the specified file. The file is usually an external text file. This mechanism guarantees the probability of picture descriptions and the availability of pictures at several installations.

load_picture(File_name)

It loads all pictures from the specified file to the PROLOG data base. The pictures were defined and saved to the external file in a former session and perhaps at another system. Note that the external file can also be built without using the define_picture and save_picture predicates using a standard text editor and following the syntax of the picture definition described above.

show_picture(Name)

This predicate starts a picture interpreter. It executes components as PROLOG goals; as a result the picture appears on the screens of all active workstations (figure 3). The main function of this predicate is to execute the parameters of the geometric transformations and attribute setting functions. All such transformations and attributes are local, i.e. they are valid only in the picture in which they are defined. If they are set outside the picture definition list, they change the default values of the transformation and attribute parameters. The predicate show_picture executes all goals appearing in the picture list, including cut and fail in the proper way. This means the control mechanism for the picture predicates are the same as for any other PROLOG predicate. In other words, the picture predicate shows proper behaviour on backtracking.

The picture interpreter plays a central role in the picture concept. As shown in figure 3, it is a link between the PROLOG picture definition and the GKS function level. The picture interpreter treats picture predicates in the same way as the top level PROLOG integer treats the other predicates. Therefore, the integration of this picture interpreter into the PROLOG interpreter should be realized in the future by directly implementing the picture predicates in PROLOG.

The picture predicates can be used in connection with GKS control and transformation functions. They are not added to the picture definition list because the functions are not directly picture-oriented like, for instance, attribute settings. However, it is possible to include these functions in the picture definition list. In this case their parameters can appear as arguments in the picture name.

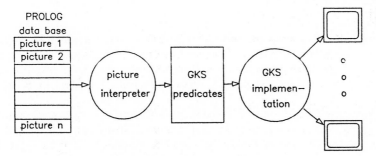

Figure 3 The Picture Interpreter

It is important to note that our picture concept differs from the concept of a fixed graphical object. Using parameters in the picture definition list can make the picture independent of some of its geometric characteristics, for example position on the screen and size. Thus, the parameters description of the picture is closer to the integral logic structure than to the real graphical appearance on the screen.

5   An Implementation of the PROLOG-Graphics Interface

An available PROLOG interpreter [6] and a GKS implementation [7] have been used for the integration of graphics in PROLOG. Both run on a PCS CADMUS 9200 workstation under the UNIX operating system, which enables different programs (processes) to communicate through special files called pipes. This mechanism is used for the PROLOG-GKS connection instead of implementing graphical primitives directly in PROLOG.

The GKS functions used are linked in a FORTRAN program, which communicates with PROLOG using the pipe mechanism. The PROLOG lower level graphics primitives and functions are implemented as predicates sending the codes of GKS functions and their parameters throgh a pipe to a transformer written in FORTRAN. This FORTRAN program interprets these codes, transforms the parameters into suitable forms and calls up the corresponding GKS functions of the GKS implementation using a FORTRAN language binding. The pipe mechanism offers many advantages, for instance easy implementation, independence between PROLOG and GKS, possibilities for easy and fast changes in both parts of the PROLOG graphical system etc.

All direct built-in predicates described in section 3 have been implemented in this way.

The built-in predicates for picture manipulation of PROLOG. Both sets of predicates are available for the user programs. This gives the user an opportunity either to build his own graphical structure or to use the predefined data structure picture.

An example for the use of the GKS-PROLOG interface is shown in the appendix. The corresponding structure of the graphical data base and the pictures produced are shown as well.

6   Trends for Future Work

The approaches described above and the current realization provide some ideas and basic tools for using graphics through PROLOG. The graphics package implemented is used as an experimental environment and a basis for the development of more complex graphics packages. For these purposes the set of graphics functions can be extended to higher level GKS versions by using the same FORTRAN-pipe interface.

The most important parts of the PROLOG-GKS system which need improvement are the graphical data base and the graphical data structures. Further efforts will focus on improving the connection between the graphical data base and the data structures used by GKS, as well as on the implementation of the graphical input primitives in combination with PROLOG input. More sophisticated graphical structures can be implemented for the purpose of geometric modelling, using the powerful

PROLOG mechanisms.

Graphics programming in PROLOG is not only a new tool for many applications, but may also be considered as a step towards graphical logic programming. We introduce this term taking into account the logical connection between the facts and rules in textual form and the graphical objects. The graphical objects can be represented as a set of facts (basic objects) and a set of rules or relations (for connecting the basic objects in order to build more complex objects). Such an object hierarchy is used in geometric modelling systems and is based on some logic operations. Following this analogy, a pure graphics PROLOG can be defined. In this context the construction and decomposition of the graphical objects may be seen as graphical tree searching with backtracking, and the PROLOG pattern matching can be extended to graphical objects as graphical patterns matching (based on pattern recognition). We mention these topics as a subject for discussion. There is a demand for extending the PROLOG capabilities towards graphical applications in the fields of picture processing and picture analysis.

The advantages of PROLOG-GKS integration are evident. It combines two highly interactive tools and also provides some powerful data processing mechanisms like tree searching with backtracking, pattern matching, and relational data bases. These are the mechanisms needed in many applications as knowledge based graphics systems [3], "intelligent" CAD-systems [4], expert systems, decision support systems and software engineering. The importance of the R&D in this field is evident in connection with the Fifth Generation Computer Project, where logic programming ("PROLOG") plays a central role.

Acknowledgements

This work was carried out while one of the authors (Z.I. Markov) stayed at the FG Graphisch-Interaktive Systeme of the Technical University of Darmstadt in the Federal Republic of Germany. We would like to express our gratitude to Prof. J. Encarnacao for his support and encouragement. We also owe thanks to M. Goebel, M. Mehl and L.A. Messina for many helpful discussions, and to M. Muth for the technical support.

References

1. W.F. Clocksin and C.S. Mellish, *Programming in PROLOG,* Springer-Verlag, Berlin (1981).

2. R.E. Davis, "Logic Programming and Prolog: A Tutorial," *IEEE Software* **2**(5), pp.53-62 (September 1985).

3. J. Encarnacao, "Incorporating knowledge engineering and computer graphics for efficient and user-friendly interactive graphics applications," in *Eurographics '85*, ed. C. E. Vandoni, North-Holland, Amsterdam (1985).

4.   J. Encarnacao, L.A. Messina, and Z.I. Markov, "Models and methods for decision support systems for evaluating and choosing CAD-Systems," in *IFIP W.G. 5.2. Working Conference on Design Theory for CAD*, Tokyo, Japan (1985).

5.   G. Enderle, K. Kansy, and G. Pfaff, *Computer Graphics Programming: GKS, the Graphics Standard,* Springer-Verlag, Heidelberg (1983).

6.   Interface Computer GmbH, *IF/PROLOG User's Manual*, 1984.

7.   GTSGRAL, *GKSGRAL User's Manual*, 1984.

8.   ISO, "Information processing systems - Computer graphics - Graphical Kernel System (GKS) functional description," ISO 7942, ISO Central Secretariat (August 1985).

9.   S.M.P. Julien, "Graphical in Micro-PROLOG," Research report DOC 8217, Imperial College-London (1982).

10.   R. Kowalski, "Algorithm = Logic + Control," *Communications of the ACM* **22**(7), pp.424-436 (July 1979).

11.   P. Sykes and R. Krishnamurti, "A Proposal for a Prolog Binding to GKS," Technical Report EdCAAD, University of Edinburgh (1985).

Appendix

In the first example a picture definition of a binary tree (the picture btree(X,Y,B)) is given. A path in this tree specified by a list of nodes (the fact l([2,3,8]) is drawn with a solid line. The other part of the tree is drawn with a dashed line. The produced picture is shown in figure 4. The second example shows the use of geometric transformations. It is typed in the file clock. The corresponding picture is shown in figure 5.

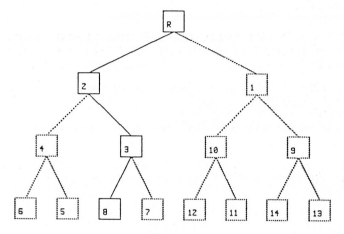

Figure 4

Figure 5

```
?- g_open(3,1000), g_open_wk(1,3,8), g_act_wk(1).

yes
?- g_set_wn(1,0,0,1000,1000), g_set_vp(1,0,0,1,1).

yes
?- g_selnt(1).

yes
?- consult(binary_tree).
picture(b(_,50,_),[ ]).
picture(b(X,Y,S), [n(X+S,Y-100), g_pl([X+S,Y-100,X,Y]), n(X-S,Y-100),
g_pl([X-S,Y-100,X,Y]), P is Y-150, b(X-S,P,S/2), b(X+S,P,S/2)]).
picture(n(X,Y), [retract (n(N), lt(N), sq(X,Y), g_txt (X-15, Y-40, N),
M is N+1, assertz(n(M))]).
picture(sq(X,Y), [g_pl( [X-25, Y, X+25, Y, X+25, Y-50, X-25, Y-50, X-25, Y])]).
picture(root(X,Y), [sq(X,Y+50), g_txt(X-15, Y+10, 'R')]).
picture(btree(X,Y,B), [root(X,Y), b(X,Y,B)]).

n(1).

lt(N):-l(L), member(N,L), g_set_lt(1),!.
lt(N):-g_set_lt(2),!.

yes
?- assertz(l([2,3,8])).

yes
?- show_picture(btree(500,500,200)).

yes
?- g_clear_wk(1,1).

yes
?- consult(clock).
picture(c(13),[ ]).
picture(c(X), [g_pl([0,140,0,190]), rotate(30), Y is X+1, c(Y)]).
picture(small, [g_pl([0,0,0,100])]).
picture(big, [g_pl([0,0,0,130])]).
picture(small(X,Y), [rotate(X*30+Y/2), small]).
picture(big(X), [rotate(X*30/5), big]).
picture(clock(X,Y), [translate(500,500), c(1),
small(X,Y), big(Y)]).

yes
?- show_picture(clock(12,32)).

yes
?- g_deact_wk(1), g_close_wk(1), g_close.

yes
?-
```

A Proposal for an ALGOL 68 Binding of GKS

R. R. Martin and C. Anderson

1 Introduction

This paper puts forward a proposal for an ALGOL 68 binding to GKS. It is hoped that this can be the basis for producing an internationally accepted binding of GKS to ALGOL 68, after discussion and review, in order that programs which use graphics from ALGOL 68 may easily be transported between different computer systems.

2 Practicality of the Binding

It is intended that this binding will be of practical use in as many different versions of ALGOL 68 as possible. Thus, as well as taking into account the formal definition of ALGOL 68 as in the Revised Report [4], details of particular implementations of ALGOL 68 will also be considered where appropriate, so that we end up with a useable binding, rather than one which is formally correct but not realizable. Two general points are mentioned below, and other more specific ones will be mentioned later.

One area where ALGOL 68 is usually extended is to provide modular compilation. There seem to be two main methods of doing this: for example, ALGOL 68C has environments [1], while ALGOL 68R uses KEEP lists [5]. ALGOL 68RS has a wide variety of methods of modular compilation, incorporating both of the above concepts [6]. Fortunately, it seems as though the binding will be able to be carried out in the same way in both cases. However, in the former case, internal GKS variables will be in scope in the user's program. This is not as important as it may seem, because these variable identifiers will not be known to him, and if he declares an object with the same identifier, his new identifier will be used in preference to the one defined at the outer level. Nevertheless, there is the small problem that he may use an identifier with the same name and mode as an internal GKS one, and forget to define it himself. We suggest that all GKS internal identifiers start with the letter 'g', thus considerably reducing the possibility of such a conflict.

A second place where problems may occur is in the length of identifiers - for example, the ALGOL 68R compiler only considers the first 12 non-blank characters for determining uniqueness of identifiers. Thus, when creating abbreviations for GKS function identifiers this must be taken into account.

3   Mapping of GKS Functions to ALGOL 68 Procedures

It has been our aim, wherever possible, to follow the rules given in annex C of the ISO Draft Standard on GKS [2] for language bindings. We have avoided the approach taken for Pascal [3], where several GKS functions are mapped to one Pascal procedure. For example, they use procedures like

SetRepresentation (*Polyline*,...)

to replace the six basic GKS functions used for setting representations, like

set polyline representation (...)

In their proposal, there is a very large number of data types, which then allows them to use a greatly reduced number of procedures. We have chosen to adopt a strict one-to-one correspondence between GKS functions and ALGOL 68 procedures, and to use a small number of data types, which we feel will benefit both the implementor and the application programmer alike.

3.1   Procedure Results

These procedures will deliver a result of mode **void**, except for inquiry functions, which will return a value of mode **int** corresponding to the error indicator argument. This will easily allow the application programmer to deal with error conditions by means of an **if** or a **case** statement. The single exception is *inquire operating state value*, which does not have an error indicator. This approach has been chosen rather than to deliver a structure containing the results produced by the procedure, as in some cases the procedures return many values simultaneously. This would result in many different structures being defined, which would be unwieldy for the application programmer to remember and use.

It was also considered whether to return an enumerated value for those input functions which deliver a status of *ok* or *none*, and while this would have similar advantages to the above, it was felt in the end that the treatment given to input functions would be more uniform if all values returned by the functions were passed through the argument list.

3.2   Procedure Arguments

In general the arguments of procedures will be in one-to-one correspondence with those given in the Draft Standard. However, see section 4.6 for a description of two new modes which have been defined, which serve to group arguments together in a logical way in special cases. Because of the ability in ALGOL 68 to find out the size of arrays by means of the operators **upb** and **lwb**, it has been decided to leave out arguments which give the size of input arrays. Output arguments which return array sizes are retained, however, for the convenience of the programmer. It avoids the need for him to calculate array sizes using **upb** and **lwb**, by letting GKS do this work instead. It is up to the user to supply an array of sufficiently large size for his purposes when an output array is required. If he does not then the following new error message is designed to cope with the problem:

  901 Output array provided too small

The *set aspect source flags* function will use an array argument for the source flags (to improve readability over a long list). If the array does not have the expected size, then the following error will be generated:

  903 Wrong number of aspect source flags supplied

A further problem arises for the escape and gdp functions. These will be discussed separately later.

3.3   Procedure Names

Bearing in mind the problem mentioned previously about identifier lengths, it is necessary to abbreviate the GKS function names for use as ALGOL 68 procedure identifiers, so that each identifier is uniquely specified by its first twelve characters. As we have more flexibility at our disposal than the six characters allowed by FOR-TRAN, and as Pascal does not have one-to-one correspondence between GKS functions and Pascal procedures, we do not use the same procedure names as either of these languages. The abbreviations are meant to be as mnemonic as possible for the application programmer, and have been created in as regular a way as possible from the original GKS definitions, for simplicity and ease of use. Note that we do not have strict consistency of name-mapping. The rules below do not show uniquely how to generate the ALGOL 68 procedure names, but rather work the other way round: given an ALGOL 68 procedure name, they allow it to be equated to the appropriate GKS function (for example, both *viewport* and its abbreviation, *vpt* are used in the binding, in different places). The main abbreviations used in forming the ALGOL 68 identifiers are given below:

ALGOL 68 ABBREVIATIONS

acc	accumulate
aspect	aspect source
att	attribute
av	available
char	character
class	classification

conn	connection id
dd	device data
df	default
dim	dimension
expf	expansion factor
facs	facilities
fill	fill area
gdp	generalized drawing primitive
id	identifier
ind	individual
init	initialise
line	polyline
marker	polymarker
max	maximum
mod	dynamic modification
no	number
ntrans	normalization transformation
op	operating
pd	predefined
q	inquire
refpt	reference point
rep	representation
sf	scale factor
state	state values
sty	style
tables	state tables
trans	transformation
type	item type
update	update states
vpt	viewport
ws	workstation

4   Mappings of GKS Data Types to ALGOL 68 Modes

The Pascal proposal has a great many data types, especially those with a limited range of values, which allows much checking to be done at compilation time. ALGOL 68 does not have this facility, and even if it did, we feel that such extensive use of it may not be justified, as it places a great burden on the application programmer to remember all of these new data types. We feel overall that it is better to have a small number of new modes.

4.1   Basic Modes

The data types integer, real and string can all be mapped directly to the ALGOL 68 modes **int**, **real** and **string** without any problems.

4.2 Mode Point

The GKS data type point can be mapped directly to an appropriate ALGOL 68 mode defined as below:

mode point = **struct**(**real** x, y);

Note that in various places, the standard uses a pair of x, y values for other entities than a point, for example as a vector, or as a pair of scaling values. While a structure the same as the one above would also be appropriate for such items, we have followed the standard and reserved mode **point** exclusively for values described as being of type point in the standard.

4.3 Enumeration Types

There are at least three ways of mapping GKS enumeration types to ALGOL 68. The first is to do as FORTRAN does, and use integers. This was not thought to be the best method, as it would not use the full power of ALGOL 68 type checking to assist the programmer.

The second possibility considered was to have a separate enumerated type for each possible set of alternatives, such as **mode fillstyle** with constant values of *hollow, solid, pattern* and *hatch*. This would have the advantage in that procedure arguments could be type checked to the full extent, to make sure that an appropriate value is always supplied for an argument of some enumerated type. On the other hand, it became obvious that this approach also has disadvantages: There would be a very large number of new types defined, which the application programmer would have to learn if he wanted to use enumerated values in assignments, etc. Also, this could put a heavy burden on an ALGOL 68 system with limited resources of space. A third problem with this approach is that some of the enumerated type constants are shared between different meanings: for example, *normal* is a value for highlighting, text alignment vertical, and text alignment horizontal. Thus we would like to suggest the compromise below.

There is a new mode defined: **mode enum**, with a constant for each possible enumerated value of each type. These will have the same identifiers as in the standard, except for the constants defining levels of GKS: these have been changed from 0a, 0b , ..., 2c to a0, b0, ..., c2 because ALGOL 68 requires identifiers to begin with a lower case letter, and the attributes polyline, polymarker, text, and fillarea returned by *inquire generalized drawing primitive*, which have had *attr* added to the end of them, so that they are not confused with the procedures of the same name. Although this may seem to leave open the possibility of name clashes between **enum** values, and user-defined names, in practice one of two things will happen: either the user will not wish to use the name as an enumerated value in his program anyway, in which case the fact that his definition will overrule the GKS one will be of no consequence, or he will at some point try to use the name as an enumerated value, when a compiler error message will tell him that due to his redefinition, the name is no longer of the correct mode, except in the unlikely circumstance where he himself declares the name to be an identifier of **mode enum**.

It is envisaged that **mode enum** will be implemented with a structure with a single integer field in it, as below, although this is not necessary. The only operations which the user needs for mode **enum** would seem to be assignment (which is automatically provided), and the operators for equality and non-equality, '=' ('**eq**') and '/=' ('**ne**'). The two latter operators will have to be defined for the user. Thus the suggested implementation for **enum** is in a manner similar to the one given below:

> **mode enum** = **struct**(**int** value);
> **op** = = (**enum** l, r) **bool**: value **of** l = value **of** r;
> **op** /= = (**enum** l, r) **bool**: value **of** l /= value **of** r;

where *value* is hidden from the user so that he can only use assignment, and the operators provided. Using this **struct** mechanism prevents the user from assigning integers directly to variables of mode **enum**, thus affording more type checking than if 'raw' integers were used. Each enumerated constant will then be given an arbitrary implementation-dependent integer value.

This compromise has the virtues of providing a certain degree of type checking, without any problem of overloading of some of the constant names above, and a plethora of new type names for the user to remember.

There is now one further problem, however, in that the user may supply an enumerated constant which is inappropriate, such as *wiss* where a GKS level is required. This will be catered for by defining the following new error message and number:

900 Inappropriate enumerated type constant supplied

Another possibility for dealing with enumerated values involves a treatment like the one given above, except that where a pair of enumerated values are obviously a pair of opposites, such as *on* and *off* or *ok* and *none*, these could be mapped to **bool**, which might give some advantages. On the whole, however, it was felt that the non-uniform treatment of enumerated types which would result would be more confusing than helpful to the application programmer.

4.4   GKS Name Type

The GKS name type is used for many different purposes at different points - for example, to identify a file, a procedure, a segment or a group of primitives which has been picked. It is suggested that these are dealt with separately as follows:

4.4.1   Segment, Workstation, Workstation Type and Pick identifiers

There are two distinct possibilities here. Firstly, a new mode could be defined for each of these, as below:

mode segment;
mode workstation;
mode wstype;
mode pick;

It is envisaged that they would be references (for efficiency when being passed as arguments to procedures) to complicated data structures which hold the information about that particular item. The only operations allowed for such types, other than the standard GKS procedure calls, would be assignment, and the operators '=' and '/='.

The advantage of using separate types for these, is that checking can be done at compile time to ensure that the correct type of object is supplied as required.

However, there are disadvantages with this approach. The GKS inquiry functions such as *inquire set of active workstations* would now return a set of ALGOL 68 references, rather than a set of human readable names which could be printed out at the terminal. Secondly, the sequence

segment a;
createsegment(a);

is likely to look confusing to the user - it seems as if segment *a* has been created twice. A further and worse example of this type of problem is given below:

segment a, b;
createsegment(a);

...

createsegment(b);

...

b := a;

After doing this, the second segment exists, but cannot be accessed.

Thirdly, the user will have to be careful to define all of his segments, etc., at the highest level at which they will be used, so that they will remain in scope when required, or declare them on the heap. This will in turn result in problems for systems like ALGOL 68C which do not provide garbage collection: The function *deletesegment* will not be able to free the space a redundant segment takes up if it is declared explicitly as suggested above. On the whole, we feel that these disadvantages outweigh the one advantage given above, and so we reject the above idea in favour of the suggestion below.

The other possible method of dealing with these names is to represent them by integers, or strings, as FORTRAN, and Pascal do. We feel that strings are more mnemonic than integers, and in the case where integers are easier to program with, for example, where something has to be done in a loop using several segments in succession, the names could be placed in a string array, where the array index now may be used in exactly the same way as if the segments had integer names. Thus, we feel that the binding should use strings for these names.

In the case of workstation type, it is envisaged that a set of implementation and installation-dependent constants will be provided to describe the workstation types available, such as "tek4014", "sigma5678", and "datatyped22". The possible types defined can be found be calling the appropriate inquiry function.

GKS defines one workstation of the category *workstation independent segment storage*. We suggest the strings "wiss" and "WISS" should be accepted for its denotation.

4.4.2   File Identifiers

Where a name refers to a file, it seems appropriate just to use an object of mode **file**. However, because standard ALGOL 68 transput procedures require objects of mode **ref file**, and these will need to be called internally by GKS, all GKS function arguments which denote a file will thus be of mode **ref file**.

4.4.3   Procedure Names

When a name refers to a function, as in the gdp and error handling procedures, for example, it seems sensible to handle the name as a **string** value. This is for two reasons. Firstly, the name may need to be transmitted to the external world, as in the case of error logging. Secondly, the mode of the procedure argument required will vary in different cases. In ALGOL 68 it is not possible to have an argument merely of mode **proc**, as the formal parameters and returned value must also be stated. Thus, the simplest mechanism available seems to be to pass procedure names as strings. For further considerations on escape and gdp, see section 4.5.2.

4.5   Data Records

Again, there seems to be no uniform way of dealing with data records. Although ALGOL 68 has structures and unions for dealing with records with variable fields, these are not really appropriate to the GKS concept of data record, because the Draft Standard does not define what possibilities the data record will have to cover. In effect, the data record is used as a method of transmitting arbitrary, implementation-dependent data between the program and peripherals. The three different cases in which the data record type is employed are for transactions with the GKS metafile, for escape and generalized drawing primitives, and for input devices. These will be considered separately.

4.5.1   GKS Metafile Records

The normal way of storing items in the GKS metafile, if annex E of the Draft Standard is followed, is as character strings (although an option of using some implementation-dependent binary format for numbers is allowed where reasons of economy dictate). Thus, it seems natural to use mode **string** for the data records required in this case, especially when considering the large range of possible data that the records may represent.

4.5.2   Escape and Generalized Drawing Primitive Data Records

Escape and *gdp* are essentially similar GKS functions, the distinction being that *gdp* is for geometric data, and *escape* is for non-geometric data. Data is supplied to both functions in the form of a data record of unspecified format. In addition, *gdp* takes an explicit array of input points, which is transformed before drawing.

We suggest that the data record for *escape* should be a **string** item. While this data record may conceivably contain numbers, it is more likely that the data will be a stream of characters to be transmitted directly to the hardware device controller. On the other hand, the geometric output produced by *gdp* is much more likely to be specified by numbers, and so for the data record here we use an array of **real**s and an array of **int**s. This is also the approach used in Annex E of the Draft Standard for storing a *gdp* item in a metafile.

It should be possible to handle any non-standard graphics output function as a combination of *escape* and *gdp* functions, thus eliminating the need to put numerical data in an *escape* data record, or text into a *gdp* record.

4.5.3   Input Device Data Records

The Draft Standard describes the data records for the different input device classes as having at least the compulsory components below:

Locator	none
Stroke	input buffer size in points
Valuator	minimum and maximum values
Choice	(see below)
Pick	none
String	input buffer size and initial cursor position.

For the choice device, the data record, depending upon the prompt and echo type, must contain at least the following :

Type 2   number of choices, array of off / on values for prompts

Type 3   number of choices, array of strings for prompting

Type 4   number of choices, array of strings for prompting

Type 5   segment name to be used for choosing by pick.

The other data which may be put into the data records is implementation-dependent, although it is suggested, for example, that for the stroke device, this data could be used to specify how often points are to be sampled, either in the x or y directions, or time. Because of the widely differing nature of what this part of the data record may describe, it seems most appropriate to deal with it by providing a **string**, which can then be used to pass either numerical or textual information.

However, in the case of the compulsory part of the data records, it will be more efficient and straightforward to provide objects of an appropriate mode. The only case where it is not so obvious what this implies is the choice data record. We suggest using [ ] **string** to pass the data, which caters for prompt and echo types 3 and 4 in a direct manner, while if we are prepared to specify on and off values by the strings "ON" and "OFF", it will also cover prompt and echo type 2. Prompt and echo type 5 can be dealt with by giving a single string which contains the name of the segment. Although this is perhaps not very clean conceptually, we feel that the extra complication to do it any other way will hinder rather than help the application programmer. This means that we now need a new error message, should the user give data of the wrong type for a given prompt and echo type, such as some string other than "ON" or "OFF" for prompt and echo type 2. The error message is given below:

902 Choice data record has inappropriate value for given prompt and echo type

Thus, we suggest that where input device data records are used, they are implemented as below:

Locator	**string** data
Stroke	**int** buffersize, **string** otherdata
Valuator	**real** min, max, **string** otherdata
Choice	[ ] **string** data
Pick	**string** data
String	**int** buffersize, **point** initcursorposn, **string** otherdata

(Note that these are not **struct**s, just collections of data.)

It should be noted that the Draft Standard contains a small error with regard to the inquire default device data routines: in these, the number of available prompt and echo types is described as being n integers. This should, of course, be a single integer, giving the number of items in the following argument, list of available prompt and echo types. Thus, in this binding, the former argument is omitted, as it just serves to give the size of an array.

4.6   Other Modes

While the data types listed above are strictly the only ones called for by the Draft Standard, it seems to us that it will benefit the implementor and application programmer alike to introduce the following additional modes:

> **mode rectangle** = **struct**(**real** xmin, xmax, ymin, ymax);
> **mode colour** = **struct**(**real** red, green, blue);

The former will be useful for defining rectangular regions in a variety of circumstances, especially when specifying windows and viewports. (It is not used, however, for *cell array* and *inquire pixel array dimensions*, where two points are used to specify a rectangular region, as the order of the points is significant; nor in *inquire text extent*, as the rectangle returned is not necessarily aligned with the axes.) Mode **colour** is not really necessary, but it seems quite likely that if it were not defined as part of the binding, many programmers would invent some such mode anyway, which is why we include it.

5 ALGOL 68 GKS Binding

Bearing the preceding points in mind, the following binding of GKS to ALGOL 68 is suggested. The enumerated constants (apart from the GKS levels) are in alphabetical order, while the procedures appear in the same order as they do in the Draft Standard. For those not familiar with ALGOL 68 it should be noted that arguments which return values must have **ref** in front of their modes, so that assignments may be made to them inside these procedures, and the notations [ ] and [,] etc. are used to denote 1 and 2 dimensional arrays.

comment GKS ALGOL 68 BINDING **comment**

comment mode and constant definitions **comment**

mode enum;		**comment** defined as some suitable **struct comment**
enum	a0,	**comment** this and all other **enum** constants given suitable unique values (see section 4.3) **comment**
	b0,	
	c0,	
	a1,	
	b1,	
	c1,	**comment** GKS level numbers changed from 1c to c1, etc. **comment**
	b2,	
	c2,	
	absent,	
	active,	
	always,	
	allowed,	
	asap,	
	asti,	
	base,	
	bnig,	
	bnil,	
	bottom,	
	bundled,	
	cap,	
	centre,	
	char,	
	choice,	
	clip,	
	colour,	
	conditionally,	
	detectable,	
	down,	
	echo,	
	empty,	
	event,	
	fillareaattr,	**comment** attr added because of procedure fillarea **comment**
	gkcl,	

gkop,
half,
hatch,
higher,
highlighted,
hollow,
inactive,
individual,
input,
invisible,
imm,
irg,
left,
locator,
lower,
metres,
mi,
mo,
monochrome,
more,
ndc,
no,
noclip,
noecho,
nomore,
none,
nopick,
normal,
notempty,
notpending,
off,
ok,
on,
other,
outin,
output,
pattern,
pending,
perform,
pick,
polylineattr, **comment** attr added because of procedure polyline **comment**
polymarkerattr, **comment** attr added because of procedure
        polymarker **comment**
present,
raster,
realized,
request,
right,
sample,
set,
sgop,

      solid,
      string,
      stroke,
      suppress,
      suppressed,
      textattr, **comment** attr added because of procedure text **comment**
      top,
      undetectable,
      up,
      valuator,
      vector,
      visible,
      wc,
      wiss,
      wsac,
      wsop,
      yes;

comment other mode definitions **comment**

mode point = **struct**(**real** x, y);
mode rectangle = **struct**(**real** xmin, xmax, ymin, ymax);
mode colour = **struct**(**real** red, green, blue);

comment the operators = and /= should also be defined for each
of the modes given above **comment**

comment procedure definitions (procedure bodies omitted) **comment**

proc opengks = (**ref file** errorfile, **int** buffersize) **void**:
proc closegks = **void**:
proc openws = (**string** workstation, **ref file** connection, **string** wstype) **void**:
proc closews = (**string** workstation) **void**:
proc activatews = (**string** workstation) **void**:
proc deactivatews = (**string** workstation) **void**:
proc clearws = (**string** workstation, **enum** controlflag) **void**:
proc redrawws = (**string** workstation) **void**:
proc updatews = (**string** workstation, **enum** regenerationflag) **void**:
proc setdeferralstate = (**string** workstation, **enum** deferralmode, implicitregen) **void**:
proc message = (**string** workstation, **string** msg) **void**:
proc escape = (**string** escapefunction, datarecord) **void**:
proc polyline = ([ ] **point** p) **void**:
proc polymarker = ([ ] **point** p) **void**:
proc text = (**point** posn, **string** s) **void**:
proc fillarea = ([ ] **point** p) **void**:
proc cellarray = (**point** p, q, [,] **int** colıxarray) **void**:
proc gdp = ([ ] **point** p, **string** primitive, [ ] **int** intdata, [ ] **real** realdata) **void**:
proc setlineindex = (**int** n) **void**:
proc setlinetype = (**int** n) **void**:
proc setlinewidthsf = (**real** factor) **void**:

proc setlinecolourindex = (**int** n) **void**:
proc setmarkerindex = (**int** n) **void**:
proc setmarkertype = (**int** n) **void**:
proc setmarkersizesf = (**real** factor) **void**:
proc setmarkercolourindex = (**int** n) **void**:
proc settextindex = (**int** n) **void**:
proc settextfont = (**int** font, **enum** precision) **void**:
proc setcharexpf = (**real** factor) **void**:
proc setcharspacing = (**real** spacing) **void**:
proc settextcolourindex = (**int** n) **void**:
proc setcharheight = (**real** height) **void**:
proc setcharupvector = (**real** xup, yup) **void**:
proc settextpath = (**enum** textpath) **void**:
proc settextalignment = (**enum** halign, valign) **void**:
proc setfillindex = (**int** n) **void**:
proc setfillstyle = (**enum** style) **void**:
proc setfillstyindex = (**int** n) **void**:
proc setfillcolourindex = (**int** n) **void**:
proc setpatternsize = (**real** scalex, scaley) **void**:
proc setpatternrefpt = (**point** p) **void**:
proc setaspectflags = ([ ] **enum** aspectflags) **void**:
proc setpickid = (**string** pick) **void**:
proc setlinerep = (**string** workstation, **int** index, type, **real** widthsf, **int** colindex) **void**:
proc setmarkerrep = (**string** workstation, **int** index, type, **real** sizesf, **int** colindex) **void**:
proc settextrep = (**string** workstation, **int** index, font, **enum** precision,
            real expf, spacing, **int** colindex) **void**:
proc setfillrep = (**string** workstation, **int** index, **enum** style,
            int styleindex, colindex) **void**:
proc setpatternrep = (**string** workstation, **int** index, [,] **int** pttnarray) **void**:
proc setcolourrep = (**string** workstation, **int** colindex, **colour** c) **void**:
proc setwindow = (**int** transformno, **rectangle** r) **void**:
proc setviewport = (**int** transformno, **rectangle** r) **void**:
proc setvptinputpriority = (**int** transformno, retransformno, **enum** relativeprio) **void**:
proc selectntrans = (**int** transformno) **void**:
proc setclipping = (**enum** clipindicator) **void**:
proc setwswindow = (**string** workstation, **rectangle** r) **void**:
proc setwsviewport = (**string** workstation, **rectangle** r) **void**:
proc createseg = (**string** name) **void**:
proc closeseg = **void**:
proc renameseg = (**string** oldname, newname) **void**:
proc deleteseg = (**string** name) **void**:
proc deletesegfromws = (**string** workstation, segment) **void**:
proc associatesegwithws = (**string** workstation, segment) **void**:
proc copysegtows = (**string** workstation, segment) **void**:
proc insertseg = (**string** segname, [,] **real** transformation) **void**:
proc setsegtrans = (**string** segment, [,] **real** transformation) **void**:
proc setvisibility = (**string** segment, **enum** visibility) **void**:
proc sethighlighting = (**string** segment, **enum** highlighting) **void**:
proc setsegpriority = (**string** segment, **real** priority) **void**:
proc setdetectability = (**string** segment, **enum** detectability) **void**:

proc initlocator = (**string** workstation, **int** device, **point** initposn,
        int initntransno, prompttype, **rectangle** echoarea, **string** data) **void**:
proc initstroke = (**string** workstation, **int** device, [ ] **point** initstroke,
        int initntransno, prompttype, **rectangle** echoarea,
        int buffsize, **string** otherdata) **void**:
proc initvaluator = (**string** workstation, **int** device, **real** initvalue, **int** prompttype,
        rectangle echoarea, **real** min, max, **string** otherdata) **void**:
proc initchoice = (**string** workstation, **int** device, initchoice, prompttype,
        rectangle echoarea, [ ] **string** datarecord) **void**:
proc initpick = (**string** workstation, **int** device, **enum** initstatus,
        string initseg, initpick, **int** prompttype,
        rectangle echoarea, **string** data) **void**:
proc initstring = (**string** workstation, **int** device, **string** inits, **int** prompttype,
        rectangle echoarea, **int** buffsize, **point** initcursorposn, **string** otherdata) **void**:
proc setlocatormode = (**string** workstation, **int** device, **enum** operatingmode, echoswitch) **void**:
proc setstrokemode = (**string** workstation, **int** device, **enum** operatingmode, echoswitch) **void**:
proc setvaluatormode = (**string** workstation, **int** device, **enum** operatingmode, echoswitch) **void**:
proc setchoicemode = (**string** workstation, **int** device, **enum** operatingmode, echoswitch) **void**:
proc setpickmode = (**string** workstation, **int** device, **enum** operatingmode, echoswitch) **void**:
proc setstringmode = (**string** workstation, **int** device, **enum** operatingmode, echoswitch) **void**:
proc requestlocator = (**string** workstation, **int** device, **ref enum** status,
        ref int ntransno, **ref point** position) **void**:
proc requeststroke = (**string** workstation, **int** device, **ref enum** status,
        ref int ntransno, **ref int** npoints, **ref** [ ] **point** stroke) **void**:
proc requestvaluator = (**string** workstation, **int** device, **ref enum** status, **ref real** value) **void**:
proc requestchoice = (**string** workstation, **int** device, **ref enum** status, **ref int** choice) **void**:
proc requestpick = (**string** workstation, **int** device, **ref enum** status, **ref string** segment, pick) **void**:
proc requeststring = (**string** workstation, **int** device, **ref enum** status, **ref string** s) **void**:
proc samplelocator = (**string** workstation, **int** device, **ref int** ntransno, **ref point** position) **void**:
proc samplestroke = (**string** workstation, **int** device, **ref int** ntransno,
        ref int npoints, **ref** [ ] **point** stroke) **void**:
proc samplevaluator = (**string** workstation, **int** device, **ref real** value) **void**:
proc samplechoice = (**string** workstation, **int** device, **ref int** choice) **void**:
proc samplepick = (**string** workstation, **int** device, **ref enum** status,
        ref string segment, pick) **void**:
proc samplestring = (**string** workstation, **int** device, **ref string** s) **void**:
proc awaitevent = (**real** timeout, **ref string** workstation,
        ref enum inputclass, **ref int** device) **void**:
proc flushdeviceevents = (**string** workstation, **enum** inputclass, **int** devicenumber) **void**:
proc getlocator = (**ref int** ntransno, **ref point** p) **void**:
proc getstroke = (**ref int** ntransno, **ref int** npoints, **ref** [ ] **point** points) **void**:
proc getvaluator = (**ref real** value) **void**:
proc getchoice = (**ref int** choice) **void**:
proc getpick = (**ref enum** status, **ref string** segment, pick) **void**:
proc getstring = (**ref string** s) **void**:
proc writeitemtogksm = (**string** workstation, **int** type, length, **string** record) **void**:
proc getitemtypefromgksm = (**string** workstation, **ref int** type, recordlength) **void**:
proc readitemfromgksm = (**string** workstation, **int** maxreclength, **ref string** record) **void**:
proc interpretitem = (**int** type, length, **string** record) **void**:
proc qopstatevalue = (**ref enum** opstatevalue) **void**:
proc qlevelofgks = (**ref enum** level) **int**:

comment in this and subsequent procedures, all results delivered are error indicators **comment**
proc qavwstypes = (**ref int** navwstypes, **ref** [ ] **string** wstypes) **int**:
proc qwsmaxnos = (**ref int** maxopenws, maxactivews, maxwsassocseg) **int**:
proc qmaxntransno = (**ref int** maxntransno) **int**:
proc qopenwss = (**ref int** nopenwss, **ref** [ ] **string** workstations) **int**:
proc qactivewss = (**ref int** nactivewss, **ref** [ ] **string** workstations) **int**:
proc qprimitiveattvalues = (**ref int** lineindex, markerindex, textindex,
            ref real charheight, charupx, charupy,
            ref enum textpath, halign, valign, **ref int** fillindex,
            ref real pttnsizex, pttnsizey, **ref point** pttnrefpoint, **ref string** pick) **int**:
proc qindattvalues = (**ref int** linetype, **ref real** widthsf, **ref int** linecolindex, markertype,
            ref real markersf, **ref int** markercolindex, font,
            ref enum precision, **ref real** charexpfactor, charspacing, **ref int** textcolindex,
            ref enum fillstyle, **ref int** fillstyleindex, fillcolindex, **ref** [ ] **enum** aspectflags) **int**:
proc qntransno = (**ref int** ntransno) **int**:
proc qntransnos = (**ref** [ ] **int** ntransnos) **int**:
proc qntrans = (**int** ntransno, **ref rectangle** window, viewport) **int**:
proc qclipping = (**ref enum** clipindicator) **int**:
proc qnameopenseg = (**ref string** segment) **int**:
proc qsegnames = (**ref int** nsegments, **ref** [ ] **string** segments) **int**:
proc qmoreevents = (**ref enum** moreevents) **int**:
proc qwsconntype = (**string** workstation, **ref file** connection, **ref string** wstype) **int**:
proc qwsstate = (**string** workstation, **ref enum** state) **int**:
proc qwsdeferralupdate = (**string** workstation,
            ref enum deferralmode, implicitregen, dispsurfempty, frameupdate) **int**:
proc qlineindices = (**string** workstation,
  ref int nlineindices, **ref** [ ] **int** lineindices) **int**:
proc qlinerep = (**string** workstation, **int** lineindex, **enum** typeofanswers,
            ref int linetype, **ref real** widthsf, **ref int** linecolindex) **int**:
proc qmarkerindices = (**string** workstation, **ref int** nmarkerindices,
            ref [ ] **int** markerindices) **int**:
proc qmarkerrep = (**string** workstation, **int** markerindex, **enum** typeofanswers,
            ref int markertype, **ref real** markersf, **ref int** markercolindex) **int**:
proc qtextindices = (**string** workstation, **ref int** ntextindices, **ref** [ ] **int** textindices) **int**:
proc qtextrep = (**string** workstation, **int** textindex, **enum** typeofanswers,
            ref int font, **ref enum** precision, **ref real** charexpfactor, charspacing,
            ref int textcolindex) **int**:
proc qtextextent = (**string** workstation, **point** textposition, **string** s,
            ref point concatpt, txtxt1, txtxt2, txtxt3, txtxt4) **int**:
proc qfillindices = (**string** workstation, **ref int** nfillindices, **ref** [ ] **int** fillindices) **int**:
proc qfillrep = (**string** workstation, **int** fillindex, **enum** typeofanswers,
            ref enum fillstyle, **ref int** fillstyleindex, fillcolindex) **int**:
proc qpatternindices = (**string** workstation, **ref int** npttnindices, **ref** [ ] **int** pttnindices) **int**:
proc qpatternrep = (**string** workstation, **int** pttnindex, **enum** typeofanswers,
            ref int pttnsizex, pttnsizey, **ref** [,] **int** pttnarray) **int**:
proc qcolourindices = (**string** workstation, **ref int** ncolindices, **ref** [ ] **int** colindices) **int**:
proc qcolourrep = (**string** workstation, **int** colindex, **enum** typeofanswers, **ref colour** c) **int**:
proc qwstrans = (**string** workstation, **ref enum** updatestate,
            ref rectangle reqwindow, curwindow, reqviewport, curviewport) **int**:
proc qsegnamesws = (**string** workstation, **ref int** nsegments, **ref** [] **string** segments) **int**:

proc qlocatordevicestate = (**string** workstation, **int** device, **enum** typeofanswers,
        ref enum opmode, echoswitch,
        ref int initntransno, **ref point** initlocposn, **ref int** prompttype,
        ref rectangle echoarea, **ref strinstring** data) **int**:
proc qstrokedevicestate = (**string** workstation, **int** device, **enum** typeofanswers,
        ref enum opmode, echoswitch,
        ref int initntransno, **ref int** npoints, **ref [ ] point** initstroke, **ref int** prompttype,
        ref rectangle echoarea, **ref int** buffsize, **ref string** otherdata) **int**:
proc qvaluatordevicestate = (**string** workstation, **int** device,
        ref enum opmode, echoswitch, **ref real** initvalue, **ref int** prompttype,
        ref rectangle echoarea, **ref real** min, max, **ref string** otherdata) **int**:
proc qchoicedevicestate = (**string** workstation, **int** device, **ref enum** opmode, echoswitch,
        ref int initchoice, prompttype,
        ref rectangle echoarea, **ref [ ] string** datarecord) **int**:
proc qpickdevicestate = (**string** workstation, **int** device, **enum** typeofanswers,
        ref enum opmode, echoswitch, initstatus, **ref string** initsegment, initpick,
        ref int prompttype, **ref rectangle** echoarea, **ref string** data) **int**:
proc qstringdevicestate = (**string** workstation, **int** device, **ref enum** opmode, echoswitch,
        ref string inits, **ref int** prompttype, **ref rectangle** echoarea,
        ref int buffsize, **ref point** initcursorposn, **ref string** otherdata) **int**:
proc qwscategory = (**string** wstype, **ref enum** category) **int**:
proc qwsclass = (**string** wstype, **ref enum** class) **int**:
proc qmaxsize = (**string** wstype, **ref enum** devunits, **ref real** maxx, maxy,
        ref int rastermaxx, rastermaxy) **int**:
proc qmodwsatts = (**string** wstype,
        ref enum linerep, markerrep, textrep, fillrep, pttnrep, colourrep, wstrans) **int**:
proc qdfdeferralstate = (**string** wstype, **ref enum** dfdefl, dfregen) **int**:
proc qlinefacs = (**string** wstype, **ref int** nlinetypes, **ref [ ] int** types,
        ref int nwidths, **ref real** nominalwidth, minwidth, maxwidth,
        ref int nlineindices) **int**:
proc qpdlinerep = (**string** wstype, **int** lineindex, **ref int** linetype,
        ref real widthsf, **ref int** colindex) **int**:
proc qmarkerfacs = (**string** wstype, **ref int** nmarkertypes, **ref [ ] int** types,
        ref int nsizes, **ref real** nominalsize, minsize, maxsize,
        ref int nmarkerindices) **int**:
proc qpdmarkerrep = (**string** wstype, **int** markerindex, **ref int** markertype,
        ref real sizesf, **ref int** colindex) **int**:
proc qtextfacs = (**string** wstype, **ref int** nfontsprecs, **ref [ ] int** fonts,
        ref [ ] enum precisions, **ref int** nheights, **ref real** minheight, maxheight,
        ref int nexpfactors, **ref real** minexpfac, maxexpfac, **ref int** ntextindices) **int**:
proc qpdtextrep = (**string** wstype, **int** textindex, **ref int** font, **ref enum** precision,
        ref real charexpfac, charspacing, **ref int** colindex) **int**:
proc qfillfacs = (**string** wstype, **ref int** nfillstyles, **ref [ ] enum** fillstyles,
        ref int nhatchstyles, **ref [ ] int** hatchstyles, **ref int** nfillindices) **int**:
proc qpdfillrep = (**string** wstype, **int** fillindex, **ref enum** fillstyle, **ref int** styleindex, colindex) **int**:
proc qpatternfacs = (**string** wstype, **ref int** npttnindices) **int**:
proc qpdpatternrep = (**string** wstype, **int** pttnindex, **ref int** pttnsizex, pttnsizey,
        ref [,] int pttnarray) **int**:
proc qcolourfacs = (**string** wstype, **ref int** ncolours, **ref enum** colouravailable,
        ref int ncolindices) **int**:
proc qpdcolourrep = (**string** wstype, **int** colindex, **ref colour** c) **int**:

proc qavgdps = (**string** wstype, **ref int** ngdps, **ref** [ ] **string** primitives) **int**:
proc qgdp = (**string** wstype, primitive, **ref int** nattrs, **ref** [ ] **enum** attrsused) **int**:
proc qmaxlengthwstables = (**string** wstype, **ref int** maxline, maxmarker, maxtext,
        maxfill, maxpttn, maxcol) **int**:
proc qnosegpriorities = (**string** wstype, **ref int** nsegprios) **int**:
proc qmodsegatts = (**string** wstype, **ref enum** transchg, vischgvtoi,
        vishgitov, highltchg, segpriochg, addprim, segdelimm) **int**:
proc qnoavinputdevices = (**string** wstype, **ref int** nlocator, nstroke, nvaluator,
        nchoice, npick, nstring) **int**:

comment Note section 4.5.3 about a small error in the Draft Standard affecting
the next six procedures **comment**

proc qdflocatordd = (**string** wstype, **int** device, **ref point** dfinitposn,
        ref int nprompttypes, **ref** [ ] **int** avprompttypes, **ref rectangle** echoarea,
        ref string dfdata) **int**:
proc qdfstrokedd = (**string** wstype, **int** device, **ref int** maxbuffsize,
        ref int nprompttypes, **ref** [ ] **int** avprompttypes,
        ref rectangle echoarea, **ref int** dfbuffsize, **ref string** dfotherdata) **int**:
proc qdfvaluatordd = (**string** wstype, **int** device, **ref real** dfinitvalue,
        ref int nprompttypes, **ref** [ ] **int** avprompttypes, **ref rectangle** echoarea,
        ref real dfmin, dfmax, **ref string** dfotherdata) **int**:
proc qdfchoicedd = (**string** wstype, **int** device, **ref int** maxchoices,
        ref int nprompttypes, **ref** [ ] **int** avprompttypes,
        ref rectangle echoarea, **ref** [ ] **string** dfdatarecord) **int**:

comment the number of data record strings is determined by the number of
choices **comment**

proc qdfpickdd = (**string** wstype, **int** device, **ref int** nprompttypes,
        ref [ ] **int** avprompttypes, **ref rectangle** echoarea, **ref string** dfdata) **int**:
proc qdfstringdd = (**string** wstype, **int** device, **ref int** maxbuffsize,
        ref int nprompttypes, **ref** [ ] **int** avprompttypes, **ref rectangle** echoarea,
        ref int dfbuffsize, **ref point** dfinitcursorpos, **ref string** dfotherdata) **int**:
proc qassociatedwss = (**string** segment, **ref int** nwss, **ref** [ ] **string** assocworkstations) **int**:
proc qsegatts = (**string** segment, **ref** [,] **real** transfm, **ref enum** visibility, highlighting,
        ref real priority, **ref enum** detectability) **int**:
proc qpixelarraydim = (**string** workstation, **point** p, q, **ref int** xdim, ydim) **int**:
proc qpixelarray = (**string** workstation, **point** point, **int** dx, dy,
        ref enum invalid, **ref** [,] **int** colindices) **int**:

comment Here, exceptionally, integers dx and dy are used to specify how much of the
output array is to be filled **comment**

proc qpixel = (**string** workstation, **point** p, **ref int** colindex) **int**:
proc qinputqueueoverflow = (**ref string** workstation, **ref enum** class, **ref int** device) **int**:
proc evaltransmatrix = (**point** point, **real** shiftx, shifty, rotation, scalex, scaley,
        enum coordinates, **ref** [,] **real** transmat) **void**:
proc acctransmatrix = ([,] **real** transmatin, **point** point,
        real shiftx, shifty, rotation, scalex, scaley,
        enum coordinates, **ref** [,] **real** transmatout) **void**:
proc emergencyclosegks = **void**:
proc errorhandling = (**int** errorno, **string** procedure, **ref file** errorfile) **void**:
proc errorlogging = (**int** errorno, **string** procedure, **ref file** errorfile) **void**:

5.1   ALGOL 68 GKS Binding Error Messages

This summarizes the new error messages generated by the binding process. Note that ISO GKS defines that they should be given error codes in the range 900 onwards. However, American ANS GKS suggests the use of error numbers from 500 onwards for this purpose. Thus in an American version, 400 should be subtracted from the numbers below:

900 Inappropriate enumerated type value supplied
(see section 4.3)
901 Output array provided too small
(see section 3.2)
902 Choice data record has inappropriate value for given prompt and echo type
(see section 4.5)
903 Wrong number of aspect source flags supplied
(see section 3.2)

6   Examples

In order to illustrate the binding, we give below two examples from annex F of the Draft Standard in their ALGOL 68 form. Note that the original examples were incomplete, in that some of the variables were not explicitly initialized; further, some of the GKS functions used were not given suitable arguments. These are commented on below as necessary. We have made the examples below follow the originals as closely as possible, even though other features of ALGOL 68 may have been more suitable for expressing the algorithms, in order to assist comparison. Note that the 'repeat... **until** *condition*' construction has been replaced with '**while**...;**not** *condition* **do skip od**'.

6.1   Example 2 from the Draft Standard

begin

file file1, ddplt, errfile;

string item array;

int item array length;
    comment initialize to some suitable installation dependent constant **comment**

int item type, item length;

int eoftype; **comment** initialize depending on local file conventions **comment**

open gks(errfile, n);
    comment the original omitted arguments, but an error file, and
    buffer size are needed. 'n' should be replaced by a suitable installation
    dependent constant. **comment**
open ws("GKSM_IN", file1, "GKSM_INPUT");

```
open ws("PLOTTER", ddplt, "FLAT_BED_PLOTTER");
activate ws("PLOTTER");

while
    get item type from gksm("GKSM_IN", item type, item length);
    read item from gksm("GKSM_IN", item array length, item array);
    interpret item(item type, item length, item array);
    item type /= eoftype
do
    skip
od;

deactivate ws("PLOTTER");
close ws("PLOTTER");
close ws("GKSM_IN");
close gks
end
```

6.2   Example 4 from the Draft Standard

```
begin

file dddis, ddseg, ddplot, errfile;

rectangle windowbounds, comment this must be initialised comment
            viewportbounds; comment and so must this comment

enum status;

[1:n]point p; comment 'n' must be replaced by an integer sufficiently large to hold
            all expected points comment

point p1, p2;

int trans, trans1, trans2;
int ch;

[1:2,1:3]real matrix, matac;

int colour1; comment initialized, for example to 1 comment

real sx, sy; comment these must be initialized comment


open gks(errfile,n); comment see comment in previous example comment
open ws("DISPLAY", dddis, "3"); comment ws type was 3 in original comment
activate ws("DISPLAY");
open ws("SEGSTORE", ddseg, "WISS");
activate ws("SEGSTORE");
```

```
set window(1, windowbounds);
set viewport(1, viewportbounds);
set vpt input priority(1, 0, higher);

create seg("POLYGON");
set line index(3);

int next := 1;
request locator("DISPLAY", 1, status, trans1, p[1]);
        comment original example has the arguments in an order inconsistent with the
        body of the Draft Standard for all calls to request locator comment
select ntrans(trans1);

while
    next := next + 1;
    request locator("DISPLAY", 1, status, trans, p[next]);
    not (status = none or trans /= trans1)
do
    skip
od;
p[next] := p[1];
polyline(p[1:next]);
close seg;

evaltransmatrix((0,0), 0, 0, 0, 1, 1, wc, matrix);
bool ch equals 12or3 := true;
while
    request choice("DISPLAY", 1, status, ch);
    if status = none then goto endloop fi;
    case ch
            in
            begin
                comment shift is a choice of 1 comment
                request locator("DISPLAY", 1, status, trans2, p1);
                if status = none then goto endloop fi;
                request locator("DISPLAY", 1, status, trans, p2);
                if status = none or trans /= trans2 then goto endloop fi;
                select ntrans(trans2);
                acc transmatrix(matrix, (0,0), x of p2-x of p1, y of p2-y of p1,
                                0, 1, 1, wc, matac);
                set segtrans("POLYGON", matac)
            end,
            ..., comment zoom is a choice of 2 comment
            ... comment rotate is a choice of 3 comment
            out
                comment any other value of 'ch' comment
                ch equals 12or3 := false
    esac;
    update ws("DISPLAY", perform);
    ch equals 12or3
do skip
od;
```

```
endloop:
deactivate ws("DISPLAY");
deactivate ws("SEGSTORE");
open ws("PLOTTER", ddplot, "FOURPENPLOTTER");
activate ws("PLOTTER");
set colourrep("PLOTTER", colour1, (1,0,0));
set linerep("PLOTTER", 3, 1, 1.5, colour1);
set textrep("PLOTTER", 2, 1, stroke, 1, 0, colour1);
    comment the original example did not agree with the draft standard in the
    number of arguments given comment
set wsviewport("PLOTTER", (0,sx,0,sy));
copysegtows("PLOTTER", "POLYGON");
set text index(2);
set charheight(0.1);
text((0.5,0.5), "This is a polygon");

deactivate ws("PLOTTER")
close ws("PLOTTER");
close ws("DISPLAY");
close ws("SEGSTORE");
close gks
end
```

References

1. S. D. Bourne, A. D. Birrell, and I. Walker, *ALGOL 68C Reference Manual,*
    Cambridge University Computer Laboratory (1975).

2. ISO, "Information Processing - Graphical Kernel System - Functional description," Draft International Standard DIS 7942 (1983).

3. M. Slater, "Pascal Interface for GKS 7.2," BSI OIS/5/WG5/207, BSI Working
    Group on Computer Graphics (1984).

4. A. van Wijngaarden et al., "Revised Report on the Algorithmic Language
    ALGOL 68," *Acta Informatica* **5**, pp.1-236 (1975).

5. P. M. Woodward and S. G. Bond, *ALGOL 68R Users Guide,* Her Majesty's
    Stationery Office London (1972).

6. P. M. Woodward and S. G. Bond, "Guide to ALGOL 68 for Users of RS Systems," ISBN 0 7131 3490 9, Edward Arnold.

Contact Addresses

K. W. Brodlie   Computer Centre, University of Leicester, University Road, Leicester LE1 7RH, U.K.

R. Buhtz   Konrad-Zuse-Zentrum fuer Informationstechnik Berlin, Heilbronner Strasse 10, D-1000 Berlin 31, F.R.G.

D. A. Duce   Informatics Division, Rutherford Appleton Laboratory, Chilton, Didcot, OXON OX11 0QX, U.K.

J. L. Encarnacao   FGRIS, Technische Hochschule Darmstadt, Alexanderstrasse 24, D-6100 Darmstadt, F.R.G.

R. Gnatz   Institut fuer Informatik der Technischen Universitaet Muenchen, Arcisstrasse 21, Postfach 20 24 20, D-8000 Muenchen 2, F.R.G.

M. Goebel   Fraunhofer-Arbeitsgruppe AGD, Bleichstrasse 10-12, D-6100 Darmstadt, F.R.G.

I. Herman   Insotec Consult GmbH, Franz-Joseph-Strasse 14, D-8000 Muenchen 40, F.R.G.

W. Huebner   ZGDV, Bleichstrasse 10-12, D-6100 Darmstadt, F.R.G.

A. Kotzauer   Wilhelm Pieck Universitaet Rostock, Sektion Informatik, Albert-Einstein-Strasse 22, DDR-2500 Rostock, German Democratic Republic.

R. Krishnamurti   EdCAAD, University of Edinburgh, Department of Architecture, 20 Chambers Street, Edinburgh EH1 1JZ, U.K.

R. Lindner   FGRIS, Technische Hochschule Darmstadt, Alexanderstrasse 24, D-6100 Darmstadt, F.R.G.

R. R. Martin   Department of Computer Mathematics, University College Cardiff, Mathematics Institute, Senghennydd Road, Cardiff CF2 4AG, U.K.

A. J. Matthew   Computer Centre, University of Leicester, University Road, Leicester LE1 7RH, U.K.

S. P. Mudur   National Centre for Software Technology, Gulmohar Cross Road No. 9, Juhu, Bombay 400 049, India

G. J. Reynolds   School of Information Systems, University of East Anglia, Norwich NR4 7TJ, U.K.

J. Rix   Fraunhofer-Arbeitsgruppe AGD, Bleichstrasse 10-12, D-6100 Darmstadt, F.R.G.

K. Singleton   (now Mrs K. Wyrwas) Computer Graphics Unit, Department of Computer Science, University of Manchester, Oxford Road, Manchester M13 9PL, U.K.